MW01518058

Transgenerational Trauma and the Aboriginal Preschool Child

New Imago: Series in Theoretical, Clinical, and Applied Psychoanalysis

Series Editor

Jon Mills, Adler Graduate Professional School, Toronto

New Imago: Series in Theoretical, Clinical, and Applied Psychoanalysis is a scholarly and professional publishing imprint devoted to all aspects of psychoanalytic inquiry and research in theoretical, clinical, philosophical, and applied psychoanalysis. It is inclusive in focus, hence fostering a spirit of plurality, respect, and tolerance across the psychoanalytic domain. The series aspires to promote open and thoughtful dialogue across disciplinary and interdisciplinary fields in mental health, the humanities, and the social and behavioral sciences. It furthermore wishes to advance psychoanalytic thought and extend its applications to serve greater society, diverse cultures, and the public at large. The editorial board is comprised of the most noted and celebrated analysts, scholars, and academics in the English speaking world and is representative of every major school in the history of psychoanalytic thought.

Titles in the Series

Relating to God: Clinical Psychoanalysis, Spirituality, and Theism, by Dan Merkur
The Uses of Psychoanalysis in Working with Children's Emotional Lives, edited by Michael O'Loughlin
Psychodynamic Perspectives on Working with Children, Families, and Schools, edited by Michael O'Loughlin
Working with Trauma: Lessons from Bion and Lacan, by Marilyn Charles
Hypocrisy Unmasked: Dissociation, Shame, and the Ethics of Inauthenticity, by Ronald C. Naso
Searching for the Perfect Woman: The Story of a Complete Psychoanalysis, by Vamık D. Volkan with J. Christopher Fowler
In Freud's Tracks: Conversations from the Journal of European Analysis, edited by Sergio Benvenuto and Anthony Molino
Desire, Self, Mind, and the Psychotherapies: Unifying Psychological Science and Psychoanalysis, by R. Coleman Curtis
Transgenerational Trauma and the Aboriginal Preschool Child: Healing through Intervention, edited by Norma Tracey

Transgenerational Trauma and the Aboriginal Child

Healing through Intervention

Edited by Norma Tracey

Foreword by Ursula Kim

ROWMAN & LITTLEFIELD
Lanham • Boulder • New York • London

Published by Rowman & Littlefield
A wholly owned subsidiary of The Rowman & Littlefield Publishing Group, Inc.
4501 Forbes Boulevard, Suite 200, Lanham, Maryland 20706
www.rowman.com

Unit A, Whitacre Mews, 26-34 Stannary Street, London SE11 4AB

British Library Cataloguing in Publication Information Available

Library of Congress Cataloging-in-Publication Data

Transgenerational trauma and the Aboriginal preschool child : healing through intervention / edited by Norma Tracey ; foreword by Ursula Kim.
p. ; cm. – (New imago)
Includes bibliographical references and index.
ISBN 978-1-4422-3549-6 (cloth : alk. paper) -- ISBN 978-1-4422-3550-2 (ebook)
I. Tracey, Norma, editor. II. Series: New imago.
[DNLM: 1. Child, Preschool–Australia. 2. Oceanic Ancestry Group–psychology–Australia. 3. Stress Disorders, Post-Traumatic–psychology–Australia. 4. Intergenerational Relations–Australia. 5. Social Environment–Australia. 6. Transference (Psychology)–Australia. WM 172.5]
RJ506.P66
618.92'852100994–dc23
2014037064

∞ ™ The paper used in this publication meets the minimum requirements of American National Standard for Information Sciences Permanence of Paper for Printed Library Materials, ANSI/NISO Z39.48-1992.

Printed in the United States of America

Dedicated to the Aboriginal people of Australia,
the past, present, and future custodians of this land.

Contents

Foreword

Ursula Kim

Before I address the value of this amazing book for preschool teachers everywhere, I would like to take this opportunity to tell a little about myself and who I am and what I believe my being Aboriginal is about. I grew up on the riverbank. The river was our playground, and it taught us many things—but most of all how to survive in this environment. My mother would call us ducks because we as children learned how to swim in the river and to play and to become aware of what was happening around us. In our early years numeracy was something easily learned by playing with stones and sticks to create play, as for example with the little rooms we called cubbies, in games, and leaving landmarks when walking in the bush. This taught us how to live off the land and respect for nature. During flood time our parents would teach us not to approach the river because of the danger in the strength and force of the water. I have many stories but my experience of our culture was that we as children had a lot to learn and it was from our own experiences. And this gives us the connection to our land.

This book also gives us a voice. It gives us the right to speak about our feelings, and it shows the pain inflicted on us as a vulnerable people.

I know that one of the most important things for the traumatized people of my culture is to regain their identity. Every morning I stand at the entrance to my preschool, which has one hundred and twenty Aboriginal families, and I say "good morning" and I greet each of them by name. Just to be acknowledged and to have a feeling that they belong is healing in itself. If I am going to do the talk I want to do the walk as well.

Through this book, Norma Tracey helps us tell our story and speak of our pain and the pain of our children. Some people will not want to know. They will ask, How can a non-Aboriginal understand us? How can people from the United States write about us? They can because we all need to see ourselves as human beings, all suffering and struggling in our lives. Some of the things they write about in this book are things our ancestors have known for more than 40,000 years. Things like the Dadirri circle and like The Dreaming stories. We can be proud of having something to give the newcomers to our ancient land.

It is fitting that Norma and two of her colleagues have been awarded the title and role of Reconciliation Ambassadors to the Aboriginal people on behalf of the Australian Association of Social Workers. We want reconciliation on both sides, and it is books like this one that will give us that reconciliation.

This book about Gunawirra's work has two levels. One is really supportive and nourishing—it is an environment where there is a rich and lively discussion of things that concern us all, Aboriginal and non-Aboriginal—yet the other is about a deep underlying layer that is full of really frightening trauma that is there too. This book is not afraid to name that and it is not afraid to attempt a healing through reconciliation at a level of cultural understanding, as well as a healing in our own unconscious through a psychoanalytic understanding of our problems.

Ursula Kim
Director Minimbah Preschools, Armidale, New South Wales
Gunawirra Board Director

Acknowledgments

The miracle of Gunawirra has always been alive in the common spiritual energy and vision of every person involved. That spirit is present in this book with each of our authors—Aboriginal and non-Aboriginal, teachers or students, clinicians or academics.

To acknowledge all our contributors would fill a book but I want to thank especially the parents and little children who have allowed the use of their material here. Gunawirra thanks Poet's Corner and Gunnedah fro their immense contribution to our work and for the partnership with Gunawirra which have given rise to the work of this book.

I also thank my analyst Ron Brookes, who recently died, my supervisor David Buick, and, for his years and years of support, Mike Eigen; they form the spirit of this book.

I must especially thank my wonderful "readers," Jackie Stewart, Maria Losurdo, Ursula Kim, and our Gunawirra cultural advisor, reader, and contributor Graham Toomey.

My dear friends and colleagues Jeff Eaton and Marilyn Charles have been helpful and supportive throughout as has Michael O'Loughlin. At our publishers Rowman & Littlefield, Amy King, Kelly Blackburn, and Francinia Williams have been generous with their time and support, as has our indexer Robert Swanson.

I want to acknowledge Louise Gyler for her consultations, Joysna Field and Anton Aronson for their supervision of the child therapy cases, and especially Tessa Philips for her supervision of the parent work, which we could not in the end include in this volume. I want to thank Josephine Pretorius for the use of her case material in chapter 4.

The person to whom I owe most thanks is Sigrid Asmus. Her years of publishing experience and her care for language have made her the perfect midwife for this book. We authors salute her for bringing our project to fruition.

In addition I want to acknowledge the Board of Gunawirra for always supporting our work. I thank the book's funders, including The Trust Company, and Vincent Fairfax Family Foundation.

We acknowledge the Law firm Gilbert & Tobin, whose lawyer Darren Fittler and corporate social responsibility lawyer Michelle Hannon have given such excellent pro-bono services to Gunawirra. We thank Danny Gilbert whose generosity has given Gunawirra its legal basis for existence.

Gunawirra especially acknowledges the support of the Aboriginal and Torres Strait Islander Healing Foundation. We thank the Healing Foundation for funds granted under its training and education programs stream. They made this book possible.

Special thanks go to Judith Atkinson who was too ill to write for us but whose support and writings over the years have been a guide and inspiration to us all.

Finally, thank you John my dear husband and companion, and Paul and Sally, my family, for your ever-present support.

Norma Tracey
Sydney, Australia

Introduction

Norma Tracey

Our hope for this book is to create a preconceptive space where the possibility of understanding between the many different imported cultures and our primal culture of First People may be conceived. We in Australia best experience ourselves as a country through integrating the spiritual, psychic, and cultural contribution of the First People of this land.

Multiple authors give many different perspectives here, but this book focuses on the transgenerational trauma experienced by Aboriginal preschool children who carry the loss suffered by generations of their people within their young psyches. When over 250,000 of us walked arm in arm in the Corroboree 2000 Bridge Walk across Sydney Harbour Bridge on May 28, 2000, we symbolized the bridge crossing we make countless times in this book, as we came to understand how our little children of Aboriginal culture and race are carrying the pain of their people and family over generations.

This book and its choice of authors and chapters tell the story of our own search for direction and meaning through many different voices. Our hope is to create a space in which to find one's own voice while understanding and seeing how issues of transgenerationally transmitted trauma have left indelible wounds. We make apologies to our Koori brothers and sisters if our "whitefella" approach, or our narratives and interpretations fall short of the reality of their experiences. We cannot truly know, we can only surmise. We apologize too that our thinking space is not confirmed in academic sureness, for we are all still learning about healing, the learning their ancestors have had for more than 40,000 years.

For us this book represents a *psychic space*, akin to a psychic womb, similar to a space in the mother's body but also in her mind, a space for receiving, listening, creating, and with promise of emotional growth. We take this idea to the space in the child care centers we work with. Therapists and preschool teachers learn "to welcome and receive the children's primitive communications of distress; they learn to bear the negativities projected onto them"[1] not only by the children, but by vulnerable parents who see their children as exposing their inadequacies.

The capacity to accept the reality of pain is central to all our work in Gunawirra. We know the potential to live, to negotiate life for oneself, may be lost if a real-life situation is truly awful. Fear and terror foreclose creative space, killing imagination, causing a kind of internal deadness, a concretization of living. Most obvious are the loss of meaning and the capacity to symbolize. With meaning lost, an autistic deadened space, psychic death, and even suicide are distinct risks. All this the preschool, by its purpose and vision, works against.

The preschool's very special environment, with its focus on experience and expression, becomes the psychic space where *creation dreaming* can occur. It is the space where the small child can fantasize, symbolize, and imagine through free play, creative arts, music, drama, growing gardens, and through just being.

The preschool center is for many children a place where the damage is already evident, and it creates terrible pain for those Aboriginal preschool teachers who may have experienced similar traumas in their own childhood. Revisiting does not by itself cause healing. The desperate effort of the Aboriginal people to revisit their trauma often fails because it recreates the trauma without the possibility of its healing.

HOW IS TRAUMA HEALED?

The *Dadirri* circle (a space of deep soul listening), together with *The Dreamtime* spirituality stories, create the soul of this book. The healing available from and generated by ancient Aboriginal cultural wisdom, with its understanding of and approach to healing, forms the basis of our work and of our understanding. Through this form of listening the Aboriginal people caused their own healing. They bring that healing to us to use today.

The Dadirri circle became the place where the one in trauma would cry for help. A formal ritual circle would be formed. Its purpose was to bear witness to the suffering of this community member at the deepest soul level. All in the circle sat in silence, holding and acknowledging the pain of their fellow man. Through connection to land, spirits, ancestors, dreaming, totems, creation of identity and story, healing occurs. And through this we as psychoanalytic therapists have been gifted a cultural and spiritual basis to our work that is respectful to the ancestors and enhancing of our own profession in every way.

The two ancient ways of Dadirri and The Dreaming given to us by the first people of this land join forces with psychoanalytic understanding to form the psyche of this book. These ways of thinking give enrichment and depth to all our values as an organization. We do not "own" our way of working, it is evolving; we do not own our way of thinking, that too is evolving. We view psychoanalytic thinking not as the precinct of a few middle-class, insightful, able to afford it clients, but as belonging to all of us who work at the coal face of man's suffering, the place where there is the essence of man's humanity, as well as man's inhumanity to man. For this we use the marriage of these two ways of thinking. There is the possibility that a deep reflection and understanding of ancient wisdom may not merely add to psychoanalytic thinking, but perhaps inform or change it. We are open and welcoming of this. We seek it.

We want to ask the hard questions. We want to ask what makes a man deprive himself of the right to live, to create, to be? What makes him kill himself—as so many of our Aboriginal youth are doing? Can we change it in any way by using one of the greatest thinking methods of modern life—psychoanalysis—to make sense of our destruction of one of the oldest cultures known to man? Is our stripping of culture, spirituality, land and family, the stripping of the meaning of life for a whole race? Is that why it is better to be dead, or at least numbed by alcohol and drugs? Can we reverse this? Can we learn the basis of dealing with trauma? Because from time immemorial the Aboriginal people had the answers in the symbology of their Dreaming stories and in their circles of listening. Can we from this create a spiritual basis, a soul space where pain and suffering are not only heard but are taken in, processed, and neutralized, in the same way it was in the Dadirri circle, and in the same way every mother does for her infant as she takes in, absorbs, and transforms the infant's pain in a way that makes it bearable, sufferable?

We address trauma in the little preschool children as they battle to negotiate their crazy world in which loved ones may well take drugs, use alcohol, and even abuse the boundaries of their body. Or a child's loved ones might be simply too lost in their own unresolved and continuingly increasing pain and suffering to be available to the child's needs.

ART AS A MEDIUM FOR HEALING

At its core this volume offers a path-breaking discussion of the way trauma comes to be manifested at the deepest psychic level in the lives of 3- to 5-year-old children. A growing body of literature, now extending over many years, has highlighted both the many causes and the widespread extent of domestic violence and sexual abuse, suicide, poverty, unemployment, physical illness, lack of education, racism-induced stress, substance and drug abuse (including alcoholism and petrol-sniffing)—all elements that continue to devastate indigenous families and other marginalized communities. These problems contribute to social isolation as well as to loss of identity and self-esteem in early childhood. The transgenerational trauma carried by any race dislocated from its culture, concomitant with the loss of its tribal basis in communal living, its ancient lands, and its spiritual values attached to the earth, brings shame and a sense of deadness.

The animating spirit of this book is the attention it gives to creating a space in which to listen to the voices of traumatized children, and that gives those voices relevance; it is a space in which to hear the voices of the parents; and it is a space in which to hear from professionals and academics around the world, making their own voices heard in the analyzing and understanding of trauma. In this we continue to carry forward the deep soul listening practiced since ancient Aboriginal times in the Dadirri circle, where the community sat together, listening to the pain of another. This space for listening has become the template we use in this book.

We have based our book on the belief that future harm can be prevented by early treatment of trauma and its understanding. The intrinsic human impulse to enact or depict a drama, tell a story, and to know that one has an audience to witness, is essentially a form of psychotherapy that helps to order personal and social experience. In finding and creating some simple but effective models of treatment through using art as a therapeutic medium both for preschool children and their traumatized families, we have provided a well-supported model that can be used by all those who work to heal the trauma suffered by preschool children, which has until now been largely ignored.

My intention as editor has been to produce a book that will be used by those Aboriginal and non-Aboriginal workers and teachers who deal daily with traumatized children in their communities and schools. We want this book to make a difference, because of the usefulness of its model, the depth of its thinking, and the intensity of its methodology. And, most importantly, because hearing the voices of the little children and their parents presents us with a truth we cannot capture in any form of pedagogy.

THE IDEA FOR THIS BOOK

The idea for this book was born out of the understanding we received when we began working with projects in more than forty country preschools throughout the state of New South Wales, Australia. We were unprepared for the response to our work, and for the use the children could make of just ten one-hour weekly sessions of psychotherapy using art as the primary medium. We were also not prepared for the enthusiasm of the teachers, both Indigenous and non-indigenous, who filled our seminar on Trauma for the Preschool Child, with some sixty-seven teachers attending from as far away as 600 kilometers (about 375 miles). We were not prepared for the generous influx of top world leaders in their field who donated time and energy to come to our center here in Sydney from the rest of New South Wales, and from Washington State, Massachusetts, New York, London, and New Zealand, bringing their expertise to us without pay or reward because they were aware of the importance of understanding the task at hand.

While in our historical past the concentration has been on "learning" and getting an education, little has been done to help children be emotionally ready to learn. No one wants to hear of the possibility that a 4-year-old can be traumatized.

NAVIGATING THE BOOK

Our introduction offers a map for the book, describing the authors and subjects chosen for the individual chapters and how they meet and relate to each other. Each contributor will discuss the interface of trauma and education where we work, knowing that the relief of trauma allows learning because learning needs curiosity, a capacity to contain fear of the new, to imagine and to dream.

When as editor I asked for a history of Aboriginal life since the white man came, I was not prepared for a voice from the heart that told of the suffering endured by a race of people, suffering so traumatic that even the reading of it was often too much to bear. Jackie Stewart and Maria Losurdo's chapter is a passionate and heartbreaking story of a life lived in pain and hardship created by man's inhumanity to his fellow man. This chapter creates the spirit of the book. It is the canvas that serves as a backdrop that affects our thinking throughout the following chapters.

Against that background and infused with that chapter, I have tried in the simplest way to give meaning to the idea of Gunawirra and the thinking out of which it was conceived. I describe how this organization moved from a dream to become a living reality, and of how a joint vision of elders and professionals throughout NSW took form to become the vital and rich organization that Gunawirra is today.

It seemed fitting then to bring in Jeffrey Eaton's beautifully written and painstakingly prepared material. Jeff felt this important task was for him also a sacred journey. He is one of our foremost child analysts and has gifted us a model on which to think and work, and to use as a direction finder. How does one build a floor for experiencing? How do we think about the child's experience? He offers descriptive metaphors drawn from his own training and work as a psychoanalyst to help orient the worker to the child's inner world, expressed through action in the therapy play setting. Jeff is the weekly supervisor by Skype for our individual therapy work with Aboriginal preschool and early school children. He helps Gunawirra understand and view "the child's picture of the world" as it is expressed and enacted in our sessions. Our hope is that workers of all kinds will be able to recognize, tolerate, and welcome the deeper levels of the child's experience as a result of absorbing this chapter. Jeff and I have exchanged thinking in Michael Eigen's online groups for some years, reaching across distance and space to share our interchanges. It is right, then, that my chapter on understanding trauma follows Jeff's chapter.

My chapter is predicated on two significant gifts from Aboriginal peoples: the concept of The Dreaming, and the most ancient form of treating trauma, known to every Aboriginal group as Dadirri, or for modern Aboriginal people the healing circle. From ancient times we as humans imbued our external world and its events with meaning drawn from the contents of The Dreaming—our internal world. We create boundaries for this meaning and we draw symbols from it. This chapter includes the narrative of a child's therapy. Central to this chapter is an analysis of how meaning is lost for the small child as a result of trauma. The small child who closes down emotionally as a result of trauma may employ an autistic defence, but if that breaks down then chaos, envy, and rage come alive with ensuing primitive enactment. The central psychosis of terror—terror of being, or of being annihilated—is neutralized and dispelled by psychic holding. The mother does that for her infant, the healing circle does that for the traumatized person in their midst, the good-enough therapist does that for their patient, the preschool teacher does that for her children.

No book on early childhood trauma could ignore the neurobiological effects of trauma. Shiri Hergass has given us a living chapter detailing the effects of trauma on the micro-architectural processes of the child's neurobiology early in life. Trauma experienced during early childhood may alter the brain's biology and functioning; the pain caused by the disruption to the child's brain-mind-self system may result in abnormalities in behavior and cognition, including the ability to adapt to society. This is important to our understanding of the relevance of protecting the small child from experiences beyond their capacity to digest and integrate. Children react to the stress of trauma in one of two ways: with a hyperresponsive mode of unruly or uncontrolled anxiety and hyper-reactivity or with a hyporesponsive mode characterized by social and emotional withdrawal. Damage to the brain's right hemisphere through early trauma is associated with difficulties in both the perception and communication of affect, which in turn creates problems in establishing relationships. Traumatic experiences may also cause physiological damage in vital organs such as the heart and lungs, and can correlate with diabetes, asthma, a weakened immune system, and premature death.

Shiri's chapter moves toward a model of the whole child, addressing the child's pain as part of a brain-mind-self system. It seeks a language that speaks of the whole child and the embodied child, not just the brain. This focus on the holistic is one of the main lessons drawn from indigenous traditions, where there is less separation not only within the person, but also between person and environment (or world). Shiri describes how art therapy is a promising treatment for preschool children who have experienced traumatic events, giving special attention to trauma-focused art therapy as a therapeutic intervention.

From this we move to the intergenerational transmission of trauma and its effects on identity development in the preschool child, as presented by Marilyn Charles. Marilyn has been our guiding light, our carer, supporting us all with her sensitivity and understanding. She has played a significant role in emotionally supporting me during the writing of this book. Marilyn visits Gunawirra each year to share with preschool teachers in special groups her empathy toward their work with their traumatized children. She understands how trauma that is insufficiently worked through is passed along the generations in infancy via the transmission of deficits in the parents. The mother who is absorbed in her own distress is not easily available to recognize and attend to the needs of her child. Moreover, denial of the impact of trauma increases the likelihood of reenacting it with the next generation. When trauma has affected an entire culture, as has happened with our Aboriginal people, the situation becomes more complicated because of the negative cultural identity that becomes internalized.

Marilyn uses case illustrations from Gunawirra's preschool project where she supervised the work of our therapists with the children. From this she introduces some of the ways in which trauma impedes the integration of a solid sense of identity, and also shows ways in which an empathically attuned therapy environment can begin to loosen the constraints of such a legacy and allow the child to open to the greater curiosity and exploration so important for healthy identity development. The second part of her chapter offers illustrations drawn from the work of clinicians working with preschool children in the Gunawirra project. Her chapter concludes with some illustrative therapeutic strategies based on her understanding of the importance of child therapy.

The next chapter, also by Marilyn, explores the topics of trauma, childhood, and emotional resilience. She sees the development of resilience as dependant on the child's ability to remain engaged and curious about his or her experiences. Trauma interferes with these capacities, both by making the child fearful about venturing out into the unknown, and also, more importantly, by interfering with the development of the affective and cognitive capacities so crucial to healthy development. In this chapter, Marilyn describes the development of emotional resiliency and the ways in which trauma interferes with that development, and then continues to look closely at case illustrations from Gunawirra's work with preschool children in order to discuss ways in which play therapy provides the type of facilitative environment in which the child can develop greater emotional resilience.

Celia Connolly and Judy King's moving account lets us see and hear a child whose world cannot be held because she cannot experience herself as held and contained. The child's fear of falling apart is obvious. For anyone who has read Winnicott on holding or Bion on containing and the container–contained, this chapter could not offer a better window into what those concepts look and feel like in the moment-by-moment world of a child who has never had the security of being really held. Both Conolly, the supervisor, and King, the art therapist, are superb observers and writers, and have the gift of giving the reader a close-in, accessible sense of what Kylie's moment-to-moment actions might mean and convey. Kylie too speaks, and we watch how expressing her own emotions both in words and through the unifying force of creative art gave her an improved sense of who she was and of enjoyment in being. Together, the three voices in this chapter show how the capacity to just *be* without fear of disintegration depends so centrally on that inner sense of being "someone," and how that sense is dependent on being contained by an internal caring object. As Conolly and King tell us, "Trauma robs children of their fundamental right to feel trust in good things being sustained in their world; it leaves them vulnerable to the feeling that at any time things could go terribly wrong again and it could all be lost. If there is nowhere to put your feet on solid ground, then it's hard to learn how to stand on your own two feet." How poignant it is to understand that a traumatized child can never take anything in life for granted; it all seems to spill away. Yet as this chapter so sensitively shows, it is not only the capacity to hold oneself together that is important, but the possibility of being able to fall apart and experience the faith that one can come together again.

In the next chapter, the account by Judy King and Celia Conolly of Judy's art-therapy work and Celia's supervision of therapy with a young Aboriginal girl gives us an intimate glimpse into the work we do. As in the previous chapter, Judy is an art therapist with psychoanalytic thinking in her background, and her supervisor and companion during this work was Celia Conolly, a well-known child psychotherapist. Here, they present Lola, a young preschooler who seems to struggle with the concept that things in her world can be sustained. Over and over she tries to find ways to "leave her mark," as if needing to prove that she herself will continue to exist and be remembered. She seemed compelled to choose art materials that were fragile and would not survive her art-making activities, as if they too could not be expected to survive or continue. She repeatedly asked her teachers, "When's my painting time? When's my painting time?" as if it were hard for her to believe that her therapy could continue and that her special relationship with her art therapist could be sustained. Through giving us the child's own statements, the therapist's notes as she watched and listened to her communications about her experiences, and the supervisor's analysis of elements underlying work with this child, the authors allow us to see how therapists can begin to think about what the child needs from the adults in her life to help her to hold onto her feelings in a safe, contained way.

Shiri Hergass and I have been companions on the journey of developing The Five Big Ideas, an approach born out of the last five years of working in outback communities. From our listening and learning we created the website www.trackingthemilkyway.com as a place to formulate and communicate practical ways of working. In Gunawirra's work with the preschools, we use—with our skilled teachers directing us—art, music, literature, and drama to play a strong role in helping children recover from early trauma. This program is led by preschool teachers, designed by preschool teachers, and brought into practice by preschool teachers. Our and their experiential learning methods are informed by psychoanalytic thinking, underpinned by Reggio Emilia thought linked with and brought into the here and now by the Marte Meo method, create a powerful mix in the experiential teaching center of preschool work.

We knew the program had to be from within the community, and as a result of weeks, months, and years of sharing, the Five Big Ideas were born—health and hygiene, nutrition, my culture my identity, handling troubles at home, and care of my country. We needed something for our Aboriginal community that would address their hurts and their needs adequately, in a way that was enjoyable to the children and acceptable to parents and teachers. We wanted to create links for the children about how to care for themselves and negotiate their lives. We wanted to create links between the teachers and children; links from the preschool to the parents and community. The Five Big Ideas used mediums that Aboriginal healers traditionally used—techniques of repetitive rhythmic patterns such as drumming, singing, and touch—powerful and direct ways to counteract the effects of trauma on children.

Ionas Sapountzis was inspired to help the preschool teachers by bringing the Weaving Thoughts concept into their group to begin to "think" about the children as a form of a deeper understanding and a form of knowing the children. His chapter is fascinating as his thought moves toward the notion of "convergent and divergent associations around early childhood trauma." Judy King is the same art therapist who appears in the Mr. Carrots chapter, and her work really enriches the book. His chapter reviews the work of a Weaving Thoughts peer-process group in responding to a child session conducted by Judy King as part of the Gunawirra Project. The Weaving Thoughts process is a method for generating associations around a case or a child, without the peer participants having any background information on the case they respond to.

The aim of this method is not to reach a level of consensus among participants or to generate an understanding that is superior to that of the therapist, nor is it to serve as a supervising session. Rather, its aim is to increase the potential space that exists between preschool teacher and child, and to enable the teacher to become more sensitive to possible blind spots in her working with a child. By virtue of being unfamiliar with the underlying dynamics of the case, the peer participants' associations can only emerge from their own inner dynamics. Their associations thus resemble dream-thinking, in that when they are woven together they can help highlight unconscious dynamics and elements the teacher may not have been aware of. We saw this as a significant chapter because it invites a "thinking about"—thinking about our work with a child, thinking about a child, thinking about the process of what goes on between a child and teacher. We think we will have arrived when we can create similar processes of "thinking about" in all our preschools.

It is appropriate that one of the most significant chapters in the book should come toward the end as it asks "Who cares for the worker, as the worker cares for the child?" The authors of this chapter are Ingo Lambrecht and Aretha Paterson, one a social work student on placement in Gunawirra, the other a psychoanalyst with deep experience in working with autistic and traumatized children. They discuss one of Aretha's sessions with a child traumatized by profound domestic violence in his home just days before his session. Underneath the child's rage is his obvious suffering. The description and analysis of these events enters into the very core of the origins of trauma in the small child. What kind of splitting takes place as he cuts off the traumatizing experience from his usual life experiences? Here is an analysis of trauma in its rawest unprocessed state. This child's acting out of his terror and rage on a toy and his student child therapist affects her deeply. Its effect on her working with this child, and on all those who were to later share the experience, demonstrates the power of trauma to affect the unconscious of all those who are in close contact with traumatized children. This becomes one of the most powerful stories in the book as it lays bare the suffering of all who work with the pain of small children and why so often we as professionals close ourselves off from a pain that is too much to be seen or felt or experienced.

Bringing Aboriginal spirituality to the conclusion of this book is Graham Toomey's sensitive and deeply felt chapter on art as the opening of a door into culture and identity. We in Gunawirra see Graham as representing our soul and as a constant reminder of what we are there for. The meaning with which Graham has imbued his chapter raises us above the ordinary in the human spirit, above the suffering, and allows us to glimpse the true nature of spirituality in the Aboriginal people. We are humbled by this, even as we never cease to be amazed by the giftedness revealed in his artwork.

Last week, as I wrote this, Graham held an art exhibition that was launched by the Governor of New South Wales. It was time for speeches; Graham's wife and children were around him, but we could not find his mother, who was shyly hiding in the next room. The governor refused to begin the speeches and instead went and found her. Hand in hand they stood together, two mothers, two grandmothers, holding hands and applauding her gifted son. I hope in humility that our book approaches the people of this ancient race always with that same deep respect. We salute two grandmothers holding hands, we salute our Aboriginal children, our leaders of the future, and we thank all our Aboriginal people and elders for the ancient culture of this land that they give to us. It is appropriate that Graham's words end this introductory chapter and also stand at the beginning of this book.

> When I do a painting, I know it is my ancestors' spirit not me—their spirit, my hand, painting their stories. Up country, where my people came from, as I paint I hear the children laughing and playing in the stillness near the creek as the water washes down on the rocks. This is not a made-up thing. I can hear them. I think too of how this changed from a happy place to a place of blood and death. We black people all have shame in us, but when I do this painting work I have pride in who I am. I write our stories in paintings—better than in words. The spirits of the children and the spirits of my ancestors are alive in me when I paint.[2]

NOTES

1. Jeffrey Eaton, private communication, 2007.
2. From Norma Tracey and Graham Toomey, "The Sense of Loss and the Search for Meaning," in Michael O'Loughlin, ed., *The Ethics of Remembering and the Consequences of Forgetting: Essays on Trauma, History, and Memory* (Lanham, MD: Rowman & Littlefield, New Imago Series, in press).

Part 1

History and Background

Chapter One

Mirrored Images

The Story of Many Reflected in One Aboriginal Family's Journey

Jackie Stewart and Maria Losurdo

This story is set against the historical context of colonization that has influenced the lives of Aboriginal people in Australia for nearly 250 years, and both the official and unofficial social policy that has enshrined and enforced social control over time. Victoria was the first state in Australia to formally establish such legislation under the Board for the Protection of Aborigines in 1869. Similar legislation was then passed in other states: New South Wales in 1883, Queensland in 1897, Western Australia in 1905, and South Australia in 1911. These boards were progressively empowered to control and direct the lives of Aboriginal people, including the removal of children from their families. In Queensland, where this particular story started, The Aboriginal Protection and Restriction of the Sale of Opium Act allowed the "Chief Protector" to remove local Aboriginal people onto and between reserves, and to hold children in dormitories. From 1939 until 1971 this power was held by the Director of Native Welfare. The director was appointed as the legal guardian of all Aboriginal children, whether or not their parents were living, until 1965. Under this legislation, Aboriginal people were effectively confined to reserves and banned from towns. These reserves were administered by government agencies or missionaries and for Aboriginal people every aspect of life was controlled, including the right to marry, guardianship of children, the right to work outside reserves, and the management of assets.

In this story we follow the journey of just one Aboriginal family and their life experiences over six generations from the late 1800s through the present day. This is a journey of great struggle that reveals the deep wounds caused by the colonization of this country and the social and emotional restrictions, controls, and abuses that have shaped history and changed Aboriginal lives and culture so dramatically.

It is a story mirrored over and over again in one form or another for all Aboriginal families and communities. It is an invisible tattoo at the heart of the thoughts, feelings, and behaviors of each and every Aboriginal person you are likely to meet. Sometimes it is reflected in ongoing trauma and struggle, sometimes in humor and resilience, sometimes in determined achievement and success, and sometimes just in a kind of silent rumbling, a background hum that doesn't really have a name or conscious face.

We ask you to hold not only this family with care and respect, but all Aboriginal people with that same respect as you read these words. To notice where you want to shy away from their pain, where you want to blame or find fault, where you want to minimize or distract yourself. In that noticing try also to reflect on how non-Aboriginal Australians as a whole might be playing a collective part in keeping these stories out of sight and out of mind. In particular you are asked to enter the worlds of the children, as it is perhaps through their eyes that we can learn the most about what they were forced to do to make sense of their lives and to survive, and how this carried into their adult life and then passed onto each new generation.

This journey starts with a little boy named Victor when his life was irrevocably altered at 5 years old, and travels eighty years and beyond through little Rose and others at that same age. What might it have been like for these children and all the others like them in this and other Aboriginal families? Do you have a 5-year-old child in your life? Do you know them well enough to notice where they feel most able to be themselves? Do you marvel at watching them navigate and make sense of the world around them as they grow and learn? Hold to that knowing in your mind as you read about Victor's story and as you go on to learn about his family's journey through the children and adults of the following generations.

The names of the living relatives of this family have been changed, but their stories and experiences are real. Details and all direct quotes have been drawn from interviews with living family members and from official government records from Queensland and New South Wales that was sourced by Link Up Queensland (at www.link-upqld.org.au/) on the family's behalf.

The impetus for telling this story at this time comes from a woman we call Rose, as part of her own journey as an Aboriginal woman making sense of and healing from her own experiences. Over time Rose has turned more and more directly to her cultural pride and identity as the source of that healing. In doing so she has offered the opportunity of this healing to her family and the broader Aboriginal community. Rose told us that she has always felt the presence of her ancestors in her life but only in more recent years has she come to know with certainty who this presence was and how much they have helped her to survive and thrive. She wants to give back to them now by bringing them to life, telling their story and speaking up for them as determinedly as they stayed close to and protected her.

VICTOR DANIEL JOHNSON

Victor Daniel Johnson was born in Forest Vale near Mitchell in Queensland on August 9, 1900. Victor was the son of Ida and Daniel Johnson. Ida was described as a "full blood" Aboriginal woman. Daniel Johnson was described as a "white man," although some paperwork also referred to him as "half caste" Aboriginal. In 1904 Ida and Daniel had a second child, Mabel Johnson.

Sometime during late 1905, at the age of 5, Victor was removed from his family by government authorities from the Office of Protector of Aborigines. Victor was "charged with the offence of being an illegitimate and neglected child" and was taken to the Mitchell watch house, where he was held until July 1906 when he was formally sentenced to seven years' detention at Barambah Industrial School (a juvenile detention center), which was located approximately 500 kilometers (about 310 miles) from Victor's home and family.

After his sentencing, Victor's father Daniel formally petitioned the government, with the assistance of local solicitor George Lethbridge, to have Victor transferred from Barambah to Tufnell Orphanage, which was located 600 kilometers (nearly 373 miles) away from home. Based on this application Victor was transferred to Tufnell Orphanage on October 15, 1906, where he spent the next seven years of his life. Daniel Johnson paid 5 shillings per week to Tufnell Orphanage for Victor's keep until his own death in 1910, at which point he left all his savings with the solicitor for Victor's care until he was 21 years old.

Victor's time at Tufnell Orphanage marked the beginning of his lifelong quest to seek exemption from the Aboriginal Protection and Restriction of the Sale of Opium Act of 1897. This legislation gave the government the power to direct and control the lives of Aboriginal people. Victor's first formal request for exemption was made on his behalf by Solicitor Lethbridge in 1912; this request was denied on the basis of his age. A second request made on his behalf in 1913 was also denied.

In 1913 Victor left Tufnell to work as a farmhand for the local police sergeant in Mitchell. Under that act, Victor's movements and wages continued to be controlled by The Office of Protector for Aborigines. In 1915, Victor's solicitor made a third request for his exemption, this time based on Victor's right to receive a full wage and to have unrestricted access to the money he earned. This application had the support of Victor's employer, who agreed to pay increased wages to Victor if the exemption was granted.

Official documents show that Victor's wages were being held by the Office of the Protector of Aborigines under what was known as a "payment agreement." Under this policy, moneys earned by Aboriginal people were collected by the police and forwarded to the Office of the Protector of Aborigines, who held the funds in bulk accounts. This office would then allocate money to pay for the worker's clothing, lodging, food and medical treatment at its own discretion. In Victor's case, these payments were often withheld or denied, despite formal requests by Victor's solicitor, on the assertion by government officials that these expenses should be coming from the trust fund left by his father.

This third request for exemption was also denied by the Chief Protector of Aborigines, who stated that he "failed to see how Victor was being hampered by the Act or would be benefitted by an exemption."

Victor remained under the control of the Act and continued to work as a station hand, during which time he met and married an Aboriginal woman named Jessie Bowman in 1919. On April 19, 1921, Victor was finally granted formal exemption, nearly ten years after his first application. For this to happen, both Victor and Jessie were forced to give up all connections to their Aboriginal culture, family, and community. Victor's affidavit read: "I do not habitually live with, or associate with, Aboriginal peoples." In response the Office of the Protector of Aborigines said Victor was "a fairly intelligent boy and can write fairly well and is of temperate habits and rarely associates with other Aboriginals."

Once exemption was granted, the Chief Protector of Aborigines handed over the amount of 60 pounds and 6 shillings. In 1921, 60 pounds and 6 shillings would have meant Victor had earned approximately 30 cents per week from 1913–1921 (eight years); today the total amount would be equivalent to about $4,400, or approximately $10.60 per week, according to information at www.rba.gov.au. This was said to be the remaining sum total of Victor's held wages from the eight years of his full-time employment.

We leave Victor's story here for a while to explore a little more about what was happening for his family throughout this time.

DANIEL JOHNSON, VICTOR'S FATHER

Not much more is known about Victor's father, Daniel Johnson. We know he was sometimes known as Anthony Chippenall, who was described as "half caste," and that he was born in Ballarat, Victoria, in 1847. Daniel came to Queensland in 1880 where he worked as a laborer and scalper (someone who caught and skinned animals and sold the fur). Daniel died at the age of 63 in

1910 from what appeared to be a heart attack while working. It also appears that Daniel and Ida went separate ways after Victor was removed from the family. From Victor's own story we know that Daniel dedicated the last years of his life to support his son and that he left all his savings in the hands of a solicitor for his ongoing care.

IDA JOHNSON, VICTOR'S MOTHER

Victor's mother Ida, also referred to as Ada, was born in 1871 and belonged to the Kongabula tribal group. Her traditional lands would have been in the region of the Carnarvon Ranges in Southern Queensland. This was about 250 kilometers (155 miles) from Mitchell, where she worked as a domestic servant and scalper.

Only two years after Victor had been forcibly removed, police came to the camp where Ida was living and threatened to take her 3-year-old daughter, Mabel. Ida became very distressed. Police documents state that she said "If anyone wants to take away my child they will have to kill me." The police left without taking further action at that time. Less than a year later, on December 15, 1908, Mabel was removed and sentenced to Barambah Industrial School for the same charge as Victor, that of "being an illegitimate and neglected child."

Ida married an Aboriginal man named Prince Alfred under tribal lore. Ida had a total of four children in her care at that time: Nancy, Dolly, Amis, and Cyril. It is not known how many of the older children were Ida's by birth, and how many were other peoples' children that she had taken into her own care. Ida went on to have one child with Prince Alfred, named Prince Albert. In 1913, all five children, by then aged between 22 months and 11 years, were also removed for what official records state as "their own care and protection."

In June 1914 Ida was arrested by police and officially charged "on suspicion of being of unsound mind" and committed to a mental institution where she remained for an unknown period of time before returning to her husband in Mitchell.

In 1921, the same year Victor was granted exemption, Ida—now 50 years old—was formally removed by government authorities from Mitchell and taken to Taroom Aboriginal Reserve, 255 kilometers (about 158 miles) away, because she was said to be "destitute and unable to obtain employment." Soon after this, Ida was readmitted to the Willowburn Asylum in Toowoomba. It is unclear how long Ida spent in the asylum or when she died, but records show Toowoomba as her place of residence at the time of her death.

MABEL JOHNSON, VICTOR'S SISTER

Mabel Johnson, Victor's little sister, appears to have spent her entire sentence at Barambah, and in fact her whole life, living on and around the Cherbourg mission, where Barambah was located. It is known that Mabel's first two babies died as infants and that she went on to have four more children. There is no information as to what contact Mabel had with her parents after her removal, or why Daniel didn't also advocate for his daughter. It is also not known if Daniel knew about Mabel's whereabouts, or if he was still in contact with Ida by the time Mabel was removed. It is known, however, that Victor called his firstborn child Flora Mabel, so it appears Victor did remember his sister with some fondness. Mabel died in 1975 at the age of 71 from cancer of the uterus.

VICTOR'S ADULT YEARS

Returning now to Victor's journey, we come back to 1921, when he was granted exemption. Victor and his first wife Jessie were together for eight years, during which time they had three children: Flora, Victor (later known as Arthur Miller), and Judy.

In 1927 Victor left Jessie and began a relationship with a woman named Annie Turner, whom he later married. Victor and Annie had at least nine children together and lived together in Augathella, Queensland, until at least 1941. This information was recorded in official documents relating to child endowment entitlements, in which the family is described as living in a "well-kept hut," and which stated that "the father maintains the family by doing station work and is nearly always in employment."

The next known account of Victor's whereabouts was from the mid-1950s, when his granddaughter Ellen remembers going to visit a property in Queensland where there were "lots of kids" and meeting a man who she was told was her "grandfather." This was the first and only time they met. Police records confirm Victor lived in the Charleville District in Queensland until at least April 1958.

By 1959 Victor had moved to Walgett in New South Wales. By moving states, Victor lost his Queensland exemption status and found himself again under government control, this time under the New South Wales Aboriginal Welfare Act and Regulations. Victor engaged a solicitor to act on his behalf to now apply for a New South Wales exemption. Authorities questioned Victor's eligibility for exemption because of his alcohol use. Investigations were made with the Queensland police and past employers, and the Queensland Native Affairs Director found Victor had four previous charges of "gambling and drunkenness" in Queensland between 1951 and 1958, although he was never convicted of these charges. Police at the time recommended that Victor's application for exemption be declined because he "was addicted to liquor and encouraged other Aboriginals to drink and gamble" and that he "had little to no knowledge of financial matters and although he had been afforded every opportunity he had failed in the upbringing of his family." His application for exemption was declined. From this time we lose track of Victor's life. His living family are still searching for information on the remaining years of his life and the date and place of his death. Perhaps the greatest irony of all is that Victor's fight for exemption in an effort to protect him and his family would later leave him at odds with the broader social movement by Aboriginal people for recognition and respect. This is a legacy shared by many Aboriginal families, in which it became a shameful family secret to have a past family member who had denied their culture.

JESSIE BOWMAN, VICTOR'S FIRST WIFE

A related family story from these times comes from records on the life of Victor's first wife, Jessie. In 1942 Jessie was living in a little town called Blackall, in Queensland, with her then teenage children. At that time her son with Victor, known by that time as Arthur Miller, had been drafted into World War II, and Jessie was writing to the Director of Native Affairs on his behalf. Her exact words have been taken from a copy of her neatly handwritten letter still held in the State Archives in Queensland:

> 11th of September 1942
>
> Dear Sir,
> Just a note to ask you does this war service strictly apply to full blood and half caste Aboriginals? I am a half cast woman with two grown up daughters and one son, and he is my only supporter as I am not in the best of health. I also have another draw on hand and that is my eldest daughter who is more often under a doctor than able to work But never the less it seems unfair to me as only a few miles different is another town there are dark people there, with sons about seven or eight of them, and they tell me they don't have to go, so why is it I am not allowed my one and only son? Why is it he has to go to active service and fight for something he has no rights to, nor will he ever have, if he and the rest of us should live to the next century? Please let me know why he is getting raw deal and not left to look after the ones he loves so dear?
>
> It is not only him in the coloured race, why are they to go to war? Anyone of the black people of the country have to always take back seats, be given all the left overs, be barred from most theatres or an amusement. We one and all have had the colour line drawn when it came we might like a little fun, but the black is looked down on as the dirty brute. So why not then be the same now when all the whites are in trouble? The want all the boys of my kind to help,

> well I think it should be thought back to all notable days such as Captain Cook days.
>
> I do hope you will see my side of the story and grant me my dear and only son, Arthur Miller, from this awful thing they call war which takes but never returns.
>
> (Jessie) Ellen J Miller
> Mother of Arthur
> P.S. My son is only 18 years of age.

The first response sent from the Director of Native Affairs to the Protector of Aboriginals in relation to Jessie's letter states: "I shall be glad if you will cause an investigation to be made into the circumstances of this woman's position and furnished with any desired recommendation. It would be advisable to have Mrs Miller informed that her tone of letter is not conductive to sympathetic treatment of her case and in any further correspondence she would be advised to moderate the expression of opinion. Seemingly, her views are those of an agitated mother, but if the investigating officer is of contrary opinion he should advise his views on this also."

Six weeks later the Director of Native Affairs sent his final response directly to Jessie: "Enquiries have been made into the matters raised in your letter of the 11th of September and you are advised that this office is not prepared to make any move with respect to the 'Exemption from Military Service' of your son Arthur Miller. This office is satisfied that you are not living under any disabilities comparable with any other citizens of this State."

THE NEXT FIVE GENERATIONS

From here the family's journey moves over 80 years through to the current day as you are introduced one by one to the lives and voices of Victor's daughter Judy, granddaughter Ellen, great-granddaughter Rose, and great-great-granddaughter Laura. The life experiences of these women, as their lives carry on from Victor's experiences and those of previous generations, provides a very personal and often shocking window into the layered and ongoing characteristics and impacts of intergenerational trauma. Even though this is just one family's story, it is paralleled by many thousands of Aboriginal families from that time to today. Every Aboriginal family has a Victor, Ida, Daniel, Mabel, and a Jessie at the root of their psyche and heart. Every Aboriginal family today lives not only with the troubles and trauma of their current lives but also with the troubles and trauma of the lives of all those who suffered before them, whether they have access to those stories and memories or not.

VICTOR'S DAUGHTER JUDY

Victor's daughter Judy was born in 1925 in Tambo, Queensland. She was 2 years old when her mother Jessie left Victor and moved her to live with Henry Miller, where she became known as Judy Miller.

Judy and her siblings never attended school but did receive education through home schooling from her mother, Jessie. Police reports from 1938 record a number of incidences of domestic violence between Henry and Jessie. These documents also reported close monitoring by the Protection Board as to whether Judy and her siblings would be allowed to stay with their parents.

Living family members remember stories of the family continuously moving to avoid the children being removed. In these stories Henry is remembered as a strongly identified Aboriginal man who always seemed to know just a few days in advance when the government authorities were coming to the camps to take children. As part of these safeguards the children were never allowed to talk about anything related to Aboriginal identity, culture, connections, or family.

In 1942, Judy, aged 17, married Irving Plummer, a white man thirty years her senior. They went on to have six children between 1944 and 1952. From all accounts Irving was a devoted father and husband, but in 1960 Judy took her children and left her husband because her 16-year-old son was in trouble with the police for stealing and Irving thought he should be punished under the law. One can only imagine what this meant for Judy, who had lived her whole life in fear of the police and the risk they posed to Aboriginal children and families. Even though Judy never returned to Irving, he continued to support her and the children financially.

Judy went on to have a relationship with an extremely violent man named Fred, who emotionally, physically, and sexually abused Judy, her children, and then her grandchildren over the next thirty or more years. Judy became an alcoholic in her late thirties, at which time she also took on the care of her baby grandson, who was the child of her 15-year-old daughter. Her daughter was sent to Brisbane to have the baby and was given a false birth certificate by her mother to stop the baby being taken from her at birth. The year 1974 was one of great loss for Judy, when her now 25-year-old son was killed in a horrific car accident, and with her ex-husband Irving dying three months later, and her mother Jessie dying a few months after that.

Between 1982 and 1994, after her own children had grown up and left home, Judy had the care of up to fourteen grandchildren at any given time. From 1994 to 2005 her great-grandchildren also came in and out of her care. Even though the laws regarding the government's control over Aboriginal peoples' lives had changed considerably over time, Judy still lived in mortal fear of her grandchildren, and her great grandchildren being taken. She never allowed them to associate with Aboriginal children or people, and she never talked about her Aboriginal culture or childhood history. Her living grandchildren have memories of her often telling them "You're not allowed to play with the blacks from Mount Druitt."

After her grandchildren left home, Judy cared for her abusive partner until 2002, as he spent the last years of his life slowly dying from cancer. Judy herself passed away in hospital in May 2012. She was 87 years old.

VICTOR'S GRANDDAUGHTER ELLEN

Victor's granddaughter Ellen was born on the July 7, 1950, in Longreach, Queensland; she was the daughter of Judy and Irving. One of six children, Ellen was the fifth child of four boys and two girls.

Ellen's childhood was filled with significant loss and suffering. She was close to her father and missed him greatly when the family separated, spending time living between her parents over the next years. Ellen's mother moved around a lot, sometimes living in caravans or in the local pub, sometimes moving back in with her own grandmother, Jessie. The children were often sent to different families and friends when her mother was, at times, virtually homeless.

When Ellen was about 14 years old her life became a living nightmare, as her mother's boyfriend Fred became more and more abusive toward her mother, to her siblings, and to Ellen herself. Also hanging over her head during this time was her mother's ongoing fear of her children being taken and the enforced silence and disconnection from her Aboriginal identity and culture: "Mum never talked about being Aboriginal and we weren't allowed to ask questions about it."

Ellen's adult life consisted of poverty, constantly moving from place to place, ongoing threats of having her own children removed, and ongoing domestic violence. In all Ellen had six children to three different men.

In 1965, when Ellen was 15, she met her first partner, John, and had her first child. The couple was together for just a few years. Ellen said John went away for work a lot and they didn't see each other much, eventually drifting apart. But John and other family members appear to have been caring and supportive of Ellen, which enabled her to avoid her first baby being removed:

> I had my first baby at Longreach hospital. The Matron at the hospital wouldn't let me see the baby and was trying to get me to sign adoption papers and I wasn't allowed to leave unless I did. Two weeks later my brother Ronnie came to the hospital to see me and demanded to know which baby was mine. At first they tried to stop him but he said he would take all the babies if they didn't given him the baby, so they gave him the baby and he walked us both out of the hospital, I was still wearing the hospital gown.

> Then when the baby was just 6 weeks old the police came to the house to try and take him away again. The only way I could stop them was to agree to give the baby to his father and sign him over legally. I agreed and John took the baby, but after the police left he brought him back to me. We still had to go through with the paperwork signing the baby over to his father, but then John filled in extra paperwork to put him back in my care.

Ellen had four more children with her next partner, Graham, who she met in 1969. Graham was emotionally and physically violent toward Ellen and the children for the next five years. Her escape was able to happen only when Graham went to jail in 1974. During this same year Ellen lost her brother, her father, and her grandmother.

In 1975 Ellen's life took a further turn for the worse when she began a relationship with a man named Robert, with whom she had her sixth child. Robert was a violent alcoholic who emotionally, physically, and sexually abused Ellen and all the children. Even after they separated, he continued to abuse Ellen and the children. This abuse continued for more than twenty years and went on to include grandchildren as well.

Ellen made numerous attempts to leave Robert and tried to get help from the police on many occasions but was only ever met with mockery and blame. From an account in her own words Ellen talks about her attempts to leave Robert and her desperate attempts to get the children away from him. This situation ended up in her relinquishing the children's care to her mother in 1982, although this did not ultimately stop the ongoing abuse.

> When I left Robert we were living on a stud farm at Calliope, Queensland. I moved to Gladstone and stayed at my brother's place. It was crowded, as Bert and Sue had 7 children (including their adult child) and then me with my own 6 children. My oldest son wanted to go back to the farm where he worked so I let him, about 6 weeks later the stud farm owner, Doc, offered him a job so he could train him as a jockey.
>
> We were at Bert's for nearly 12 months when [the] housing commission came through and we moved in. I had all the furniture except a bed for me by then. My other son [was] already in high school and I only had to change the girls' school. It was about 2 weeks later the school had rang to say Robert had picked the girls up from school. It was a Friday afternoon and he kept them till Sunday. I went to the police station and they reckon they couldn't do anything. Then he started picking them up Wednesday morning. I went to the police again they told me they couldn't do anything because I was drunk, I asked them to take a blood test to see if I was drunk but was told I would be drunk by the time the children got out of school. This was about 11a.m.
>
> I also got AVO papers against him but this was a waste of time. At that time I would only drink when I went to the raffles for 2 hours and it would be lucky to be 3 middies. When I did go to the raffles Sue would come over and mind the children. One night Sue rang me to say that Robert had locked her out. So I got a cab home and as soon as I walked in the door Robert slammed it

> on Sue. The next thing I remember is Sue and my son was pulling me back, I had a butchers knife in my hand its tip had broken skin in Robert's guts. (From that day to this I still don't remember getting the butchers knife.) I realised that I was at breaking point, so I went to the doctor and he put me on Serepax [oxazepam]. But a few weeks later mum turned up for a visit so I borrowed $4500 [in Australian dollars] and put mum and the 5 children on the next train back to Sydney. I thought that I had solved the problem but Robert had beaten me to Sydney. Robert was down there within two weeks and started causing trouble for mum by ringing children's services on her. It took me longer to get there because I had to pack everything and send it down and I also had to sell everything I had in the house.

The children shifted back and forth between staying with their grandmother and periods of time with their mother for the remainder of their childhood. Ellen became an alcoholic in her later thirties and went on to have a series of relationships with other violent men. Ellen maintained connections to her children in varying degrees. At times relationships were very strained, especially during court custody proceedings relating to her youngest daughter's disclosure of sexual abuse in 1991. Ellen's oldest son committed suicide in 2000 as a result of the abuse he had suffered as a child, which prompted other siblings coming forward to make formal charges against Robert, all of which further fractured the already strained relationships in the family.

Ellen is now in her sixties and lives in a housing commission complex outside of Sydney. She stopped drinking a number of years ago and has re-established relationships with some of her children and grandchildren. She also reconnected with her mother Judy, caring for her for a number of years before she died. Ellen lives with a number of serious health issues including cirrhosis of the liver and diabetes, which require ongoing medical intervention and monitoring. Ellen has spent a number of years reconnecting to her Aboriginal culture and identity, finding out about her ancestral connections to the Carpet Snake Clan of the Kongabula Tribe and Country, as well as sourcing other family history documents. She has passed this information on to her children, who have extended on it through their own research. Ellen has been very supportive of her family's story being told in this book as she feels it could be helpful to other families who have been through the same thing.

VICTOR'S GREAT-GRANDDAUGHTER ROSE

Victor's great-granddaughter Rose was born on February 14, 1978, in Blackwater, Queensland, and is the daughter of Ellen and Robert, an Aboriginal man from Queensland. Robert was a violent alcoholic. Rose had two brothers and three sisters on Ellen's side and two sisters on Robert's side who lived with a different mother.

The first four years of Rose's life were spent moving from farm to farm between Blackwater and Roma in Queensland, with Robert following work and avoiding the police. Rose's early years were spent living in tents and campsites, her crib consisting of a forty-four gallon drum cut in half, and later sleeping in makeshift beds on the side of the road or in the car. Rose's first recollection of sexual assault from Robert was at the age of 2; this continued over the next thirteen years. Rose remembers Robert being physically abusive toward Ellen from a very early age: "When I was about 18 months old I remember my mum holding me in her arms and Robert punching her in the face." When asked about this, Ellen remembered an argument over challenging Robert for being drunk and driving the car dangerously.

In 1982 when Rose was 4 years old, she and four of her siblings were removed from Ellen by her grandmother Judy, whom she had never met before, and taken to Sydney, New South Wales. "I remember being scared, and crying on the train, my brother was holding me close to him, I was so scared and I didn't know what was going to happen." After a short stay in Kings Cross, Judy was offered a housing commission property in Penrith, west of Sydney. This house was initially occupied by Judy, her partner Fred, and the five children, but over time there would be up to fourteen children living there, and many other adult relatives coming and going.

Rose's first memories in Sydney were of racism and discrimination, as neighbours from surrounding streets took out a petition to have the family removed from the neighbourhood for being "too black." Rose remembers asking her grandmother, "Do I have to move? I'm not black like the other kids, I've got light skin."

Over the next five years Rose would cry many nights, missing her mother, and only seeing her a few times in this period. Robert on the other hand was a regular visitor at her home with her grandmother.

> I remember Robert often coming to the house and staying overnight. He would come to the house with a bribe of either money or alcohol for my Nan. Each time he would choose which child's bed he was going to share. It was an unspoken fear running through all us kids on who would be suffering that night.
>
> But this is only part of what was happening at that time. Nan's partner Fred would give my Nan money to go to the pub every Friday night so he could be alone with us kids. He did what he wanted to us. He also took money off at least one other man and then gives me to that man who hurt me too. I was about 4 or 5 years old at the time. These experiences continued for many years. I knew my Nan wasn't doing the right thing letting it happen, but somewhere I also knew that because of her us kids got to stay together and I really appreciated her for that.

Over the next twelve years Rose moved about twenty times between and in NSW, Victoria, Queensland, and the Northern Territory. By the time she left school at the age of 14, she had been to more than eight different primary schools, and thirteen different high schools. At each move Robert would follow the family, as would his abuse, along with the abuse from a series of her mother's boyfriends. Rose shared some specific recollections from this time in her life.

> In 1987 mum and her current partner, Kurt, came to the house while Judy was out and packed all us kids and our clothes into a black station wagon and we moved to Melbourne. We were there about twelve months. Kurt was really violent and would bash up mum. Robert arrived soon after too, and kept doing what he'd always done. I changed schools a few times there and then we headed back up to Queensland until Kurt tried to attack my sister with a broken bottle, when mum moved us all back to Nan's place.

By the time high school started for Rose her grades had dropped, her behaviour had become extreme and sometimes violent, and she became very disconnected from people.

> I loved it when I first started school, I loved learning and I did really well, straight A's all the time, but by the time I got to high school my grades were well below average and I would verbally and physically abuse teachers and other students, I left in year 9. It took me many years to find my love of learning again, which didn't happen until my late twenties when I went back to school at TAFE [Technical and Further Education] to study welfare and community services. Since then I've gone on to do lots of other courses at both Certificate IV and diploma level. I am back to getting mostly distinctions which means so much to me. Lately I've been thinking about going to university.

In 1990, when Rose was 14, her oldest brother paid for her to come and live with him and his family in Darwin. Rose hadn't seen much of her brother since she was 4 years old as he had already left home before the other children moved to Sydney with their Nan. Rose told her brother and his wife and someone at school what had been happening to her. It was at this time that Rose's brother told her he had also suffered sexual abuse from Robert before the family was separated. No formal action took place following the report made to the school. The living situation in Darwin broke down, and Rose moved back to Sydney. Unable to stay with her grandmother, or her mother, or her now young adult sisters, she ended up living with Robert. By early 1991, after changing schools several more times, concerned relatives came and took Rose to live with them in Orange, New South Wales. Rose again disclosed the sexual abuse to a school teacher at her new school. This time a formal child protection report was made. A few weeks later Rose came back to Sydney for the holidays and ended up living back at Robert's after her sister's pleading insistence that she come home.

Several weeks later officers from the Department of Community Services came to the house and took statements from Rose and her sister who also confirmed the abuse. Rose was left in the house for a further month until police came to take her to her mother's house. During this time Robert put pressure on Rose to stay silent by leaving large knives in her room, on her bed, under her pillow and in her bathroom. All this was put in Rose's police statement for court. No finding could be made on the issue of abuse as family members would not back up Rose's story; however the judge did hand down a decision that Rose must not continue to live with Robert.

After the hearing all of Rose's family members left, as did the child protection workers, leaving Rose alone waiting outside the courthouse. After a number of hours her sister came back to collect her and took her to live with her mother in an already crowded house. A few months later Rose left her mother's care and went back to live with her grandmother and her abusive partner Fred. By this time Rose had left school, was looking for work, and receiving a payment from Centrelink. It was also at this time that Rose first accessed counselling, which she paid for herself.

In 1994 Rose met Brett, a 31-year-old man who offered her an escape from the world in which she was living. Brett had three children not much younger than Rose when she moved in with the family and took on their full-time care. Two years later Rose fell pregnant with her first child. This became an important emotional turning point, about which Rose said, "I now had a purpose in my world for the first time in my life and I knew that I would protect my kids from the life I had endured."

The next eighteen years of Rose's life were spent in an often disrupted and sometimes violent relationship, caring for her three stepchildren and then three children of her own. The situation was dramatically fueled by conflict with Brett's mother, who featured strongly in their lives and who constantly voiced her racist views about how "all Aboriginal people were lazy, they were drunks, and they were all drug addicts and would steal from anyone."

Rose faced many hardships during these years. The older three children were allowed to speak and act however they liked toward Rose, and the eldest son could bring alcohol, drugs, and friends to "party" at the house against Rose's wishes. This often triggered past traumas for Rose, and she would swing from being very angry to sinking further into depression. Brett became more and more absent from the family, unable to deal with the conflict between Rose and his mother, leaving Rose to deal with the escalating behavior of the troubled older children and the demands of her own young family. As Brett's presence decreased, his mother's involvement in the family increased, as did the constant degrading and criticism of Rose and her parenting. When Rose was pregnant with her third child, Brett started an affair with Rose's sister. He moved out for a period of time but then moved back again and Brett and Rose reestablished their relationship. The cyclic buildup and explosions of conflict, violence, and other forms of abuse continued and were interspersed with more stable periods of less conflict.

> Brett never used drugs or alcohol but he would get very angry at me and the kids, he would yell and say really degrading things to me all the time, nothing me or the kids did or said was ever right. And even though Brett's income was pretty high, most of the money was spent on motorbikes and cars and money available for food was really strictly budgeted. And even when I got a victim's compensation payout for the abuse from Robert, all this went into Brett's car purchases too.
>
> And there were other things too, like sometimes in the mornings before Brett would go to work, he would have sex with me while I was asleep, but I'd learnt to block out these memories for such a long time I just continued to do it with Brett, got by just kind of pretending it never happened.

In November 2000 when Rose was 22 years old her oldest brother committed suicide due to the impacts of his own childhood trauma from sexual abuse. The deep grief and distress of this experience galvanized the determination of Rose and one of her sisters to seek out justice. Together they walked into a local police station and gave joint statements about Robert's ongoing abuse. This prompted a formal investigation with the police taking statements from everyone in the family, including the extended family.

It took three years for the charges to get to court; in all, five family members came forward with personal stories of abuse. Three of these cases went on to court stage, each was conducted separately. In the first case Robert took the stand to defend himself against charges of the sexual abuse of his grandson. The court case was conducted quickly and he was found guilty on all charges. The second court case took much longer; Robert again denied all charges but this time was instructed not to take the stand. Rose spent ten days being cross-examined by Robert's solicitor. The failure to prove the abuse in the earlier court case, when she was 14 years old, was used to discredit her testimony and resulted in a finding of not guilty. In the third court case Robert pleaded guilty to abusing Rose's sister, for which he was convicted and sent to jail. Robert has since been released but no one in the family knows of his current whereabouts.

Rose left her relationship with Brett in 2010. She has moved on to set up a home of her own for her three children and works in the community services sector, where her role is focused specifically on supporting the Aboriginal community.

VICTOR'S GREAT-GREAT GRANDDAUGHTER LAURA

Victor's great-great granddaughter Laura was born at Nepean Hospital in Penrith, New South Wales, on March 27, 1996. Laura's mother had just turned 18 and her dad was 33. Laura had two half-brothers aged 12 and 5, and a half-sister aged 11. She went on to have a younger sister and brother.

In many ways, Laura's life was quite different from her past generations. Neither of her parents drank and her mother Rose had made very conscious and active choices to protect her from the things that she had herself gone through as a child. This included disconnecting from much of her extended family, never leaving her children alone with anyone, and never withholding the truth from them. Unlike the children in the broader family tree who continue to suffer trauma to this day, these actions had the effect of dramatically increasing resilience and protective factors for Laura and her younger siblings. These were not sufficient to fully protect Laura, but they did mark a significant shift in the level of trauma suffered, how it was dealt with, and ultimately the depth of harm that was caused.

The issues of greatest distress in Laura's life have revolved around ongoing family conflict and disruption, periods of domestic violence, and the confusion involved in confronting racism at a family and social level.

Laura lived in a household filled with the conflict of a blended family, and with older siblings carrying the traumatic impacts of their earlier lives. She was also witness to her father's verbal and at times physical abuse toward her mother from an early age. This was compounded by the confusion caused by her father's affair and significant conflict in her broader family network. One incident that Laura said she has never forgotten is the time her dad asked her to lie to her mum:

> I remember when I was 6 and my dad took me with my nan (his mum) to McDonalds. When we arrived, there was a relative and her two children, and my dad asked me to lie to my mum about spending time with another woman and her children. He said to me "If you tell your mum you won't be able to play with the kids again and I will get yelled at by mummy, you don't want daddy to get into trouble do you?" I did not understand the concept of my dad having an affair at that age but I did understand lying and I know mum always said to me nothing is worse than the lie you tell me. So when dad took me home I told mum everything, my dad was so angry at me and there was a big fight in our house, [but] my mum said to me "Laura, no matter what happens you are not to blame, you did the right thing telling me the truth."

Laura had moved houses seven times by the time she was 9 years old, which also included several changed schools. During this period the family spent some time living with her grandmother on her dad's side, periods that were particularly volatile. Laura remembers her grandmother making constant comments about how "all Aboriginal people are drunks, they don't like to work, they are lazy, they all steal" and the fights this would cause—her mother getting angry and defending herself, her father yelling at everyone in the house, Laura herself never really knowing what was happening or what it meant for her own identity.

Laura's first memory of racism, outside that of her grandmother's opinions, was from her first year in high school in 2008. Her science teacher at the time was addressing the class about Aboriginal people and she said "Aboriginal people get everything for free and the government are always giving handouts." Laura stood up in front of the whole class and said, "I am Aboriginal and my mum doesn't get anything for free, my mum and dad both work." The teacher sent Laura to the principal's office for being disrespectful. The principal then called Rose to the school to deal with Laura's "bad behaviour." When Rose confronted the teacher, she denied being racist and said Laura had misunderstood the discussion, but after that the teacher would make Laura sit at the back of the class. After a number of similar incidents Rose moved Laura to a different school.

Laura had a better experience at her new school. When she was 13 she started working part-time at McDonald's and other local fast-food outlets. After completing year 10, Laura left school and increased her part-time work.

Shortly after leaving school, Laura experienced a sexual assault from a boy her own age in a date-rape situation that involved her being set up by a girlfriend at the boy's request. Laura was distraught and rang her mum who came and got her straightaway. After comforting and reassuring Laura, Rose encouraged her to make a police statement, which she did with both her mother and her father's support. Rose also arranged counselling for Laura and supported her to move through her distress at her own pace as she reestablished her normal daily life and work activities. The boy was not convicted of the crime, but Laura came away from this experience feeling heard, believed, and supported; all the ingredients needed for genuine healing and moving on.

Later that same year things at home came to crisis point on a night that Laura remembers vividly:

> It was a Thursday night and mum was planning our weekly outing dinner at the local tavern. When mum arrived home from work Dad was yelling at her about cooking chicken for dinner, [and] she said "We always go to tavern on Thursdays I am not cooking tonight, but if you don't want to come, there is chicken there if you want to cook it." Dad got real angry and started yelling at mum about cooking him dinner: "I have been at work all day and have to cook my own f&%king dinner, while you piss off to the pub." Mum reacted angry as well, [but] after about five minutes of yelling mum went into the kitchen to start cooking, Dad snatched the knife from mum and told her to get out of the kitchen . . . Mum said "I am cooking dinner for you." He then pushed the knife

> into the side of her arm and told her to get the f&%k out of the kitchen. When mum walked away from the kitchen she said something under her breath and Dad ran and grabbed at her, I went to jump in between them and my dad pushed me into the wall and called me names. Yelling at me "Your mother is good for nothing."

After this last incident, Laura's parents separated completely, and while arguments and conflict between her parents continued things at home became a lot less stressful for Laura after her father moved out of the house. She is still in contact with her father and while he doesn't contribute to the children's ongoing care in any way he has supported her to buy a secondhand car, which he helped get on the road by doing the repair work needed to make it roadworthy.

Laura continues to live at home playing a significant role in helping to take care of her younger siblings now that her mother works longer hours to support the family. She has had a number of jobs since leaving school and is currently exploring her options for further study to increase her future employment prospects.

GENERATIONAL LAYERS OF TRAUMA

The story of this one family highlights the harsh realities of the impacts of colonization on Aboriginal peoples and their culture for the past almost 250 years. It gives a window into the devastating and sometimes brutal conditions that were forced on Victor and all those like him. The struggle to stay alive, to keep your family together, and to somehow hold onto your cultural, spiritual, and even human identity when that is what put you in danger. These are tangible fragments of the lasting impacts of an earlier world, where the building of a new nation was based on an unquestioned belief that Aboriginal people were somehow less than human, and where "breeding out the black" was the proudly articulated goal set to assimilate Aboriginal people into a "civilized" society.

This story also highlights the critical issues and lasting pain that need to be spoken, heard, believed, and understood for collective healing. A healing that needs to start with developing a deeper understanding of an experience that has cycled and expanded child after child, adult after adult in each new generation. A genuinely felt appreciation of what it must have been like for Victor and all those that followed, as a child and then as an adult, to experience these kinds of assaults on their world and personhood, trauma after trauma, disappointment after disappointment, heartbreak after heartbreak, shame after shame. Rose described it this way:

> There are so many traumas mixed up through the generations it's hard to know which trauma belongs in which generation and then by the time you get to the present day the trauma has become that thick there's no clear path to move through. With all this going on, when you don't even really know it is going on, where do you get to learn who you really are? Where do you get to learn about how to be a parent? How do you access that level of connection when the most important thing on your mind is just surviving . . . when your spirit has been so broken, when you're carrying so much pain you can only think from a state of crisis?

Each layer of this story reveals more and more of the compounded nature and the deepening pain and confusion of transgenerational trauma. A significant aspect of this complexity can be found in the shifting relationships between cultural identity and survival. For Victor, the ongoing fight for exemption played a big part in keeping his family safe and keeping his own children from being removed. But this also meant he was forced to give up all visible connections to his Aboriginal identity, to his family, friends, culture, spirit, and ancestors. To a large extent Victor achieved what he wanted for his family, but by making this choice he was also making a choice to take these things away from his children and future generations. This became an added shame and confusion for his descendants, one that current living relatives still struggle to defend and regain to this day. An irony is bought into sharp contrast when comparing Victor and Rose's personal experience of identity. In Victor's time, he needed to carry an "exemption card" that would in theory allow him to live outside of segregation and social control and be part of accepted "white" society for the well-being of his family. In current times, Rose lives and works in a world where she too is asked to provide paperwork about her identity, but now it is to prove that she is Aboriginal.

It is true that for Rose and some of her family things are starting to turn around, but even within this one family there are many who continue to suffer greatly. Adults and children still living with the unresolved effects of abuse, violence, poor mental health, and drug and alcohol addictions, babies and children at risk of being removed, and families living with poor health, unemployment, and poverty.

While all people know what it is like to suffer and experience loss, this culturally shared experience of loss and the multiple layering and thickening of trauma over time has had a distinctive impact on Aboriginal people as a whole. It has caused a kind of collective broken heart that sits underneath current daily life regardless of how known these stories are to the individual. This experience continues to be compounded by the ongoing inequalities and injustices embedded in the broader Australian psyche, and social systems that also continue to exist.

The complex and ongoing nature of these issues needs to be more deeply understood for lasting healing and change to take place for both Aboriginal people and Australian society as a whole. If these broader understandings do not become more fully embedded in our efforts to respond to the individual struggles and distress of Aboriginal families, we risk deepening these wounds rather than healing them by continuing to focus on individual circumstance.

From an Aboriginal perspective, these stories remind us that this shame we carry, whether we have a name for it or not, is not our shame, and that it should not define who we are or who we can be. From a non-Aboriginal perspective, we are offered the invitation to consider what role we might unwittingly play personally and collectively in keeping these painful stories at arm's length at the expense of Aboriginal peoples' right and need to be heard.

THE HEALING POWER OF STORYTELLING

The telling of this story involved not only pain and tears but also a window into itself. This journey has allowed some family members to make new sense of and talk about their experiences in ways not so weighed down by personal shame, guilt, and blame. A fundamental shift in family dynamics took place that saw older family members start to share stories of culture and life experiences with younger family members in ways that had never happened before. It is a journey that has offered a place of deeper respect, appreciation, and knowing within the family, which is perhaps best described by Rose herself:

> When starting this storytelling journey with my living relatives I was terrified, bringing up and naming past and current pain and suffering, I didn't know what would happen, or what it would mean for my family's future. Then as we started turning the pages of history and inspecting then reinspecting what was happening at that time for each generation, a new understanding came out about what was happening for them personally, what was being carried from the generation before, and what was happening socially that impacted decisions and choices. By bringing a generational view to the family it has given us access to a place of healing we had not been able to see or reach before. For me, this came by seeing the courage it took my ancestors to stand up and protect their children, even when political and social odds were against them. It's helped me see that it's not just pain that has been passed down but also survival, courage, resilience, strength . . . reminding me that I am part of a deep cultural connection that has lived on for over 40,000 years before any of this ever happened.
>
> I know I have been blessed to be able to find and hold onto my connection to spirit, to land, to ancestors, and at knowing that this has not been taken away and that our ancestors were waiting for the right time to bring spirit back to our family. Last night I could hear the Ancestors singing to me, strong women voices as I drove down the road. I stop and look at the sky. I am shown seven

women: Ida, Mabel, Jessie, Judy, Ellen, Rose, and Laura gathering at sunset surrounded by the darkness of storm clouds that couldn't touch them. They were singing and celebrating in ceremony. The cloud formation changed to what I can only describe as a protective ceremony circle. My heart filled with honour knowing that sharing our family's story is healing not only generations past but also bringing the possibility of healing to children today and tomorrow.

Chapter Two

Gunawirra and the Gunawirra Trauma Project

A Background

Norma Tracey

GUNAWIRRA

Gunawirra means "the invisible seed from which all creation occurs." It is the name we chose for our organization, which was conceived in the minds of our Aboriginal elders and professional people for many years before we formed ourselves into an organization. We spent that first day we met asking ourselves, "How can a race who had customs of communal care for their little ones and all kinds of protective boundaries now find themselves in this awful and undeniable situation?" We knew that this people's traumatic history had had such a severe impact on present-day Aboriginal parents that they could not always deliver what they wanted for their children. We were aware that Aboriginal mothers and fathers, like all parents, want the best for their children. What we didn't know and what we may need generations to properly understand is this: If we were the perpetrators, how could we now join with them to become the healers? Our very naming of the shame was in a sense an opening of the wound. How could we—caring professionals, caring elders—translate our work into something real and meaningful? Continually facing what many of our white colleagues denied—the suicides, unending domestic violence, and pedophilia (committed not just by white and Aboriginal men, but also by Aboriginal boys now preying on children younger than themselves, just as they had been preyed on). We could see and hear the disastrous results of years of racism, subjugation, and denial of meaning for a proud and even more resilient people today.

One answer was to go back to that which worked and was such a gift to all peoples in their own culture. The other was to talk with them, know their problems and needs, and identify how our professions could bridge this gap.

COLLABORATION

On our first meeting in May of 2008, we invited elders and professionals to spend a day thinking about what was needed for our Aboriginal children from pregnancy to age 5. Twenty-two were invited, including six elders from outback New South Wales, Aboriginal country preschool directors, and the best childhood health professionals we had to offer in the areas of psychoanalysis, psychotherapy, social work, psychiatry, and psychology. On that amazing day, with the elders advising us, we felt we had reached an agreement on the root of many problems faced by their people today. What kind of assistance was needed, and what could we provide by forming an organization?

Attachment and problems of attachment very early on became the theme, introduced by the people who knew best: the elders and teachers in Aboriginal preschools. Displacement from the land, for a people who experienced themselves "as the land"; loss of the depth of their own spirituality and culture that made sense and gave meaning to their lives when that was replaced by a questionable substitution of a faith steeped in Western culture, foreign to them; a total disruption of kinship through the Stolen Generations, when children were forcibly removed from their parents; children conceived as a result of intercourse with a member of a race they hated, and which despised them—all this was a rupturing, dislocating loss of cataclysmic proportions. This litany, so often repeated, sometimes offensively, gave us an understanding of the enormous task ahead.

GUNAWIRRA'S TWO PILLARS

In our search we were surprised to find the rich center of all Aboriginal culture. First *Dadirri*, the most ancient form of treating trauma known to every Aboriginal group, or, for modern Aboriginal people, the *healing circle*. Dadirri is the capacity to wait, to create a space of deep listening and awareness of the depth of being. The other concept is that of *The Dreaming*. In the ancient contents of The Dreaming, Aboriginal people imbued their external world and events with meaning from their internal world; they created boundaries and symbols for this meaning. We have based all Gunawirra work and this book on these two significant gifts from ancient Aboriginal peoples—Dadirri, to heal trauma, and The Dreamtime stories, as a spiritual path through which we can imagine and create of the world around us what we want it to mean.

We understood that, with the stripping of all they had, we had also stripped away from these people the meaning of life. Was it this that caused so many suicides? If life has no meaning are we better dead? We knew that a growing body of literature, extending over many years, had highlighted both the many causes and the widespread extent of elements that continue to devastate Aboriginal families and other marginalized communities. Today these problems contribute to social isolation and loss of identity and self-esteem, even in early childhood. The transgenerational trauma carried by any race dislocated from its culture, concomitant with the loss of its tribal basis in communal living, its ancient lands, and its spiritual values attached to the earth, often brings shame and a sense of deadness. No wonder the latest statistics show Aboriginal suicide to be seven times more prevalent than in the mainstream population.

We began a search for a framework of thinking that would help the forty-three preschools where Gunawirra now has projects to have a foundation on which to build a practice for the healing of early childhood trauma. We found much in the recent literature on education for this age group, but much less on how infants and toddlers cope with stress and trauma as individuals.

SERENDIPITOUS BEGINNINGS

One day at Mass, an old woman I had spoken to the week before about our ideas tapped me on the shoulder. "I know someone who can help you! You can find him in the telephone book, Danny Gilbert."

When I went home I began to look. My husband said, "Are you mad! A little old lady taps you on the back in Mass and you actually believe her?"

She proved absolutely right! With unbelievable courage I called and got his personal assistant the next day. I could not believe it when she said, "Oh I am sure he will help you!" Well he did and I think always will. We were so fortunate to find Gilbert and Tobin, his very large law firm. They funded us, wrote our Constitution, and are still our guides in all legal processes and our support in countless ways. Our lawyer, Darren Fittler, is a blind social worker who then trained in law. Because of this law group, Gunawirra now enjoys the highest status as a Public Benevolent Institution, all our legal processes are in absolute good order, and we are protected as an organization at every turn. With a dedicated board, Gunawirra is well set up.

Gunawirra is an unusual organization. It has not lost a single professional from those first days. The shared vision made up for the small stipend paid. We knew that every person there was there because they wanted to be there. In the early days we did run short of funding. We feared we would close down, but the workers formed a group and came and said, "Just cut our contract fees." Each one then earned only a token fee. A membership-based Constitution meant every worker "was" Gunawirra. This and the shared vision in the work we do supported our togetherness, in a way much as the early communal system had cemented the relationship of kin in Aboriginal culture. (It also fitted the culture of my Lebanese parents where all migrants would group together to help each other and live communally in this foreign land.) With the foundation so well laid on the underlying vision, the hope born out of a hopeless situation, and masses of work to be done, it meant no one had time for the kind of infighting, envies, and jealousies that plague most human institutions. In the six years of Gunawirra's existence, the way we brainstorm and work creatively to resolve the best way to work for our children remains in the mind of each of us. We cannot idealize our organization because every worker knows how hard it is to focus in the way we do, to share our thoughts in the way we do, to humbly seek help from more skilled others from all over the world in the way we do, to humbly seek understanding from the people we serve in the way we do.

One thing we were all agreed on: Our projects needed to be small, focused, provide what is requested, and be financially affordable, well researched, and simple enough to be disseminated and shared wherever possible! We had to learn to "cut our cloth accordingly."

UNIFYING VALUES

As our website states, "Gunawirra, through its high-impact programs, works with parents and their children towards a world where respect and dignity matter." The website adds, "Gunawirra designs unique, innovative, and transformational programs to empower young Aboriginal parents with children aged zero to five years to intervene early in their children's lives, breaking the life cycle of trauma caused by loss of country, community, culture, and family."[1]

Our work is aimed squarely at Aboriginal children assuming their full and rightful place in Australian society by having the kind of early childhood that allows them to develop to their full potential. Of the preschool centers where we have projects, most are community based and council- and government-supported. Eleven are Department of Education and Training (DET) "Designated Preschools in Aboriginal Communities," and are attached to the local public schools. They were established by the government in response to the *Deaths in Custody Report* of 1998. They operate in areas designated as having the highest rates of suicide and death in custody. The government got it right. The wisdom of beginning by working in preschools to prevent adult problems is well known to all of us. Yet in addition to our focus on preschools, another sixty-eight or so preschools with Aboriginal children have been granted access to Gunawirra through our website initiative, http://trackingthemilkyway.com/. We are expecting to roll out the programs to these preschools as funding makes it possible.

So we at Gunawirra work today at the interface of healing, trauma, and education in around forty-three Aboriginal community member preschools across New South Wales and in Redfern, Sydney. Gunawirra has developed long-term relationships with these preschools. We work closely with them to tailor our programs to their particular needs and they are the key to the distribution of all our programs. In 2013 we invited twenty preschool teachers and directors to a two-day seminar titled "A Time for Healing: Treating Trauma for the Preschool Child." Sixty-seven came and in all eighty-nine attendees were present. Some had never left their towns before.

We are made up of Aboriginal and non-Aboriginal professionals working side by side. We have Tax Concession Charity and Deductible Gift Recipient status. Our website at http://gunawirra.org.au/ has a summary of all our projects, which range from high-level discourse and publications in psychoanalytic journals and booklets to giving toys to 3,000 Aboriginal children every Christmas and growing gardens as a community effort in more than thirty Aboriginal preschools, or in community preschools caring for Aboriginal children. In November 2013 Gunawirra was granted the status of a Public Benevolent Institution (PBI). This is the highest status level for a charity in Australia.

Self-help, professional support, intense research, and evaluation—together with wide distribution—form the basis of all Gunawirra work. Gunawirra funding relies almost solely on donations from high-wealth individuals, foundations, and charitable organizations. It has no government funding.

RESEARCH

All Gunawirra's programs are designed by a team of top-level, experienced professionals, continuously consulting with the community they serve to create models of excellence, which are subjected to rigorous evaluation by independent researchers and then disseminated at no cost. Gunawirra also has working relationships with various faculties at four Sydney universities. For example, Professor Jane Ussher of the University of Western Sydney has been commissioned to formally review the effectiveness of the Five Big Ideas program. Gunawirra has four to five social-work students from the Australian Catholic University and the University of New South Wales each year. Our three social worker managers officially have the title of Reconciliation Ambassadors of the Australian Association of Social workers.

GUNAWIRRA'S ACTIVITIES

Gunawirra's signature programs, born out of our thinking around the trauma research, are the *Young Aboriginal Mothers Groups* and the *Five Big Ideas*.

Young Aboriginal Mothers Groups

Gunawirra has two mothers groups in Redfern, an inner-city suburb of Sydney with a large Aboriginal population and a history of Aboriginal people who moved here from country areas when they were freed from the missions and given the right to vote in the 1960s. Our groups have pregnant young women and mothers with newborn babies in one group, and an older group that began like this but now has children aged about 3 years. Their work has deep psychoanalytic thinking at its base and a psychotherapist is the group leader, but the groups also extend into areas of Aboriginal art, pottery, filming, and photography—and there is a special focus on cooking each week. (One in three Aboriginal people has diabetes; many purchase fast food seven nights a week.) We have a Psychotherapy clinic which sees our mothers in individual therapy and sees six children weekly in intense psychotherapy, and we have the beginning of art therapy in schools and preschools for groups of up to six children chosen by the teachers because they have problems.

The Five Big Ideas

The Five Big Ideas are specially designed education modules that have been developed as an answer to the pervasive daily challenges this marginal group faces; the modules emerged from active collaboration with the directors and teachers of the Gunawirra childcare centers.

The five modules are: *Personal Health and Hygiene*, *Nutrition*, *Healing Trauma at Home*, *My Identity, My Country*, and *My Environment*. These are very much practical, grassroots programs that impart living skills in a supportive environment, with an underlying message of emotional healing at the heart of each of them.

The Five Big Ideas (which are discussed in more detail in chapter 10) combine a number of activities, including community days, the planting of vegetable gardens, nutrition programs, famous Dreamtime stories, and our Gunawirra puppets speaking of trauma for the little ones, all of which serve to create a rich and culturally relevant means of reaching the children and community.

Gunawirra has an ongoing source of wooden toys, created in a culturally sensitive way by fourteen retired men in a special place up country where they make giant blocks with alphabet letters, numbers, clocks, doll bassinets, a rainbow serpent, and large wooden puzzles. These are distributed along with pre-literate (pre-lit) books to most of our preschools. Up to 3,000 toys are distributed at Christmas time and more that 2,000 pre-lit books are distributed annually.

THE GUNAWIRRA TRAUMA PROJECT

This book is predicated on this single project, taking place over six months in a far west country preschool and an inner slum suburban preschool. Our aim is to make the work of the Gunawirra Trauma Project—in creating a space to hear the children's voices—form the core of this book.

The Purpose

The project's purpose was to understand and better treat traumatized Aboriginal preschool children, and to describe, define, and seek a theoretical construct and a way of working that would form the basis of our thinking and our programs. Everything in Gunawirra is continually born out of a two-way process in which we form our practical and clinical work from a theoretical basis; in turn, that theoretical basis and its constructs inform, underpin, and influence our work.

The Project

Gunawirra was awarded a special funding from The Healing Foundation for $100,000 over two years to carry out a project on art as a medium for the healing of early childhood trauma for Aboriginal preschool children. Three other large benefactors gave further funding.[2] From this we created a model that could be used in more than one hundred preschools in New South Wales. We would like the whole project to be operating in twenty preschools by the end of this year.

This project approaches trauma from a transgenerational perspective, spanning back to the early colonization of Australia and what that event has historically meant for the country's indigenous population and its culture, and how that history has continued to traumatically propagate through subsequent generations.

In linking analytic thought with both art and play therapy, we sought to create a basis for thinking about trauma for the preschool child. We based our thinking on two particular philosophies that seemed to be the best fit for us. We used an early-intervention model called *High Scope*, used with indigenous people and in poorer areas in the United States, and a particularly appealing philosophy called *Reggio Emelia*, which, although Italian in concept, seemed to have so much in common with Aboriginal culture and thinking. We found the *here and now* aspects of focusing on hearing the child as in the *Marte Meo* program (its name means "under one's own power") invaluable, even though their sophisticated ideas of studying video were well beyond our small, overworked preschools, who lacked in any case the technical skills.

Underpinning everything was our own grounding in psychoanalytic thought and theory. All our workers were trained in this, and all our supervisors were child psychotherapists or psychoanalysts.

BASIS OF THE PROJECT'S THINKING

The animating spirit of this project was the creation of a space in which to listen, a space where the voices of traumatized children could be heard in a way that gives those voices relevance. It would also be a space in which to hear the voices of the parents, and in addition a space in which to hear the voices of the teachers. We wanted to have at its core the process of deep soul listening, present since ancient Aboriginal times in the Dadirri circle, where the community sat together, listening to the pain of another. This space for listening has become the template of all Gunawirra work. We wanted, too, the other pillar of our work: the capacity to imagine, and The Dreamtime myths. We saw these as the cultural and spiritual basis of all Gunawirra's work, which informs us on how ancient people came to use the world around them in ways that gave their life and existence on this earth meaning, a way that allowed curiosity and imaginings, because both of these are lost to the traumatized child. How could we use art, and our understanding of its emotional meaning for them, to restore imagination to its rightful place became the research question.

DESIGNING AND IMPLEMENTING THE TRAUMA PROJECT

The project consists of fifty-minute sessions of psychotherapy with eight children, seen individually, and delivered over ten weeks. Two of the workers were specialized art therapists; one of the therapists was a child psychotherapist and one was a social worker in training with a particularly sensitive awareness of small children. Four of the children came from a small country town in Southern NSW two hours from the nearest airport. This preschool had more than a hundred preschool children, half of whom were Aboriginal. The other four children came from a preschool in the inner suburban slums of Sydney with a large Aboriginal population. Every session was supervised and evaluated weekly by a highly specialized child analyst, with each therapy session recorded on tape and written up in detail each week. The session with the supervisor was digitally recorded and transcribed.

Parents were interviewed before the program began, midway, and after the program ended. They were supported and encouraged to focus on their child and to report any changes in the child's emotions, attitude, and behavior, both through a questionnaire and in an interview with a trainee social worker or a psychologist. These sessions were also written up in detail and the supervision of these sessions was digitally recorded and transcribed. All sessions were further discussed in a group with two psychoanalysts from the United States who are specialists in childhood trauma.[3]

The teachers chose the children for the project. They were children who had experienced trauma: sexual abuse, domestic violence, alcohol abuse. They were children with low self-esteem and a poor sense of body image.

Each child's teacher was interviewed by a social worker. The supervision of these interviews was digitally recorded. It was these that we were to give special attention to at a later time as we realized how many of the teachers were themselves victims of trauma.

All the workers and supervisors in this project wrote the material for this book, seeking the salient issues that would assist us in our thinking about early childhood trauma and the role of the preschool as a perfect place to heal this trauma and prepare these little ones to negotiate their lives.

From this work we developed the Five Big Ideas, wrote two books, four booklets, and designed programs on health and hygiene, identity, nutrition, trauma, and environment that could be used in every preschool. This would be a simple, usable model for both professional health workers and preschool teachers. A DVD film of puppets addressing the issues was created from the narratives of the children, directing us to their needs and expressing their problems in a palpable way. We created a PowerPoint presentation on first aid and nutrition, and provided care packs with ordinary things like soap, toothbrushes, band-aids, disinfectant, and underwear. We developed music and dance events and later a very special program on Aboriginal art for Aboriginal preschool teachers to use with Aboriginal preschool children. We put our material on our www.trackingthemilkyway.com website and presented our work through seminars, tutorials, and supervision in NSW, with a later hope for this program to become nationwide.

WHY ART THERAPY?

Our thoughts about using art therapy were based on the recognition that a child's most intense thoughts and feelings, hidden in their subconscious, can find expression in their own painted or drawn images rather than in words. Their art gives children the opportunity to express powerful emotions when the speaking or writing of words with emotional meaning may be beyond them. The images created in art sessions are not unlike a fingerprint, telling where the child is at in that particular moment. Images allow a chain of emotions and feelings to surface. The process of creating art opens doors to a different kind of communication that later becomes talking and understanding. It creates a bridge between the therapist and the child.

The child is telling him or herself and the therapist something they both do and don't want understood or known about them. This is the area of *telling and not telling* that creates confusion for every small child. Walking the tightrope carefully is the central skill of every child therapist. For children the age of our little ones, the art not only tells a story, it enacts an experience. When Tom takes a piece of broken plastic and runs around the room screaming, "I'll kill you, you c . . t," he can tell himself and his therapist, "That is what my dad did to my mum last night." Later we hope that out of his pain, anguish, and anger he can paint or draw in a way that will depict this and not cause him as much angst as did the enactment. That is another step forward.

It is easier for the child to talk about the image than about him or herself. This important work allowed each child to explore feelings and ideas, and mostly our focus was on an increasing ability to experiment and bring feelings through art. We felt that just creating the space allowed their creative minds permission to exist along with their inner pain. We knew with this they would also be freed to learn.

We later included art sessions for our mothers groups and for our children's parents, understanding the need to include them and make them a living part of the process so as to facilitate the child's connection between home and school.

RESULTS

The results of the program were evaluated by John Prince of Social Compass, a research organization supported by The Healing Foundation; our thinkers, senior psychoanalysts and psychotherapists in Australia and the United States, and our workers were able to analyze the material from these art sessions and from them develop an understanding. Later our resident Aboriginal artist and cultural advisor was to be an important contributor to this.

Research questionnaires were given to all parent, worker, and teacher participants before, during, and after the project, with documentation of changes listed from none to many. Qualitative interviews of all participants in the project were made. The Social Compass researcher reported: "Essentially, the surveys and the interview data point towards some interesting and useful changes against the 14 indicators/result areas."

For the children, some of the important and encouraging outcomes that came as a result of thinking through and analyzing the questionnaires are:

1. Enjoying experiences and being more responsive with teachers;
2. Relating better with peers;
3. Relating better with siblings and friends;
4. Showing an interest in art as a means of expression and repeating art at home;
5. Feeling more relaxed and not as frustrated;
6. Showing reduced levels of uncertainty or anxiety with improvement in capacity to express emotion through art;
7. Showing improvement in learning and in emotional mood as related to learning generally;
8. Offering a deeper understanding of the meaning of trauma, for us.

The greatest gain was the message found in some of the teacher and parent answers: That the children seemed more aware of when they were disruptive or doing something unacceptable and could feel shame or embarrassment for it.

As a result of this study, giving professional training courses for preschool teachers, social workers, medical students, and therapists in the area of Aboriginal health became important to us. The development of our website, www.trackingthemilkyway.com, became central to our contact with the preschools. Our workers from Gunawirra who were visiting and telephoning the preschools were also a result of this project. The best research data, we realized, will be this book itself, where we use qualitative data to analyze some of the more distinctive cases.

SUPPORTING THE TEACHERS

Supporting the teachers continually means that they are encouraged to support the parents. We know that lost or never-established links are damaging our children, and through this program we began to understand how art creates the needed bridge.

Responses created by the research were to shine the torch on one very significant area. *How traumatized were our teachers themselves?* How much had the trauma of the children entered them and affected so severely who they became to the children?

CARING FOR THE CARERS

So who takes care of the carers while the carers take care of the children? Workers need to care about themselves. Being with young children in this sensitive state of development and trauma demands a listening, supporting, and encouraging that is incredibly exhausting. Carers need debriefing and support. They need someone to talk to. They need supportive workshops. They need a sympathetic board. They need not to be used and abused. They need a good wage. They need acknowledgment of the good work they do. A supportive family life helps us, space for themselves helps, not overworking helps. Invariably workers tell the stories of their own traumas. Colleagues need to hear and respect what each of them have personally suffered. The traumatized child touches a depth of emotion in carers that exposes their own trauma. Providing debriefing for the staff in a childcare center is the role of the director. Support for the director is the role of whom? For the director, training professional staff means supporting and hearing about their work with the children, hearing their traumas, and allowing expression of them, so they no longer suffer the sense of shame that trauma brings.

We were also alarmed to find so many of these dedicated people were at an age where they are moving on, and that there simply are not enough younger-generation teachers to take their place. The singular gain from the research, from the teacher's point of view, was the interest it engendered in the parents of the children that was not there before. They refused to be defeated by the amount of red tape, which was simply getting worse and taking time away from their important interaction with the parents.

It is of great interest to us that when we are involved with the family and their child at the preschool, the teachers become involved because they have an understanding of the family. For example, one of our families—who we flew out to every week for ten weeks in a row to see their child in therapy—moved out of town to another caravan park too far away for their child to attend preschool. We were amazed when the director and a teacher drove 22 miles to talk to the parents about the value of their child having preschool. We were even more amazed that the family moved back close to the town so their child could return to the preschool.

In another case the parents of one of the children we saw wanted to quickly move the child to primary school. In primary school there is no cost, as compared to the preschool. The school called in the parents (who were separated), and the grandmother, and took a lot of time to discuss their child with them. With the teacher they decided that it was in the child's best interest to have another year at preschool and so be able to keep up when he went to school. This to us is an enormous breakthrough and will affect that child's future enormously.

A little boy was misbehaving dreadfully and was a real problem to the school. After ten sessions with us and three sessions with the parents, there had been domestic violence, and the Department of Community Services (DOCS) came to interview the child. The teacher knelt down to explain to him about DOCS, and he said, "If you will hold my hand and you stay with me I will be able to talk to them." The teacher was in tears as she told me how proud she felt of him as he gripped her hand and told the man from

DOCS: "My mum and dad were fighting something awful, my dad bit my mum on the face and there was blood everywhere. My mum said that I can't tell anyone or my dad will go back to prison and then she will cry all the time. My dad takes me fishing. My mum says he only gets cranky when he has had too many drinks. Can you help my dad not to drink too much so he won't go to prison?"

A SPACE TO HEAL

Significantly, we began to understand the potential role of the preschool as a place to heal. It had all the right ingredients: play, encouragement of imagination, music, dance, story, art—all those activities that have been used by people everywhere in all ages to understand and relieve human pain. In addition, the preschool years in a young child's life are the best time to address issues affecting the child's development, as despite even serious trauma the child's mind is then more malleable. We realized that the preschool, with its possibilities of imagination and play, could become an emotionally safe place to be, bringing a curative, healing dimension to a child's experience.

Trauma kills inner psychic space; trauma destroys our capacity for fantasy; trauma kills our dreaming. The teacher's preschool work with free play, stories, song, dance, art, growing things, and craft *recreates this dreaming space*. The presence of this work allows children to create the world as they want to, rather than through the harsh imposition of a cruel reality from without, caused by trauma.

The Preschool Center is the concept of the sacred site—a sacred, safe, secure space where trauma heals. The order in that space gives holding, its reliability gives security, the teacher's handling of stimulus that is appropriate in timing and dose allows the possibility of life and creativity in what I call *pre-creative space*.

Trauma kills dreaming! At the center of all trauma is violent emotion that is beyond the child's capacity to suffer. The sense of the good mother's internalized, containing womb is shattered. The child's internal holding psychic womb collapses and becomes a sterile womb that deadens all emotion. Central to this is a deadened and deadening internal mother. That which holds that core self, that part of us which is unknown and unknowable, is violated. Trauma ruptures this *central core self* in a way that is horrifying to conceive. It aborts the fetal self. The central core becomes a "no person." The living womb space becomes a non-living, non-thinking, autistic space. The intuitive sense of self is fragmented; negative fears are greater than positive hopes. There is no creative space. The inner world becomes a dark, frightening abyss instead of a safe and protective place. Life is rooted in abject fear and terror, freezing all emotion and joy in living. Sometimes bits of emotion do break through—but in nightmares. The child no longer has the potential to dream or sing her- or himself into existence. These children grasp reality as a defense against dreaming; grasp acquisitions because the capacity to dream is dead.

As LaMothe writes, "This is passed on to the next generation, with terrible consequences. It is passed on because the mother, not having her core self, cannot hold the child in a way that sustains the child's core self" (LaMothe, 2006, p. 450). Babies have no meaning if the psychic mother is dead; our children then lose their sacred meaning. What are left are hopelessness, depression, and lack of self-esteem, feelings of worthlessness, drugs, drinking, suicide, and sexual abuse! No dreaming left! The dead do not dream.

The preschool center is offered as a healing space—an alive womb for the child to grow in. The center holds the psychic space where the child's creation of dreaming can occur. It is the space where the small child can create fantasy and symbolism. There they can enjoy free play, through creative arts and art, through growing gardens, through just being. In this safe neutral space children can learn, be free to think without fearing the thoughts will become real, can have a space in which to experiment and test things out. This is the space the preschool center creates for healing the traumatized child. As a teacher describes N, a child in her care:

> A bright little girl trapped in a quiet body. N doesn't see the fun side of life, she is sad almost all the time. There is little expression, and she stays by herself for a lot of the day. She doesn't accept praise very well and avoids eye contact. This is her second year of preschool. Her house burnt down a few weeks ago. We didn't see a change; only that she was a bit clingier with mum. For a child in that situation, you would expect to see some abnormal behaviour. There is a lot going on in there. She surprises us. She didn't talk to us at first, but now once she starts, she doesn't stop. It has taken six months to develop trust. She is warming up; she brought a flower from home for R [staff member]. Mum says she is talking at home.

In the book by Judy Atkinson called *Beyond Violence: Finding the Dream* (Atkinson, 1990), she writes that we cannot pretend that violence is not there or that it is harmless. She writes and speaks many times of the fact that acknowledging problems such as family violence means that we must take responsibility and accept accountability in our search for solutions. These solutions then become ours. There can be no true self-determination while the Self remains unhealed.

Childhood trauma, abuse, and neglect are fundamental public health challenges—now, fortunately, widely recognized. The challenge can be largely met with appropriate prevention and intervention. We in Gunawirra have taken this opportunity to seek together a method of healing for a culture steeped in ancient art, ritual, and myth; a method including pre-literacy that will give our children a better start, using art as therapy, a garden to renew the campfire community and give ideas of nutrition and health, and reverencing the sacred earth in Aboriginal culture. To this we added storytelling in its most ancient Aboriginal dreaming forms, and drama that awakens the concepts of dreaming in all of us. This is where our workshops want to go, embedded in the real experience of the "on the ground" workers.

We know that in trauma the most primitive of defenses come into action, both at a physical and at a psychic level. One regresses to an autistic defense. Some of the questions we ask of our research are: Can a whole race revert to such a defense? Can a whole people be shut down and unable to protect themselves? We know that one of the earliest primitive protective defenses we have in infancy is this *shutdown response* to protect the vulnerable state from annihilation. I am proposing that this creates a protective shell to save one from a pain that is unbearable and a terror that is beyond words. When this does not work, the person may be in such agony that death is welcomed. This may be one of the states that lead to suicide, or destruction of self or of another.

Often it is thought that the Aboriginal or refugee is "primitive." I think it's more likely that people's defences have deteriorated to a point of primitive non-protectiveness. There is something similar in the cutoff and loss of the mother country for the refugee, and for the Australian Aboriginal, which causes a loss of one's self-respect and worth. One is left in an extraordinarily vulnerable state. In both cases the Aboriginal and the refugee become victims to the predator country, and the mother to whom they went for refuge becomes their unwelcoming destroyer. In other words, the very deepest of paranoid phantasies come to life and are enacted. The mother country that they have lost can never be refound, and with that loss comes a loss of all that is sacred to them, and, worse, there is a replacement *mother land* that fails to protect or nourish them.

ENDING TRANSGENERATIONAL TRAUMA

This project attempts to understand the way meaning is stripped away as a result of trauma. Ancient Aboriginal culture healed trauma through Dadirri, a ritualized form of *deep listening*, not an ordinary witnessing but an empathic psychic action, now known to the modern world as psychotherapy. We want to try to show how the Aboriginal people have been cut off from access to aspects of their culture that might have helped them to accommodate and recover from traumatic aspects of the current culture. We hope psychoanalytic thinking may be approaching a new way of repairing this loss. We workers observe child psychoanalytic art-therapy as symbolizing in much the same way as The Dreaming.

We have further based this important book on the belief that future harm can be prevented by early treatment of trauma and its understanding. The intrinsic human impulse to enact or depict a drama, tell a story, and to know that one has an audience to witness, is essentially a form of psychotherapy that helps to order a small child's personal and social experience as a way of healing.

In finding and creating some simple but effective models of treatment through using art as a therapeutic medium, both for preschool children and their traumatized families, we have provided a well-supported model that can be used by all those who work to heal the trauma suffered by preschool children.

Our findings are available and accessible for therapists, family workers, and preschool teachers. All these activities—art, storytelling, music, and dance—are not simply mediums of treatment but are in themselves sublimations and transformations that create a direction for recovery and have done so from ancient times in many cultures, including the art and Dreamtime stories of the Aboriginal people.

NOTES

1. Gunawirra website, http://gunawirra.org.au/ (accessed 3-2-2014). Redfern, Sydney, NSW, Australia.
2. Funders of the Trauma Project were The Healing Foundation, Vincent Fairfax Family Foundation, St. George Bank, and the Trust Company.
3. The two psychoanalysts were Jeff Eaton and Marilyn Charles, who are also senior advisors to this book.

REFERENCES

Atkinson, J., ed. (1990). *Beyond violence: Finding our dream*. Canberra, Australia: Aboriginal and Islander Sub-program, National Domestic Violence Education Program, Office of the Status of Women.

LaMothe, R. (2006). Constructing infants: Anthropological realities and analytic horizons. *The Psychoanalytic Review* 3(3): 437–462.

Part 2

A Theoretical Base for Understanding Trauma in the Aboriginal Preschool Child

Chapter Three

Building a Floor for Experience

A Model for Thinking about Children's Experience

Jeffrey L. Eaton

The purpose of this chapter is to provide *tools for thinking* for psychotherapists, teachers, and other workers who might benefit from a psychoanalytically informed point of view. I gather a number of ideas to create a framework to help begin to understand a child's emotional experience. My intention is to help orient and support workers interacting with and trying to comprehend a young child in a psychotherapy setting.

My views derive from the writings of Sigmund Freud and Melanie Klein as well as from psychoanalysts influenced by them, including Donald Winnicott, Wilfred Bion, Frances Tustin, and Donald Meltzer. I have also been inspired by contemporary writers elaborating this tradition. They include Christopher Bollas, Michael Eigen, Antonino Ferro, James Grotstein, and Thomas Ogden. I do not review all these theories here. Instead, drawing on this background, I offer the beginning of a synthetic model that intends to enhance observation for those working with and endeavoring to understand troubled children.

MODELS

One of a therapist's main tasks is to learn how to thoroughly and accurately observe a child in a clinical interaction in order to empathically lend words to the child's emotional experience. I understand a model as a strategy to help organize the rich data of observation and experience. Models should aid in this difficult task and evolve as experience accrues. In order to be useful a model must radically simplify and select among myriad factors. It is not intended to explain anything in a definitive way and it should not be used to reductively impose meaning on the complexity of experience. Instead, elements of an evolving model, like the one I will describe, should help to generate relevant questions and to foster deeper recognition of potentially meaningful patterns. A model is a tool for fostering exploration and to aid both critical self-reflection and communication.

THE PSYCHOTHERAPY SETTING

A psychotherapist begins with a specific task: the creation of an *analytic setting*. First, consider the establishment of the external conditions of the setting. These include a suitable physical space that is safe and free from interruption during a session; specific and regular times to meet with a child; a mindful selection of toys and other items available for the child to play with and to use as vehicles of self-expression and communication; and appropriate interaction with parents and caregivers in order to sustain a regular treatment schedule.

Several other important tasks include: fostering cooperative relationships with a child's parents; obtaining a thorough developmental history of the child; deeply understanding the reasons that treatment is being sought; appreciating the anxiety and concerns of the parents; and coordinating when necessary with other relevant services. All these tasks should be handled tactfully, clearly, and in a timely way in order to initiate and sustain the conditions for a successful child therapy.

A second element of the setting involves the *internal conditions* of the therapist. Many factors, both personal and professional, go into exploring what might be called a psychotherapist's sensibility. A psychotherapist must learn how to use personal experience in a professional way. In other words, the idea of internal conditions relates to the question of a therapist's skillful use of self.

This is a crucial factor when dealing with difficult-to-reach or hard-to-treat children and adolescents. It can't be ignored when considering what might help make contact with such children. I am not advocating self-disclosure (nor am I completely ruling it out). Instead, I draw attention to the elusive issue of the therapist's *quality of presence*. This theme will be addressed in various ways throughout the chapter. In this setting, the significant problem of emotional pain must first be considered.

THE PROBLEM OF PAINFUL EMOTIONS

Some children are terrified to feel and to express their intense distress. For others, their pain has already come pouring out in disturbing or violent behaviors. Little can change if you feel you must hide from your pain or if you believe that you must hide your pain from others. With this view, you will rarely ever feel confident or hopeful or creative. Instead, over time, you become increasingly rigid, cautious, agitated, and mistrustful. If you believe that your pain must be kept secret or denied you tend to isolate yourself, even from people who might show care and concern toward you.

Sometimes children don't know how to express themselves and they are afraid to try. In some cases, children can be terrified to find out what will happen if they communicate their fears and anxieties. Perhaps this is because unconsciously they recoil from becoming trapped in a kind of emotional catastrophe. They cannot bear the helplessness that seems to swallow them up when they feel their feelings. So, they protect themselves from becoming overwhelmed by the violence of their emotions and by the images and impulses that such emotions give rise to.

There are many possibilities to consider when thinking about how children unconsciously cope with what distresses them. Naturally, some children will repress seemingly dangerous feelings. On another level, they might split off their feelings and relocate them elsewhere. In yet another way they might encapsulate or compartmentalize their feelings, or even become numb and insensitive to registering any kind of feelings at all.

Some children confuse their distress with the presence of another, fearing that they will be rejected or even punished for communicating or showing any pain. Unfortunately, this is sometimes what has actually happened to them. Other children unconsciously dramatize their pain, *making a scene* that is often violent or provocative. Because such behavior is difficult for others to comprehend, the potentially communicative dimensions of it are often overlooked.

Finally there may be realms of distress that have been largely inaccessible but that suddenly and violently explode into the moment, apparently without context. Such events are often a result of *cooperating* in a deepening of the psychotherapy process, but experiences like this can leave both the child and the therapist with a feeling of dizzyingly intimidating confusion.

FOUR KINDS OF EMOTIONAL PAIN

Usually it is very difficult for anyone in extreme distress to link words to their feelings. It is helpful to track four different forms of mental pain. The following descriptions draw on insights from Bion, Winnicott, and Meltzer. The first and deepest level of fear is the *anticipation of extinction*. This fear not only involves a sense of threat to the self, but at the same time it also includes the fear of the destruction of the entire world. In this state of mind it is not just that I will cease to be, but that everything will be destroyed. This level of pain implies annihilation, and it is an important dimension to track in very young, traumatized, autistic or psychotic patients.

The emphasis in this scenario is on the environment, not just on the object. Self and environment are for some reason dedifferentiated. In these situations what happens in the environment happens to the self. For example, when listening to such a scenario, instead of hearing about a scary figure who means to do the patient harm, you will hear about *a background of catastrophe*, how nothing is safe, how everything is poisoned or dying or decaying. One of my child patients spoke of "a permanent earthquake that never stops shaking" (Eaton, 2011, p. 46).

I believe that in this kind of scenario a therapist should try to pick up on and speak not only to the danger to the self but also to the dire conditions of the environment. When this area of experience can be recognized and spoken to directly, real emotional connection can be made and steps toward comprehending a primitive agony (Winnicott) or a nameless dread (Bion) are better able to be realized.

A second form of emotional pain is characterized by a feeling of a threat to the self (persecutory anxiety). This is one of the most common forms of anxiety and should be reasonably easy to observe and recognize. It is associated with what Klein called the paranoid-schizoid position. It involves a feeling of being the object of another's hostile intent. Often, this feeling emerges as a product of the unconscious projection of a negative emotion into the image of another person. Interpretation of the process of splitting and projection is often important in lessening the anxiety of persecution that a child can feel in this state of mind, and often one can observe the operation of these unconscious phantasies as they unfold in the here and now of the child's play in the analytic session.

A third form of emotional pain is characterized by the child's dawning concern for damage done to another (depressive anxiety). This form of anxiety is associated with what Melanie Klein called the entrance into and working through of the depressive position. The quality of this form of pain involves a new awareness of the emotion of guilt. If the feeling of guilt is too intense to bear, the child may tip back into a sense of persecution. However, if the child can bear the sense of guilt, then a feeling of concern for the other and of the importance of relationship can develop. This is an important milestone that helps to change the child's picture of the world, as he moves from a world of frightening influences into a sense of greater complexity based on the awareness of relationships, not just power, presence, and absence.

Finally, a fourth form of mental pain involves the fear of not being able to think, or of feeling deeply disoriented (confusional anxiety). This form of anxiety can arise in many different ways in many different contexts. It is particularly important around experiences of transition, change, and encountering new or novel situations. I have observed with many children that the anxiety of disorientation can be one of the most painful and difficult to name or describe. Helping a child to become calm allows them to reorient themselves and to reclaim their attention. Without these basic capacities, thinking and relating to others become increasingly aversive.

Taking note of the form, flavor, and intensity of anxiety can help a therapist to draw closer to a child's experience as well as help to find more accurate words to lend to the process of transforming a child's distress. These are some of the basic functions of becoming a container for the child's pain. If a therapist can register the child's pain, reflect upon, and reply to it in a sincere, timely, and clear way, it helps the child to feel more confident in the possibility of turning toward others and of finding tangible assistance.

FROM SCREAMING TO DREAMING: FROM DISTRESS TO COMFORT

From at least birth onward an infant experiences states of distress. Various factors give rise to discomfort. Probably the earliest form of biological value involves coming to differentiate states of pain (that lead naturally to action and aversion) and states of pleasure (that increase an impulse to seek, sustain, or amplify positive experience).

When a child experiences distress, she naturally signals her mother through various forms of active behavior, most obviously through crying out and using her bodily movements to indicate her state. In a good enough situation, a mother is emotionally prepared to be receptive to her infant's signals of distress. Then she acts to address that distress. She intuitively registers, reflects upon, and replies to her infant's distress in embodied ways that help her baby to realize a movement from distress to comfort.

When this transformation is successfully repeated over and over in the first days, weeks, and months of life, an infant gradually develops faith in the caring and helping aspects of being in relationship. She learns, in other words, to turn to toward her mother when in distress, and, as time goes by, to tune into her own experience, taking an interest in it, even when it is painful, because now she anticipates that painful states can resolve into calm, alert, relaxed states once attention has been granted to them.

Watching some mothers with their newborn infants can persuasively show how strongly ordinary early vulnerability naturally calls forth a mother's capacity to sooth her infant's distress. The primal necessity to sponsor a transformation from distress to comfort can be considered a basis for developing a healthy emotional *floor for experience*. Such a floor for experience supports the development of the infant's nascent sense of self as well as the dawning awareness of the other. Finally, it also eventually promotes the discovery of various qualities of links between self and other.

In infants who do not experience this kind of positive transformation with enough continuity or efficacy it is difficult to establish an unconscious expectation of the value of the presence of another. Without this sense of the positive value of the other it is difficult to encourage contact and interaction with another. This leads to situations where the infant (and later the child and teen) will habitually turn away from the other, turn against the other, or turn inside, withdrawing into various forms of unconscious, omnipotent, isolating, or self-protective phantasies.

A CHILD'S PICTURE OF THE WORLD

It will help to understand a child to investigate her picture of the world.[1] No person simply sees the world as it is. She must continually construct and modify a dynamic picture of the world through her ongoing interactions within it. The creation and elaboration of one's picture of the world is built upon an emotional floor for experience that begins to form (adequately or inadequately) early in life. Indeed, it probably begins before birth and involves many different unconscious influences shaping it as it transforms over time through the mother–infant relationship within the context of the oedipal family.

The following sections offer descriptions intended to help orient a clinician to various elements influencing a child's picture of the world. These sections are not intended as a model for use within a session. Rather, they are meant to help stimulate thinking and reflection after a session when considering the complexity of any clinical encounter. These notes are intended to help stimulate the therapist's thinking and intuition and to support the expansion and deepening of a capacity for observation.

Brain, Mind, and Self

There is enormous interest in how the brain operates and in how its complexity contributes to generating awareness of subjective experience. It is useful to differentiate between discussions of the brain, the mind, and the self. Brains can be studied as complex real objects, while minds can be studied as functional capacities and processes. Daniel Siegel helpfully defines the mind as "an embodied and relational process that regulates the flow of energy and information" (Siegel, 2012, p. 3).

Self is a concept defined in dozens of different ways both within psychoanalysis and beyond, in areas like philosophy, theology, psychology, sociology, and anthropology. No single definition can be offered that encompasses either the history or the comparative meanings of the concept. I offer two brief contexts for the use of the concept self: (1) a neurobiological narrative of self, and (2) a psychoanalytic narrative drawn from the work of Klein and Bion.

A Neurobiological Approach to Self

A brief summary of Antonio Damasio's model provides a neurobiological approach to the concept of self. Damasio posits three levels of self. In his book *Self Comes to Mind: Constructing the Conscious Brain*, Damasio (2010) speaks of what he calls the proto self, the core self, and the autobiographical self. The basic task of the primitive *proto self* is related to preservation of life. This minimal (unconscious) sense of self concerns activity and bodily integrity. Damasio describes homeostatic life regulation as a primitive form of biological value. Primitive discrimination between pain and pleasure is related to action directed to avoidance of toxic stimuli or seeking of nourishment.

According to Damasio, as an organism develops, complex forms of signaling arise through the interaction between the organism and the environment. This dynamic interface gives rise to greater complexity. As neurons fire together and wire together, and as the brain develops, the expansion of neuronal connections generates patterns of firing from which forms of representation of both external and internal situations emerge. Damasio names this level of activity the core self.

The *core self* involves images, feelings, emotions, memories, representations, and a sense of time that is mostly dominated by awareness of experience in the here and now. All these elements evolve to further aid the organism's adaptation to the environment. Finally, in humans, the acquisition of language and the flourishing of communication furthers the evolution of consciousness and culture. These developments sponsor an emergence of an autobiographical self.

The *autobiographical self* rides, as it were, on the biological values of the proto self and core self, but it is also regulated and elaborated by new cultural and symbolic value systems. The autobiographical self is capable of becoming an agent of reflection, and of intentionally moving through space and time with self consciousness. The child can reflect upon her choices as well as remember the past and imagine the future. As she grows and develops she can communicate about and enact her desire. She can mold her circumstances and change the environment through individual and collective action. The autobiographical self is heir not only to genetic inheritance, but also to symbolic capital which is transmitted culturally through language and tradition across generations.

A Psychoanalytic View of the Self (Klein and Bion)

According to Hinshelwood, Melanie Klein tended to use the terms "self" and "ego" interchangeably. Hinshelwood (1991) quotes Klein saying that the self refers to "the whole of the personality, which includes not only the ego, but also the instinctual life which Freud calls 'id'" (p. 425). Klein's model focused heavily on the role of unconscious phantasy. *Unconscious phantasy* links primitive bodily sensation with nascent mental images. In particular, early phantasies concern the interior and contents of mother's body.

According to Klein, the early activity of introjection and projection builds up a sense of an internal world, felt to be a very real and concrete place inside the person. An unconscious phantasy of mental space becomes populated with figures who are, in essence, personifications of relationships, emotions, and drives. These personifications, called *internal objects*, have a complex interactive life. In this model, the self can be thought of as a kind of inner group or drama. There is a constant tension generated between two different countries of the mind, called the paranoid-schizoid and depressive positions, which are the stages upon which the internal object relations are dramatized. How the self navigates the passage back and forth between these differing emotional worlds colors and shapes emerging self experience and the child's picture of the world.

In his work, Bion recognizes a double challenge, both personal and interpersonal, regarding how to create, sustain, and elaborate meaningful emotional experience by transforming the raw impersonal data of sensation and primitive emotion. Bion paid particular attention to the problem of how to construct a viable capacity for thinking. Developing this capacity for thinking is not a one-person project, but, instead, involves the ongoing impact of many selves upon each other. Generative impacts occur not only through exchanging information among them but, much more importantly, by sincerely sharing attention, emotion, and imagination with others through many forms of communication.

Bion's work expands the area of his concern from unconscious phantasy to the whole of experience, both conscious and unconscious. His idea of *beta elements* is very important in this regard. In Bion's abstract system of notation, beta elements indicate experience that is not yet capable of becoming unconscious. It is experience that one is aware of but cannot use reflectively or creatively. Beta experience impinges upon awareness but with no sense of emergent meaning, generating an impulse to act in order to rid the self of accumulated tension. Bion (1962a) explains that beta elements are suitable only for violent expulsion through projection into others, into the family, into the group, or even into one's own body. The presence of beta elements points to a quality of experience that can overwhelm or undo the vulnerable self if it is not mediated and helped to be made meaningful through contact with other minds.

This situation highlights an important difference between awareness and consciousness. Bion (1962b) questions how the development of the capacity to move from rudimentary awareness of sensation to consciousness that differentiates inner and outer realities occurs. He offers a complex model (in *Learning from Experience*) about how awareness expands through the mediation of mother's reverie and how alpha function stimulates the evolution of self-consciousness. Alpha function is the name for the process that enables beta elements to be transformed into alpha elements, which Bion calls the building blocks of meaningful experience. Alpha elements combine to form what he called a contact barrier, which helps to create a creative cooperation between conscious and unconscious processes. This gives rise, in Bion's model, to a spectrum of thinking that ranges from primitive images, thoughts, and dreams into proto narratives and concepts all the way into scientific, religious, and aesthetic reflections on the mysteries of life.

Bion's theory of thinking, then, is an exploration and necessary expansion of the mystery of symbol formation. Humans are symbol-making animals. Symbols *link* many worlds, including the realms of the body; the forces of emotion, feeling, and desire; and the world of representations and dreams arising from all these interactions.

The experience of self, from this point of view, can be thought of as a spectrum of symbol development and use ranging from pre-symbol (beta elements and alpha elements) to images, dreams, myths, concepts, and beyond. Appreciating the centrality of symbol development and use allows recognition of *learning* as not just a cognitive task, but as the very fabric of the self's evolution.

In his late work, Bion pictures the self as what might poetically be called a colony of souls. One cannot imagine all the participants of this colony ever being integrated; rather, what is important is making contact and communicating across time and space with the myriad characters and energies that proliferate and gain access to consciousness. In this model, the self has a kind of kaleidoscopic complexity as an evolving process.

Psychoanalysis is particularly interested in the self, that is, in the first-person narration and expression of an individual's particular embodied experience. The psychoanalytic method, with its special setting, makes possible conditions for the expression of self-experience, and its observation, investigation, and transformation. To put it plainly, one child in therapy said to me "I like coming here because you are interested in what it feels like to be me."

EMOTIONS AND A FLOOR FOR EXPERIENCE

The development of emotional awareness and comprehension is a process crucial to establishing aspects of a child's self-experience and of an evolving picture of the world. According to Ekman (2007), basic or *primary emotions* are now recognized as part of our psychobiological inheritance. These can be reliably observed in the facial expression of people across cultures. They can also be thought of as major contributors to motivation. The primary emotions are anger, sadness, surprise, disgust, joy, and fear.

Each of the primary emotions can be understood as having a range of intensity along a spectrum. For example, rage would be a form of intense anger. Sadness could be found to vary from intense despair to a fleeting sense of loss to a complex process like mourning. Surprise might evoke many states either positive or negative. Relationships with others help us to name and differentiate emotional experience. Slowly, through interaction with others, the self develops a capacity for reflecting upon or observing emotional experience, and these primary emotions produce a kind of repertoire of basic human responses that are inborn.

In addition to the primary emotions, there is a category called *social emotions*. According to Evans (2003), the social emotions, or, as he calls them the "higher cognitive emotions," are also universal, like basic emotions, although they exhibit wider cultural variation.

The social emotions include love, guilt, shame, embarrassment, pride, envy, and jealousy. Basic emotions are thought to have survival functions, while higher cognitive emotions are thought to have social and relational functions built atop the patterns of basic emotions. They expand the range and depth of emotional response to experience.

Another important model to briefly note comes from the researcher Jaak Panksepp. In his work (Panksepp and Biven, 2012) he emphasizes inborn or inherited emotional systems that are part of the evolution of the mammalian brain. His research has revealed several systems that can be reliably triggered by electrical stimulus to various parts of the brain. Without describing the brain's anatomy here, we can say that these systems include a "seeking" system that involves interest and desire, a fear system, a rage system, a lust system, a care and nurture system, a panic system linked to sadness and separation/distress, and a play system linked to joy and social learning. Taken together, the basic emotions and the higher cognitive emotions, along with the systems described by Panksepp, form a kind of primordial palette of emotional experience and motivation that will unfold in experience-dependent and contingent ways through interactions with specific others in changing contexts.

When listening to a patient it will help to observe which of his emotions are being triggered and whether or not the patient can tolerate experiencing those emotions within himself as well as in the presence of the therapist. It will also help to consider what kinds of feelings patients have about their own emotions, and whether or not they are able to communicate them. The feelings that people have about their emotions are often clues to the nature of their internal object relations. Feelings about emotions include judgments, scenarios, scripts, wishes, and defenses. An infant learns how to feel about her emotions through the interactions and relationships she experiences. The actual interpersonal interactions are transformed in unconscious phantasy, which becomes a deeper layer of the patient's picture of the world.

A therapist can be helpful to a child in describing the relationship between the anxiety or emotion the child exhibits, the way that the child feels about or copes with that emotion, the consequences of how she feels or copes (for better or for worse), and how that whole complex pattern is played out. This can occur either in the stories of the child's relationships with others in the external world, or in the way the emotions are literally enacted in the relationship with the therapist. All of these factors contribute to a more detailed description of the child's picture of the world.

A final note on emotions. I have noticed, with many children, that they often express their emotional experience through a sensitivity to color. This is especially evident in children's drawings. It can often be helpful to simply notice the colors the child is attracted to or averse to, and to inquire in a curious way about what feelings might be linked to the specific colors. It is surprising what stories can emerge from such simple questions.

A SELF AND ITS CIRCUMSTANCES

Many clinical experiences have contributed to my evolving sense of the importance of observing various forms of self-experience as part of appreciating a child's picture of the world. Building on Bion's development of both Freudian and Kleinian theory, I favor a model of a contingent and emerging self, a self that is not a thing but rather a dynamic process or set of processes arising from our biological embodiment and its continuous, albeit always incomplete, symbolic transformation through interaction with the world and with others.

To help appreciate the complexity of a child's picture of the world I describe four different registers of self-experience. How these different registers unfold and influence each other over time is too complex a process to attempt to describe here. I will simply introduce the four proposed levels of self-experience by offering a short vignette with discussion.

Ethan

Ethan was diagnosed on the Autism Spectrum at the University of Washington Autism Center when he was 7. He is now a good-looking, slender, intelligent teen. I have worked with him twice a week since he was 9.

During our work Ethan has emerged substantially from his autistic behaviors. His changes involved, among many experiences, a prolonged period of explosive, unregulated tantrums. Eventually his rages entered the sessions and involved intense physical violence. This period was difficult for everyone to endure, especially his family, but over time Ethan was able to use my help to contain, pattern, and modulate his rage. In this process Ethan was able to discover the value of communication with an actual separate person who could tolerate him and help him to make meaning of his experience.

Now 14, Ethan is deeply interested in his own emotional experience. He has discovered a reflective relationship to his self experience as well as a much greater awareness of the actual separateness and emotional reality of others.

I will describe a recent session. Ethan eagerly enters the office and sits on the edge of the couch very close to my chair. After some initial small talk he says,

> "Hey Jeff, I had a really weird dream last night."
>
> "I'd like to hear it," I say.
>
> "Okay, it was pretty weird and it kind of scared me. I had a dream that kids were being boiled alive and then people were going to eat them. Someone came up to me and said 'Here, try some meat.' I said 'No, I won't.'"
>
> "Wow, that's interesting . . ."
>
> "Wait, there's more. I got chased by a cannibal who was going to eat me. But there was another guy there who was trying to help me and set me free. Then, I was at a kind of a carnival. Maybe it was a birthday party. I don't know. It was raining. I think it might have been a real place. But I can't remember."
>
> "Is that the whole dream?"
>
> "No, there's one more piece. I was making scrambled eggs with my brother. I think that is because I really helped make breakfast on the weekend and it was good."

"What thoughts do you have, if any, as you tell me the dream?"

"I don't know. I think it is just kind of random, you know."

"Hmmmm."

"What do you think, Jeff?"

"Let's see, as I recall, you were looking forward to spending the weekend with your cousins . . ."

"Yeah, we went swimming, and played video games . . ."

"Remind me about your cousins and how old they are?"

There is a long pause. Ethan seems to be looking up at the ceiling. I imagine he is trying to literally picture each of his cousins in his mind.

"There's Mike, he's 18, Alex is 14, and Georgie is 10."

"What was it like to be with Mike?"

"He's cool."

"Did you play with him?"

"Yeah, we wrestled and he pinned me and tickled me and I couldn't make him stop."

"Mmmmm."

"Jeff, wait, I have a thought popping up into my mind."

"What's that?"

"I think I know what the dream means."

"Tell me."

"You know, the kids being boiled might mean it is like drowning in your own worries."

"Say more . . ."

"You know, when you don't know what to do and you will just get boiled up by worrying."

"I wonder if you got really frustrated at some point over the weekend, like when Mike wouldn't stop tickling you? I wonder if you . . ."

"No, I had fun."

Ethan then tells me in great detail that he would like to be able to wake up in his dreams and control their outcome. He says that sometimes he is aware while dreaming that he is dreaming but he cannot make his dreams do what he would like them to. He asks me if I can direct the outcomes of my dreams. I tell him that, like him, I have had the experience of being aware of dreaming within a dream but that I can't guide the outcome of my dreams either. He wonders if anyone can. I say that I have heard of a few people who can, but it is pretty rare.

"Pretty rare, . . ." he repeats.

I say, "I have another idea about your dream now."

"Okay."

"You seem quite interested in controlling your dream. I wonder if that is linked to the feeling of selfishness we have also talked about recently, of wanting to have everything exactly your own way?"

"Oh! I get it."

In the remainder of the session we continue to explore the attitude of selfishness as a troubling impulse that can harden into an attitude of feeling entitled to have your own way as a defense against frustration or loss, a theme that has been important in many recent sessions.

REGISTERS OF SELF EXPERIENCE

I offer this vignette to point to differing *registers of self-experience*. I think four registers combine to create the fullness of self-experience and the child's picture of the world. Each level can be imaginatively glimpsed in this vignette. I offer these registers as possible ways to observe and make meaning of patterns of behavior.

The registers of self can be described as (1) the self as body, (2) the self as object, (3) the self as agent, and (4) the self as process. I will use the material I have just presented to abstract examples of each of these four forms of self-experience. I will then discuss the ideas broadly, rather than trying to show a process specific to Ethan's treatment.

The Self as Body

Example: In Ethan's dream he is afraid of being boiled alive.

The experience of self as body is probably our earliest form of awareness. The newborn's need to be emotionally welcomed and protected by another is profound. Almost everyone can relate to the warm feelings generated when one observes a mother sensitively and lovingly interacting with her infant. On the other hand, everyone can also feel the shock of horror at witnessing an unattended infant who has no one to comfort her distress. Our deepest fears involve exposure, exile, and the terror of not belonging to a sheltering group or, even more terrifying, of being the vulnerable victim of a group that has turned against us. Such scenarios trigger primordial predator–prey anxieties.

As the psychoanalyst Christopher Bollas (1979) has beautifully described it, before a mother is known as a stable, separate other, she is experienced as a sponsor of a process of transformation. The self as body seeks the other in order to enter an experience of transformation. From my point of view, as I have already said, the most primordial transformation is the movement from distress to comfort. This is not a psychological transformation, but initially is experienced as a psychosomatic one. Indeed, the psychosomatic transformation precedes the discovery of the realm of psychological meaning.

An infant moves from states of over- or underarousal to states of calm alertness facilitated by her mother's sensitive care. Through the establishment of this reliable transformation the infant can begin to discover how to focus her attention both on self as body experiences as well as on the influence or impact of the other, experienced primarily as an environment mother (Winnicott, 1962) in the earliest hours and days of life outside the womb.

I want to highlight what I regard as the extraordinary complexity of the journey each infant must somehow make to contact, discover, and construct an evolving awareness of the other. I think this awareness evolves over time and through myriad interactions, giving rise to perceptions that can be organized in a progression from pre-object to part object, to whole object, to awareness of another as a separate mysterious subject. This passage, one might say, is a journey across the lifespan.

This journey is not made just in the mind. It is an embodied experience that takes place through millions of complex interactions with actual others, as well as in the way those interactions become transformed through unconscious phantasy. It will not be possible here, however, to explicate the importance of each interdependent form of awareness that an infant can realize through the complex process of development.

Frances Tustin (1981) has written beautifully about a feeling of primal cooperation that arises when there is a strong fit between the mother's nipple and her infant's mouth. This fit creates a psychosomatic template of primordial shared life-giving activity. The successful coupling of mother's nipple with infant's mouth in the embodied interaction of feeding contributes to building up an experience Tustin (1986) calls a "rhythm of safety."

This primordial coupling between nipple and mouth contains within it the seeds of each of the four forms of awareness of the other described earlier. First, there is the primitive sense of self as body and its undifferentiated reliance on the mother as a holding environment. Next, there is the sense of the self as object, becoming aware of the separate part-object nipple (and breast) and its influence, both as a presence and as an absence. Then, through the initiative of sucking there is a primitive sense of proto-agency. Finally, through the sensuous contact with mother's skin, her face, and especially her eyes and voice, and her overall way of being with the infant in the intimacy of the feeding experience, one can imagine a dawning sense of the enigmatic mystery of the mother as a subject, something Meltzer (2008) beautifully describes as the *aesthetic conflict* triggered by the apprehension of beauty that is too much for the infant's immature self to process.

The experience of self as body is characterized, then, by two general trends. When a rhythm of safety can be adequately realized through interactions between mother and baby, this process naturally sponsors the establishment of a floor for emotional experience. When the rhythm of safety is obstructed, for any of myriad reasons, then, one might observe the impact of what can be called a background of emotional catastrophe.

The Background of Catastrophe

I remember an early session with an 8-year-old psychotic boy who told me he was "allergic to his own brain." I gave him paper and colored markers and asked him to draw any kind of picture he could. He drew a crude house and inside the house was a table. On the table was a telephone which had a wire that went underground to what he explained was a transmitter box. He then drew a tree in the yard and a moon. He told me that there was a monster living behind the moon that was always watching the house.

I told him I thought he hoped that I would be able to help him to deal with the monster. I said that I felt the monster must be an important part of him that for some reason had been banished far away. I said, I thought he needed my help to bring the monster back home. It was our job, I said, to figure out how to communicate with the monster.

He spent the remainder of the time drawing different sorts of monsters, and toward the end of the session he said that he wanted to take all the monsters and put them together and make a single monster. This session felt like a good beginning of establishing a floor for emotional experience. I felt a tangible relief in discovering it was possible to communicate together about what I would later learn was a severe background of emotional catastrophe involving maternal drug abuse during pregnancy.

Not all breakdowns in mother–baby connections are the product of neglect or abuse. Some babies are born hypersensitive and difficult to calm. Some have experienced fetal distress or difficulties during birth that make connecting with mother difficult. Klein's emphasis on innate anxieties, as well as on the varying proportions of envy and frustration and the child's tolerances for them, is also important to consider.

Primal Exposure

For some children, the qualities of innocence, vulnerability, and absolute dependence as an infant have been interrupted in ways that made these qualities too present and so too much to bear. One of our deepest fears is of what can be called *primal exposure*. The infant Oedipus, left to die on a hillside, represents an important mythological image of such primal exposure.

Cast out at birth by his parents, Oedipus suffers double traumas: the premature awareness of two-ness, Tustin's name for catastrophic early separation, and the experience of the presence of the other as a hostile predator—in the story, the child's murderous parents Laius and Jocasta.

Both of these forms of primal exposure are felt as severe states of bodily distress, leading first to hyperarousal (screaming and panic) and later to physiological freezing, numbness, withdrawal, and deadness.

Recalling the same young psychotic boy I just spoke of, I recognized that part of his transference involved recreating a fetal environment made toxic by maternal drug abuse. During one period of his analysis my consulting room became a place that might poison him. In other words, part of our experience involved understanding that at a deep, unconscious level he experienced my consulting room as a toxic womb, part of a powerful fetal transference. Later, he played out a repetitive scenario where he walked a tightrope above a pool of piranhas and repeatedly fell in to be devoured alive, through which he further elaborated his unconscious sense that in the very beginning of life (before birth) the environment felt as if it intended to destroy him.

Becoming an Audience

I want to emphasize a slight shift of attention here by underscoring the unconscious experience of the self as body. As the unconscious experience of the self as body becomes animated again through the emergence of an infantile transference within the therapeutic process, a background of emotional catastrophe can appear in the analytic space. This emotional catastrophe is precisely what must be tolerated, imagined, described, and discussed by the analyst. It must be held, shared, suffered, dreamt, and symbolized, and not just by the patient but within the analytic couple, which gradually becomes a *symbolizing couple* through the analyst's capacity to welcome primitive projective identifications as forms of communication.

This kind of process is often interpreted as being much more object-related than I believe it often actually is. From a technical point of view, I call this situation one of "becoming an audience" for the patient. Often the child must "make a scene" that requires an audience to welcome, witness, and recognize it. Yet while an audience is needed for this witnessing function, the audience cannot call too much attention to itself too quickly.

If the analyst can hold the space for the fragments of a psychological disaster to gather, without prematurely organizing the experience in self and object terms, then this gradually allows space for the possibility of reclaiming the experience of self as body, and subsequently of discovering the possibility of inhabiting the energetic dimension of bodily experience.

With some children, it is possible, over time, to almost literally witness the self beginning to dwell in the body again in fuller, more integrated ways that then allow for more attention to be shifted to the other and to differing qualities of links to the other.

The Self as Object

Example: In Ethan's dream he says, "I got chased by a cannibal who was going to eat me. But there was another guy who was trying to help me and set me free."

This example shows the experience of the self as object. The quality of the link to the object profoundly *influences* the experience of self (Ogden, 1990). In the first case, Ethan's experience is of being the object of a cannibal, while in the next case he is the object of someone who is trying to help.

In the paranoid-schizoid position, the sense of self is profoundly impacted by the influence of the object. The kind and quality of the link to the object transforms the sense of self. We can look at what the self does to the internal object through splitting and projective identification, and through other actions in unconscious phantasy. But we can also look at how the other impacts the self, as when the self feels like the object of the other.

At a primitive level we can consider two basic forms of self as object. The first form involves the self's link to a *projective identification welcoming object* (Eaton, 2011). In this case, the self as object feels transformed in a positive way by having its emotional experience welcomed with reverie. The projective identification welcoming object is associated with the creation of a floor for emotional experience. The welcoming object tolerates mental pain, and brings an attitude of compassion, curiosity, and confidence.

The second form involves the self's link to a *projective identification rejecting object*, as well as to what Bion (1957, p. 92) called "an obstructive object." In this case, the self as object feels transformed in a negative way. The self anticipates being attacked for communicating pain and, in the worst situations, feels endangered for having any awareness of emotional experience. In this scenario, awareness or expression of emotional pain is felt to be a provocation to the violence of an obstructive object. The projective identification rejecting object and the obstructive object are associated with emotional catastrophe, and with an atmosphere that Bion characterized as hostile and willfully misunderstanding.

With children who have suffered trauma it is extremely important to look at a potential split in their personality, which can be personified in terms of internal object relations. This split can be described as involving "a lost child" part of the self and some other form of "caretaker self" (Winnicott). There are so many different possible scenarios here. The main point is that the vulnerable part of the self becomes hidden or lost. Sometimes it becomes attached to a narcissistic object that is idealized (either positively or negatively). Sometimes the child becomes omnipotently parental (Meltzer calls this "pseudo-maturity"). Or the child may retreat into a world of virtual images or concrete sensations, using these to make barriers and walls to learning and contact with others. The main issue is that the vulnerable dependent part of the self that is capable of learning and seeking nurture from real separate parental objects is not only very hard for the therapist to contact, but it is also hard for the patient to remember, believe in, trust or have compassion for.

The Self as Agent

Example: In his dream Ethan said "Someone came up to me and said, 'Here, try some meat.' I said 'No, I won't.'"

The self as agent is a form of self that can initiate, choose, take responsibility, and to some extent begin to reflect upon experience. We could link this development to entering and working through in the depressive position. Here, the self is the subject who acts, rather than the object who is acted upon. Being able to say "No" is an important step in discovering the form of self as agent. We are always negotiating a dialectic between the experience of the self as object and the experience of the self as agent.

In early experience, agency is often mixed up with magical thinking, idealization, and omnipotent phantasy. Winnicott felt it was important for children to slowly discover their limitations rather than have them traumatically revealed. The capacity to play makes possible an arena where the child can begin to sort out reality and pretend. In work with young children it is very important to look for moments of spontaneous initiative. These are signals of the self as agent who is risking entering into a relationship and seeking to communicate.

A young, nonverbal, and deeply autistic child scribbled a picture. These were the first things that he had ever drawn. In the next session he clearly began the session by seeking the paper and colored pencils in order to draw again. It is often deeply moving when you observe the emergence of the self as agent, and begin to see the desire to communicate and to explore links with another begin to flourish.

Once you begin to see the activity of self as agent, you can also begin to track the role of conflict. Conflict arises not only between people but also within the self. Emotions compete for experience, desire and inhibition emerge, and a whole psychology well described by Freud comes to the foreground when the child is no longer trapped in a position as only the object of another's influence.

The Self as Process

Example: In his dream, Ethan becomes aware that he is dreaming while he is dreaming.

Bion suggests that we are always dreaming, even while we are awake. What would it be like to wake up within the dream of our ordinary lives?

When I think about Freud's model, I picture a model where the I (or self) operates at the intersection of four different categories of influence. These four influences are (1) the bodily energies, impulses, and drives; (2) the evolution of the ego, the superego, and the Oedipus situation; (3) the emotional experiences of daily activity, which Freud called "the day residue" in his dream theory; and finally (4) the activity of dreaming itself. All of these forces draw from the background of what Bion named O.

O is a form of notation that Bion introduced to indicate that experience exceeds what can be represented. Every form of representation is both an attempt at description and a falsification of direct experience. O simply indicates that our experience is always to some degree beyond what we can know or express. There are two fundamental reasons for this. The first is that we are too identified with concepts and forms of perception that alienate us from direct experience. The second is that even when we have brief moments of direct experience, it is impossible to communicate the nature of experience.

One model Bion uses for the self as process is the nature of dreaming itself. At night, when one is dreaming, real emotions and meaningful experiences (however weird or bizarre they may seem) are felt and lived through. Indeed, we live a second life while dreaming. However, upon waking that second life seems to disappear. Even the narration of the events of that experience, however detailed, offers only traces of the experience itself.

Where do our dreams come from? To whom are they addressed? How can we make use of them? The self can be enriched by glimpses of O, or it can be undone. What can be glimpsed from looking deeply into the process of dreaming (and of making and remaking a self) is that the self is a necessary fiction, a process in transformation, not a thing that can be said to exist in a permanent, never-changing, essential way. The self comes into being through interaction, and is carried forward in the realm of emotion (Bion's L, H, and K links), but is actually an evolving part of O. In Bion's language, a self, then, is a process of becoming O, and the traces of this process are translated into emotion and the stories we tell in the realms of L, H, and K—love, hate, and knowledge.

Patterns

To understand a child's picture of the world, consider the four different kinds of experience that are interdependent elements in an evolving model. First, there is the child's developing sense of self. Next, there are the many ways that a child perceives other people and the objects around her. Then, there are the many qualities a child feels about her relationships to others and to objects. Finally, there is the child's sense of the atmosphere generated by various complex contexts (including family, school, religious and community affiliations; political, economic, historical, and racial factors; and some kind of relationship, however tentative or alienated, to the natural world). All these influences make up an unconscious background environment of a child's emotional world. By keeping all these elements and their complex interdependence in mind, one can learn quite a bit about how a child experiences herself and her world.

To summarize the model so far, the self can be experienced in four different registers. Self as body, self as object, self as agent, and self as process. These correspond with the perception of the other as pre-object, part object, whole object, and subject. Additionally, we can describe the quality of the different links in these four registers.

Register 1. The self as body experiences the other as pre-object in the form of an environment of which the self is a part. Changes in the environment are felt as changes to the self. No real awareness of link can be described here. The anxiety that accompanies this level of experience is categorized as a fear of annihilation.

Register 2. The self as object experiences the other as a good or bad (positive or negative) part object. The nature of the link is felt as an influence on the self from the other. The dominant anxiety at this level is a feeling of threat to the self which generally has the flavor of persecution.

One can also notice a transition between Registers 1 and 2 in the form of the emergence of predator–prey anxieties. This primarily has to do with the problem of the presence of the object and the question of whether the present object will be positive or negative in its influence.

Register 3. The self as agent experiences the other as a whole object, meaning that there is a recognition that the other is not only separate from the self, but that he or she also contains good and bad, positive and negative aspects. This gives rise to an awareness of a true sense of relationship. That is, self as agent recognizes the presence of another, as well as a third experience, the relationship that exists between self and other, and the responsibility both parties have for the quality of that relationship. The dominant anxiety in this register is fear of damage to the other, which, if contained and worked through, leads to reparation of internal objects and reliable concern for others, as well as gratitude and a deepening sense of the value and meaning of relationships.

Register 4. Finally, the self as process recognizes the other as a full subject, which, by definition implies the recognition of an enigma and mystery. Just as the self is not transparent to itself, nor is the other subject transparent to the self. Going beyond recognition of the influence of the part object, and the responsibility for relationship with another, the dimension of self as subject relating to another subject implies the responsibility of deep communication, a willingness to get to know the other and to tolerate the mystery of two radically particular beings in conversation. Here, the "third" can be considered awareness of what Bion called "O," which is not only the background of the conversation, but, in fact, the ground out of which each subject arises and what each subject embodies. The anxiety that arises in this register is the fear of the turbulence of what Bion (1965, p. 11) calls "catastrophic change."

BECOMING A WELCOMING OBJECT

How can a psychotherapist encourage a child to tolerate and turn toward her own experience? What motivates a child to risk going through the pain of expressing herself? I like to speak about the psychotherapist "becoming a welcoming object." Because the child often rejects contact with her own emotions, it is important for the psychotherapist to feel a sincere commitment to welcoming whatever arises in the child's experience as potentially communicative and emotionally meaningful.

Welcoming is a notion that has deep roots in indigenous Aboriginal culture. Aboriginal writer Miriam-Rose Ungunmerr-Baumann describes something called *Dadirri*, which is translated as "deep listening":

> Dadirri is inner, deep listening and quiet, still awareness. Dadirri recognises the deep spring that is inside us. We call on it and it calls to us [. . .]

> When I experience dadirri, I am made whole again. I can sit on the riverbank or walk through the trees; even if someone close to me has passed away, I can find my peace in this silent awareness. There is no need of words. A big part of dadirri is listening.
>
> In our Aboriginal way, we learnt to listen from our earliest days. We could not live good and useful lives unless we listened. This was the normal way for us to learn—not by asking questions. We learnt by watching and listening, waiting and then acting.
>
> My people are not threatened by silence. They are completely at home in it. They have lived for thousands of years with Nature's quietness. My people today recognize and experience in this quietness, the great Life-Giving Spirit, the Father of us all. [. . .]
>
> Our Aboriginal culture has taught us to be still and to wait. We do not try to hurry things up. We let them follow their natural course—like the seasons. (Ungunmerr-Baumann, 2002)

I take inspiration from this description. The internal conditions of the therapist can express an embodied presence, which in turn creates an atmosphere *between* therapist and child that woos the child's attention into the moment, helping her move emotionally from nowhere to now-here. An attitude of deep listening implies a deep respect for self, other, links, and the world. Building on this realization one can reconnect to a natural vitality that is always already present in the recognition of now-here direct experience.

Four *locations of presence* are relevant in any session. The first is whether or not the child can attend to her own experience. Can she be present to herself? The second is whether or not she can tolerate being the object of another's attention. What does the presence of the other stimulate? Then, there is the issue of the kinds of links that might arise between self and other when the child can tolerate being in the presence of another. This third location of experience opens the possibility of *sharing minds*, which seems to be a necessary condition for transforming pain into meaning. Through opening to sharing, the child can discover herself as an agent of expression and communication. She is free to "make a scene" and to discover her own emotional experience, held by the deep listening and respect of a witness. The absence of an embodied welcoming attention combines with the child's significant anxiety, both conscious and unconscious, to create additional barriers to expression and communication.

Finally, there is a fourth level of embodied presence that involves the sudden evolution and surprise of insight, discovery, and simply a profound recognition of being, being-with, and of becoming. One can trace an evolution from being the object of another, to learning to play and share together, to becoming at one with nature and the environment, not in a regressed way, but with a sense of profound gratitude for the mystery of creation in all its sorrow and beauty. In Bion's terms this is called Becoming O. It is not something that is willed; rather, it is an experience of opening up, quieting, and welcoming, and of seeing, feeling, and sensing how experiences continue to deepen and unfold.

A welcoming object implicitly demonstrates qualities of patience, openness, curiosity, empathy, imagination, attention, respect, honesty, sincerity, and courage. These qualities are the soil in which a child can bury (or plant) seeds of worry, shame, fear, hatred, rage, helplessness, vulnerability, exposure, despair, arrogance, destructiveness, and any other emotion, fantasy, anxiety, or experience that requires being witnessed, held, comprehended, described, and discussed.

By welcoming negative emotions and letting the child plant seeds of pain in the soil of analytic reverie, the therapist helps create new conditions for emotional discoveries. Over time, realizations of connection, calmness, interest, mourning, excitement, hope, joy, and gratitude can begin to bloom. In other words, a therapist facilitates the conditions for the adventure of learning from experience to become possible in a symbolizing relationship.

When the psychotherapist can embody qualities of a welcoming object, it allows him to function in ways that become increasingly valuable to the child. The therapist can perform functions that allow him to *hold, observe, and describe*; *share and recognize*; and finally *intuit and evolve*. Each of these functions represents a condition for transformation that is related to elements of the child's experience in differing registers.

FORMS OF WELCOMING PRESENCE

At the level of self as body, the therapist "holds with reverie"—like an environment mother—the space for transformation. At the level of self as object, the therapist observes and describes the forms of influence that are impacting the self. At the level of the self as agent, the therapist shares and recognizes the evolving forms of relationship, including working through in the transference. Finally, at the level of self as process, the therapist allows for the evolution of intuition and the surprise of insight that emerges from this kind of openness.

All these levels interpenetrate and offer conditions that can help to transform experience from fear to calm, from rigidity to flexibility, from dogmatism to openness, and from emotional dread to playful aliveness. This transformation literally sponsors a movement from screaming to dreaming.

One can observe in the therapeutic process a dynamic oscillation between opening up and closing down, of expanding and contracting. This is a natural rhythm that can build and ebb, giving clues to the life of presence and its transformation. When the process is opening, the therapist can hold a space within himself and between himself and the patient for discovery and sharing and exploring. This will naturally lead at some point to the emergence of anxiety, and, at this point the therapist will naturally allow a contraction for the purpose of containing and regulating tension and intensity. Sensitivity to this back-and-forth experience of opening to exploration and contracting to tolerate anxiety is an important engine of the therapeutic process. When this kind of rhythm is not respected, exploration can lead to fragmentation, and contraction can lead to stagnation and retreat from contact.

TURNING TOWARD EXPERIENCE

Because for some children states of distress are not consistently accompanied by relief, a child may begin to become averse to registering his own experience. This can result, in extreme cases, as a feeling of hatred for emotion, and a feeling of becoming frantic when emotions are triggered. Often this situation can be combined with and complicated by an intolerance of frustration. Perhaps the seeds of destructive envy are even found in such a scenario, leading later in development to a child feeling envy for others who seem to have some secret to negotiating both their own emotions and the ability to enjoy positive relationships.

A child who is essentially afraid of his own aliveness will reject or attack his own subjective experience and blame others for aggravating him. He will often have nightmares and have trouble using his ego for learning because so much of his experience becomes organized around denying or coping with violent feelings of dread.

Instead of turning toward others, a child deprived of this primal anticipation of comfort will turn away from others, believing, often, that contact with another will only worsen the pain that he is already trying to endure. How much worse is this situation if a large portion of his community, or even generations of his community, have suffered from oppression, violence, coercion, and destruction of indigenous values and identity?

When a child turns away from others, he may also turn against others, exhibiting hostility and aggression. He may feel persecuted by others, believing that they are the cause of his pain, or even that they intend him to suffer. Another possibility is that, over time, he may turn inside, becoming lost in his imagination, in various forms of withdrawal, or, in severe cases, even becoming dissociated or psychically dead. Finally, he may become overtly self-destructive, with suicide becoming an ultimate expression of his picture of the world.

One purpose of psychotherapy is to help restore the possibility of turning toward others. When a child can unconsciously rely on the transformation of distress to comfort, she can take an interest in various forms or flavors of experience. She shows a curiosity or interest in getting to know her own experience of sensations, images, feelings, thoughts, desires, symbols, and dreams. She regains the most basic impulse to listen to her own experience, and to turn toward the experience of the world around her, making links instead of breaking or denying or building barriers to them.

The main point is that when an infant develops a belief in the transformation of distress to comfort, she seeks the presence of the other and relationship as a form of healing connection and positive feeling. When an infant cannot establish this transformation, he will lack trust or even fear the presence of another. When a psychotherapist can bring a sincere capacity for deep listening to self, other, links, and the world, then she can perhaps create the conditions, both external and internal, to allow a troubled child to make contact with and explore a wider reality, both internal and external. The child can then gradually reclaim his relationship to sensations, images, wishes, desires, fantasies, and daydreams that may lead him out of alienated "no-where" states of mind into the now-here possibilities of embodied relationship.

To realize this potential for transformation calls on the therapist to develop a capacity for deep listening, or, as Bion would say, for becoming O. As I understand it, this means having the courage to stand directly in your own experience with nothing added (for consolation) and nothing deleted (from judgment). We must learn to see ourselves and our circumstances just as they are: rich in texture and detail, saturated with beauty and pain. If the therapist can widen a space for welcoming reality within himself, then perhaps he can somehow share this space with another. It is only by freeing yourself, little by little, tear by tear, and smile by smile, of cherished habits of alienating thought and identification that you can become more at-one with the child's picture of the world and begin to comprehend her unique experience of the world. Then, from a place of deep sharing that may sometimes even transcend the role of therapist and patient, meaning, I think, that we are changed by the encounter too, you can begin to sincerely and respectfully lend words to help describe the child's picture of the world and how it may continue to transform.

NOTES

1. I have adapted the phrase "a child's picture of the world" from a book titled *Man's Picture of His World* (1961) by the psychoanalyst Roger Money-Kyrle. However, what I present here is not Money-Kyrle's model.

REFERENCES

Bion, W. R. (1957). On arrogance. Paper presented at the 20th Congress of the International Psychoanalytical Association, Paris, July-August. In W. R. Bion, *Second thoughts*, 86–92. London: Karnac, 1984.

Bion, W. R. (1962a) A theory of thinking. *International Journal of Psychoanalysis* 43(4-5). In Bion, W. R. (1967). *Second thoughts*, 110–119. London: Heinemann. Reprinted London: Karnac, 1984.

Bion, W. R. (1962b). *Learning from experience*. London: Heinemann. Reprinted London: Karnac, 1984.

Bion, W. R. (1963). *Elements of psychoanalysis*. London: Heinemann. Reprinted London: Karnac: 1984.

Bion, W. R. (1965). *Transformations*. London: Heinemann. Reprinted London: Karnac, 1984.

Bion, W. R. (1970). *Attention and interpretation*. London: Tavistock. Reprinted London: Karnac, 1986.

Bollas, C. (1979). The transformational object. *International Journal of Psychoanalysis* 60: 97–107. In *The shadow of the object*, 13–29. New York: Columbia University Press.

Damasio, A. (2010). *Self comes to mind: Constructing the conscious brain*. New York: Pantheon.

Eaton, J. L. (2011). *A fruitful harvest: Essays after Bion*. Seattle: The Alliance Press.

Ekman, P. (2007). *Emotions revealed*. New York: Owl Books.

Evans, D. (2003). *Emotion: A very short introduction*. Oxford, UK: Oxford University Press.

Hinshelwood, R. D. (1991). *The dictionary of Kleinian thought*. Northvale, NJ: Jason Aronson.

Meltzer, D., and M. Harris Williams. (2008). *The apprehension of beauty: The role of aesthetic conflict in development, art, and violence*. London: Karnac.

Money-Kyrle, R. (1961). *Man's picture of his world: A psycho-analytic study*. New York: International Universities Press. Reprinted 1978, London: Duckworth.

Ogden, T. (1990) *The matrix of the mind: Object relations and the psychoanalytic dialogue*. Northvale, NJ: Jason Aronson.

Panksepp, J., and L. Biven. (2012). *The archaeology of mind: Neuroevolutionary origins of human emotions*. New York: Norton.

Siegel, D. (2012). *The developing mind: How relationships and the brain interact to shape who we are*. New York: Guilford.

Tustin, F. (1981). Psychological birth and psychological catastrophe. In *Autistic states in children*, 96–110. London: Routledge & Paul.

Tustin, F. (1986). *Autistic barriers in neurotic patients*. New Haven, CT: Yale University Press.

Ungunmerr-Baumann, M-R. (2002). Deep listening explained. In www.creativespirits.info/aboriginalculture/education/deep-listening-dadirri (accessed 6-19-14). From M-R. Ungunmerr, *Dadirri: A reflection*. Sydney: Emmaus Productions.

Winnicott, D. W. (1962). *The maturational processes and the facilitating environment*. Madison, CT: International Universities Press, 1965.

Winnnicott, D. W. (1987). *The child, the family, and the outside world.* Reading: Addison-Wesley Publishing.

Winnicott, D. W. (1975) *Through paediatrics to psycho-analysis*. New York: Basic Books.

Chapter Four

Understanding Trauma for Aboriginal Preschool Children

Hearing Their Voices

Norma Tracey

Trauma flings us back into the terror of the initial cataclysm at the center of our psychic being. The pain of becoming becomes unbearable; the terror of dying equally so. I use this chapter to create a space where we as child therapists, preschool and health workers, can think about the links from childhood trauma to adult disturbances, even unto death, as we contemplate the number of young Aboriginal adults who die in custody and who otherwise commit suicide.

Childhood trauma results in adult trauma. That is why the work Gunawirra undertook, that of seeing eight children weekly in two New South Wales preschools over a period of ten sessions, became so important to the child therapists in Gunawirra. These children were chosen by their teachers because they were considered traumatized. No professional workers before us had ever moved the lens in so closely and used psychotherapeutic skills not only to hear their voices, but to try and understand the emotions, the responses of the Aboriginal child living in a household that might cause suffering to that child. The Healing Foundation supported our endeavor.[1] Can we enter the trauma of another race? Is such an action insensitive and of itself racist? If we are to think about emotional suffering, resulting in death, alcohol or drug addiction, domestic violence, and child sexual abuse with any chance of avoiding some of the results, it means we need to walk this tightrope, however dangerous, with some sensitivity. Aboriginal people represent only 3 percent of the total population, yet more than 28 percent of Australia's prison population are Aboriginal (Creative Spirits, 2013).

Many are not criminals, though some are. Some too are victims of racial prejudice and their crimes do not even warrant jail; some are victims of terrible trauma inflicted on their forbears, for which we all continue to pay the price. Many however are victims of early childhood trauma, and it is these I want to use this chapter to think about.

Are many of our Aboriginal children traumatized? I am afraid the answer is often "Yes." Are their parents traumatized? I am afraid the answer is often "Yes." Are the Aboriginal and non-Aboriginal staff at the centers traumatized from working directly with childhood trauma, while at the same time many may have suffered trauma in their own childhood? The answer is often "Yes!"

In this chapter, we try to understand some of the causes for this pain, but especially we try to understand how ways of healing trauma lie powerfully within a group's own cultural rites and traditions. Integral to ancient Aboriginal culture were several means of treating and healing trauma that we in therapy and in our preschools have available to us. I want to base what I have to say here on my further thinking about two of these, *The Dreaming* and the *Dadirri*, or circle of healing. Dadirri is a ritualized circle where the men or women of that community meet together to hear the pain of one of the community in silence, for hours if necessary. It was practiced in most Aboriginal communities, but very few communities continue it today. The Dreaming is a gathering of all the ancient myths of Aboriginal lore passed down orally for centuries. It is the spiritual and imaginative place in our minds, where the Aboriginal people attempted to use their thinking to make sense of the world around them just as any religion does.

THE CORE PSYCHIC SPACE IN THE CENTER OF OUR BEING

Present in all religious beliefs from before time began was the pre-creative space in which being had the potential to become. I am writing here of a neutral, safe psychic space where becoming is a possibility. In this space preconception is a dynamic that begins prior to conception in normal relationships, with both partners suffering preconceptive ambivalence. It also occurs in the psyche as a space that is the precursor of a conceived thought and that continues through every stage of life to death. It is like a womb that may or may not receive a pregnancy; it is the mind or psychic space that may or may not receive a thought. Just as in a normal state of preconception there is a womb and the possibility of a pregnancy, in our minds preconception is the possibility of a formulated thought. It is a dynamic between being and not being. This is a dreaming space, a waiting space, held by faith. Sometimes it is the faith of another, like a couple with hope of a pregnancy, or a mother's faith in her infant to grow and become. The analytic therapist's faith is like this. The preschool teacher's faith is like this. This faith holds the possibility of a spark in the darkness. So what is healing? It is a holding receptivity of this space, inside which the possibility of becoming can take form, despite previous disaster. What I am proposing is that the preschool center, its workers, and our health professionals have the capacity to hold that potential.

This safe space remains in the center of our being and we return to it many times to find nourishment, equilibrium, and the capacity to grow; it is the womb in which our psyche can form and reform through every stage of our existence. In trauma, it is this space that becomes deadened in order to defend against unbearable pain. Yet this fundamental core that is unknown and unknowable to ourselves, or to any other, is a sacred, mysterious, precious space, which must be safeguarded. It is part of the true self. LaMothe writes that "it cannot be subjugated to culture or language or the projections of theorists or anything else" (LaMothe, 2006, p. 447). This mystery of self at its core can also be found in Bion's notion of "O" as well as Lacan's notion of the "Real." In Bion's writings, O is the ultimate reality, the center of the infinite.

This space, which parents first hold, predates parental reverie. Parents hold the memory of a void before there was a container in which to dream the possibility of a child into existence. Initially there is no fetus, no child, not even a dream of a child, but only a potential space to dream into. The paradox remains that the journey back to that space is always taken alone, but cannot occur without the presence of "the other," and that the other holds the faith by their presence. It may well be the space about which Bion (1970) writes, a space that has no memory or present or future desire. This is the space that a therapist holds for a patient, and the space the preschool teacher holds for the child.

There is not only this potential for a space in which to have the possibility of creating, but also a terror at the center of human existence, of living and of dying. Bion and Michael Eigen have continuously written of the cataclysmic nature of our beginnings. I want to emphasize that that cataclysm is not only a terror of dying but also a terror of living, since living means bearing the unbearable pain, which must *paradoxically become bearable* if we are to be born. I am supposing this space becomes neutralized and safe through surviving the central terror of being and not being. I see that space as the precursor to or earliest template of what in Kleinian thought is conceptualized as the depressive position.

THE DREAMING

In Grotstein (1981), he essentially asks, How do we dream? Who is the dreamer? The dreamer within us that we do not, cannot ever know. Who does our dreaming? Who makes up who we are and imbues it with meaning for us? Ancient Aboriginals talked of singing one's self into existence. Some "self" unknown and unknowable to us is active in our unconscious, working to make up who we are, to dream us and dream those around us into existence, creating our own myths from the world we live in. This continual creating of self, of all the others in our world, and of the environs we live in, is our own Aboriginal Dreaming that goes on and on.

The whole spiritual basis of The Dreaming, with its Aboriginal cultural rituals and beliefs, gave a meaning to life and a purpose to being. The rituals, the rites of passage gave an Aboriginal person a spiritual realm and a basis for living. The capacity to symbolize present in all Aboriginal belief systems is central to life and to recovery from trauma for all mankind. If we cannot imbue the world around us from the source of our own internal mind then we have no way of communicating with the external world and owning the significance of our actions. Aboriginal culture's understanding of the value of ritual gave its community and its individuals structure born out of these symbols of belief. With subjugation and colonization of the Aboriginal peoples of Australia, their worldview was lost to them and its loss was and continues to be enormous.

THE LOSS OF THE CAPACITY TO SYMBOLIZE AS A RESULT OF TRAUMA

In trauma the unconscious is unable to process the present, which means that no symbol formation can occur. The capacity to move, for example, from "this is a rock" to consider what the rock may symbolize is lost to the traumatized. In Bion's terms, the movement of thought from unconnected bits he called beta elements through to alpha elements describes the movement of undigested things in themselves to a symbol, a model, an abstraction, and to a storage of what we could call software in our minds, making a path available to be drawn on in future experiences. It is this movement that is lost in trauma. This is the big difference between a thought that has a thinker and a thought that cannot be thought. In trauma, thought is too terrible to be thought. In the preschool setting, the child's capacity to imagine needs to be in the forefront in order to support the capacity to play, the capacity to be curious, because the capacity to sing and dance and symbolize are an integral part of the healing of trauma. These are the capacities needed for a good holding and containing space.

THE HEALING CIRCLE: DADIRRI

Another important gift from Aboriginal people is the gift of deep listening, ritualized and enacted in the healing circle called Dadirri.

In "A Reflection," Miriam-Rose Ungunmerr writes,

> NGANGIKURUNGKURR means "Deep Water Sounds." *Ngangikurungkurr* is the name of my tribe. The word can be broken up into three parts: *Ngangi* means word or sound, *Kuri* means water, and *kurr* means deep. So the name of my people means "the Deep Water Sounds" or "Sounds of the Deep." Dadirri recognises the deep spring that is inside us. It is inner, deep listening and quiet, still awareness. We call on it and it calls to us . . . When I experience Dadirri, I am made whole again. . . .There is no need of words. A big part of Dadirri is listening. . . . The contemplative way of Dadirri spreads over our whole life. It renews us and brings us peace. It makes us feel whole again. . . . Our people have passed on this way of listening for over 40,000 years. (2002)

Ungunmerr adds: "We are *putymeme*, born from the earth before time began. We are part of our land, the landforms, the trees, the animals, and the language" (Farrelly, 2003, p. vii).

THINKING ABOUT THE CORE OF TRAUMA

As described earlier in this book, Gunawirra was fortunate to be able to provide therapy using art as a medium in seventy to eighty one-hour psychotherapy sessions with Aboriginal preschool children. We include more about this in our Introduction. What I want to address here is how we and our workers were shocked at the degree and the intensity of the children's trauma. Every session was analyzed with a skilled psychoanalytic supervisor and then again in a group. We thought this was in order to understand the trauma of the child; we quickly learned it was also to understand the way their trauma entered us and gave us an opening to our own childhood traumas, to areas we would not otherwise access.

We think of trauma as being caused by an event or series of events or an accumulation of events where the degree of suffering is beyond the capacity of the child's internal world to tolerate or suffer.

Protective defenses born from internalized positive experiences collapse, boundaries that hold the vulnerable child's inner self collapse, and bad internal objects triumph over good objects, as in some science-fiction movies or *Lord of the Rings* or the Harry Potter movies. The child feels assaulted and persecuted. It is as if good is no longer stronger than evil, and the neutralized center, instead of being a potential space in which to grow, deadens everything that comes into it in an effort to deaden the pain. The child's capacity to grow simply stultifies; whatever level of growth he or she had achieved earlier ceases to be able to move forward or progress in any way. Growth is felt to be as dangerous as death by annihilation.

Trauma flings the vulnerable small child back into the terror of the initial cataclysm at the center: *the pain of being becomes unbearable; the terror of dying and the terror of living are equally unbearable.*

> To make that point clearer, using a pictorial image: a party of some five people were survivors from a shipwreck. The rest had died of starvation or had been swept overboard from the remnants of the raft. They experienced no fear whatsoever—but became terrified when they thought a ship was coming near. The possibility of rescue, and the even greater possibility that their presence would not be noticed on the surface of the ocean, led them to be terrified. Previously the terror had been sunk, so to speak, in the overwhelming depths of depression and despair. (Bion, 2005, p. 21)

I began to think about those slow deaths by suffocation. I think of suffocation as possible even in the womb rather than face the terror of being born and living. Pain cannot be suffered if it is too great; there is a "close-down" as a protection. We call this "autistic" because as a result of the close-down an area of psychic "deadness" ensues. But the close-down leaves the pain festering, unprocessed, and intrusive into all that the small child is and does. This is a universal process, one not linked to race or age, child or adult.

The fear of a cataclysm of annihilation on one hand, and a terror of being born and alive on the other threatens and intrudes on the important central space of becoming. Nothing living can enter it and live. It kills any and all efforts at life.

I propose that this closing-down is what has happened to the Aboriginal people as a result of the trauma of persecution literally to death by early colonists, which involved the loss of a spiritual basis for their existence as well as the loss of family, country, and community. Trauma ruptures the *central core self* in a way that is horrifying to imagine. It aborts the psychic fetal beginnings by killing the "holding" mother. The internal good mother's containing womb is shattered. It becomes a sterile womb that deadens all emotion. The central core is violated. The inner world becomes a dark, frightening abyss instead of a safe and protective place. Life is rooted in abject fear and terror, freezing all emotion and joy in living. The child no longer has the potential to dream.

For the Aboriginal, owing to the loss of their rituals and symbols of their culture, those feelings and that morality that give connection and meaning to life are also lost. They commit suicide, abuse their children, perform sexual actions without love or meaning . . . and "Traditions and ancient authorities nested in millions of years of trial and error unravel" (Juan Santos, personal communication, 2006).

The biological event exactly mirrors the psychic phenomenon. The autobiographical memory of trauma is thought to be stored in the right brain's orbito-frontal cortex. Neurologists have taught us that the part of the brain that accomplishes the requisite transcendence for forgiveness is the frontal cortex, its mediating, thinking part. In traumatized states, this part of the brain cannot function. Rather, the amygdala is activated, the reptilian part of the brain that registers only safety-or-danger, fight-or-flight. The experience is visceral, deep within the body, as the adrenals secrete adrenaline, norepinephrine, and—most dangerously—cortisol. We know from recent biological and neurological studies that these "stress hormones" massively interfere with reflective thought and judgment (Schore, 2003).

THE SAFE PSYCHIC SPACE IN THE PRESCHOOL CENTER

This chapter has described the idea of *psychic space*, a place in our minds for receiving, listening, and creating, a space for emotional growth. I would now like to take this idea of a space in the mind of the mother to a space in the forty-three preschool centers in NSW where Gunawirra has projects. These are both government- and community-owned, and in small or larger remote outback towns. In each at least a third of the children are Aboriginal. Some have all Aboriginal children. All are under government surveillance to keep the standards high. Special fees are available for Aboriginal children and special salaries for Aboriginal workers. These preschool centers are a very special environment that focuses on expression through art, music, and drama; they provide a space for imagination to thrive, for curiosity to be valued, and where the possibility of a negotiated life is a reality. Therapists and preschool teachers learn "to welcome and receive the children's primitive communications of distress, they learn to bear the negativities projected onto them" (Jeff Eaton, private communication, 2007), negatives projected not only by the children, but by vulnerable parents who see their children as exposing their inadequacies. In the preschools the capacity to accept the reality of pain is central to all our work. Allowing the surprise of what may begin to exist in such a space allows a potential, although it may be lost when the real-life situation is truly awful. The center can be a healing place for the traumatized child, but it can also be a place where earlier damage to the child is already evident, damage that can create terrible pain for teachers who may unknowingly have experienced similar traumas in their own childhood.

AMY

Background

Amy's preschool is in one of Sydney's poorest areas, at street level below twenty-three floors of units or apartments. The place has a sense of volatility; police cars have been there a number of times, fights are frequently observed in the streets. Because Amy's trauma is similar to that of many children in our preschools, we move the microscope in more closely here in this portion of the chapter to share material from this child, her therapist, her teacher, her carer, and a case supervisor.[2] We listen and we try to process and make sense of this child's awful fear, which threatens any capacity to relate at an intimate level.

Social Worker in Interviews with Amy's Carer

"When you first meet Amy you presume she is like any other happy four-year-old child. She is full of smiles and friendliness to strangers. She walks around talking to everyone, approaching teachers and asking questions confidently. No one scares or intimidates her. She will smile at you and ask what your name is and keep talking to you like she has known you for a long time. Ros, who is Amy's foster carer, said that Amy had a curious mind and loved to discover new things."

> In our discussion group sessions we begin to wonder if Amy has learned how to behave rather than "be" a separate person in her world and survive in it. She seems to lack fear, discrimination, "stranger" danger. There seems to be no obvious self that has doubts, that stumbles, that is "shy" or frightened.

Amy has five older siblings who are currently in their father's care. The two youngest children, Amy and her 1-year-old brother, are in Ros's care. The mother had earlier got in trouble with the Department of Community Services (DOCS), the government's statutory body for care of children, so that Ros had all seven children in her care, but after a time all the children went back to their mother. After the fourth child was born the parents separated, and the mother became pregnant by another man. She then went back to her husband and had two more children. Ros could not look after seven children in her two-bedroom flat, which is why the children are currently split up between Ros and their father. With the oldest, an 11-year-old, Ros and the father of the children organize times that the family can spend together.

Ros said that she was in shock and concerned at how the children, especially Amy, looked this time around; her face was sunken in and gaunt looking, her cheekbones were prominent. It was her aim to get the children back to a healthy standard.

> So we know Amy has been physically neglected. We know there was little or no space for her self, her being; we know the minute, negotiated, moment-by-moment care that builds the experience of who we are has been absent for her. We ask ourselves, Are children that are demanding, expectant, frightened, vulnerable . . . are these normal children struggling to make sense of their world? Are children like Amy in a way thoughtless, in the sense of having no space to think, or is thinking unbearable? We wonder what is beneath this so-obliging exterior. We have a sense of there being no internal organizer or regulator. We understand that trauma ruptures the possibility of an internal organizer. The cataclysmic chaos is too much. It is repressed rather than dealt with. We wonder if this is what has happened to Amy.

The mother visits Amy and her younger brother quite regularly. At first when the mother used to visit and leave to go home Amy would cry and scream after her. Now Amy is more relaxed and will say goodbye to her. Amy appeared very loving to Ros, her carer, and kept on coming up to give her a hug and then walking away during my interview with her.

Next Interview with Ros

"We had mum with us for a few days. It was all right at the time but messed up afterward. They thought they were going home with her—live with mum again. So stressful! I had to settle them down again. It's just the going part that mucks them up. The father is playing up now, not staying home with the bigger kids. Both the parents are very young. Amy is very active. She talks to everyone. Makes friends with everyone no matter who they are. Even if I stop pushing the pram to get a breath, she takes over so we do not stop."

> We begin to wonder at the meaning of the activity the "must keep going, must not stop." What does stopping mean? Does it mean you have to face aloneness, you have to face parts of yourself you have cut off from? You have to face and suffer real and painful feelings of aloneness and abandonment. In the absence of a single holding mother, Amy must seek holding from "friends" or from anyone she can get it from.

What of the Carer?

"I lived on the block for ages. Most of the outsiders were dangerous. But we used to sleep with our doors open. Everyone used to look after each other. Look after each other's kids. Sometimes you would look after eleven or twelve kids. They all wanted me to look after them. The dad has been leaving the other kids in their aunt's care a lot. He misses his freedom. He's in his late twenties, still young but six children. They started young."

> Here is the image of yet another carer who is caring for this child as a way of meeting her own need to be a "good" carer, a mother, without enough refer-

> ence to a real child with real needs. It almost has the quality of someone picking up stray puppies. Could this be an attempt to keep alive an internal mother by becoming her? In trauma, the internal image is lost or destroyed and one makes up for its absence by enacting it in one's own being, not identifying with it so much as becoming it.

Let us look now at some of Amy's session material and see what it reveals. None of the art therapists knew anything of the children's background during the therapy. All had ways of helping each child understand endings of sessions and the limited number of sessions. For this therapist, providing eight toy birds in a little tree, one for each session, with one ceremoniously removed at the end of each session, was the choice. (Normally there were ten sessions for each child, but for external reasons Amy's sessions began two weeks late. Therefore we knew she only had eight sessions.) Amy had no idea of how many sessions any of the other children in therapy in her center had, but for the same external reasons it was the same number. The sessions were in a small private enclosure in the preschool. We ended up putting sheets right around the area as the worker thought that seeing the fights and drunken falls in the street was disturbing to the worker–child work and relationship.

THERAPIST'S REPORTS

Amy, Session 1

She looks up at me, meeting my eyes with a steady gaze. The teacher says, "You're going to do some painting with Josephine. It's a really special time for you because you're a special girl." She comes with me readily.

I start off by showing her the art materials, pointing out various things out that she can use. "Can I do some painting?" she asks in a bright voice. Absolutely, yes, I reply showing her the water and the brushes (feeling my own keenness). "Can I use some of them now?" she says, looking intently at all the paints. She points to the colors. "This one, now this one, that one too" she says in quick succession, pointing to different colors and where on the palette she wants me to pour them into. She then says "I'll do it" and reaches out to take the small jar from me and starts pouring the paint herself. She pours slowly, carefully, with a great sense of concentration. She continues to use each color, moving around the page counterclockwise, painting one color at a time. She paints deftly and confidently, not hesitating or stopping to consider. "There we go!" she calls out in a bright voice, "make all of them," and I acknowledge she has indeed used all the colors. She has also filled the entire page (as she fills up the therapy space as the session progresses).

"Can you go and get some friends for me?" she says. (I wonder if she is over the initial flurry of trying the new materials and is now uncertain of being here with someone she does not know.) There is a tightening of feeling, is it her anxiety? She resumes painting, calling out "Let's go, let's go, let's go, that one, that one, that one!"

> *We began to wonder how much the calling for friends was an effort to avoid stopping or avoid being alone with the therapist, or to keep the action going as a way of holding herself together.*

She begins to mix up all the colors in the palette. She hums. I hum too. "You got my heart mmmm mmmm," she sings. She looks at me and smiles. I laugh softly. She sings "You know why" . . . "You know whaaaat, it's a love heaaart" she sings (the words are unclear). She asks for more paint. The palette is still full. I suggest she use that. She continues to mix paints and sing. She wants more colors again and tries to get some out of a jar that is nearly empty. "C'mon, c'mon, c'mon!" she says, banging it against the side of the palette. "More color in that, here!" she says, sounding impatient. Her feelings seem to bubble up and then recede again just as quickly. When the session ends, she walks away quickly from me toward her teacher. I say goodbye, see you next week, but she does not look back.

> What can she not tolerate? Why do we have to go and go and go? What is the danger of aloneness? A sense of intimacy that is frightening? Is that so desired and yet so threatening? Does it mean that alone you may have to face your fear of aloneness, your dependency on another, where you risk being dropped?

Amy's art therapist reports: "During supervision I speak of not feeling any warmth or sense of connection, except a for a few moments such as when Amy was singing, or pretend-pouring. I then felt physically exhausted after her first sessions, but I only felt the emotional impact later on. I wonder how this might relate to trauma."

> We were to hear such reporting many times. It was as if the therapist, unknown to herself, was receiving the trauma, but that it did not come into consciousness until much later.

Amy, Session 2

Ros called in to say Amy said she was ill and that Ros had given her Panadol, and when that happens they're not allowed to go to preschool, so she missed her session that week.

> Already a sense of fear is creeping into our thinking. Is the lack of control too much for her? Has the closeness made her sick? Is she just terrified about

"why" she is coming? We are wondering about an internal world of fear becoming exposed in what appeared to be a confident, outgoing child. Did she fear "special" meant being placed and abandoned yet again?

Amy, Session 3

Amy sees her images from Week 1 at the back of the room and says "*Those are mine*." She looks at the three images, appearing to recognize the colorful one with pleasure.

"Can I put this on?" she asks me. "Yes, of course," I say. "Can you put it on for me?" and she accepts my help with the apron. "Can I do cutting?" I say "Yes, of course you can do some cutting."

"My hands have gone! My hands have gone!" she calls out. She tells me her hands are broken and I ask "How are you going to paint with broken hands?" She repeats that they are broken and adds "now they are unbroken," and removes them from the apron. "Do it up for me! Tighter! Tight!" she says as she turns for me to secure the apron at the back. She tells me she "wants" to do some drawing and then adds that she "needs" to do some drawing. I offer her scissors as well, as she had initially asked to do some cutting. She takes some paper, a pink sheet, and places it on the floor; she then places a white sheet on top of the pink, followed by another sheet of pink. This is done quite quickly, and then she turns to gather some further white sheets to place on the table. She sits down at the table and I sit alongside her. "I just need to do some little . . . OK?" "Chop chop," I say, and she quickly "cuts" me off: "Don't say it!" "Mmm?" I say absentmindedly, as my attention is on how she is cutting, and she repeats "Don't say it"; chastened, I reply "OK." She then goes on to tell me what I think is "I teach media" but it turns out to be "I pinch Malea, my friend." I ask her why and she does not reply. "Was she upset after you pinched her?" and she replies with a soft "Yes."

She directs me, telling me exactly how to cut, and how to hold the scissors just like her, how to face the paper in the same direction and cut the same shapes and the same sizes. I ask if she wants me to cut the big piece. She replies, "I tell you, OK. Copy me. Copy me. Like this." "On a big piece?" I ask. "All right, I'm copying you like that." (I'm finding it hard to copy exactly as she is cutting so fast.) As she cuts she watches how I am cutting, making sure my cutting mirrors as closely as possible what she is doing. She then gets the box of oil pastels and starts sorting and organizing them. "I'll get the purple! I'll have to get purple! Purple! Purple! You don't know which color, you have to wait," she tells me. "That's why I do your hair," she says as she reaches up and tries to flop my fringe over my eyes. "Whoa, now I can't see anything!" I say. "That's so the coppers [police] can't see your face," she says. I ask Amy if that is because I don't want them to catch me and she says "No, no, cause them, cause . . ." She suddenly notices the door is open. I ask her if she wants me to close it and she says yes, "That's it." I say, "Then they can't see." Some discussion follows, with her trying to persuade me again to let her paint my hair. I resist and she then says, "Pretend you're at the hairdresser and so playing the game 'I agree to have my hair painted purple. Look at me!'" she says, continuing the pretend game, as though assessing her handiwork.

At the end of the session she wanted to do a bit of gluing. It was almost as though she didn't know how to use glue, she was putting splotches onto the page and then cutting a tiny sliver of pink paper and wanting to stick that onto the white page, which she did. There was a real sense of not knowing what to do with the gluing. It was clumsy and it was as if the confident child again was not sustainable. Then we started running out of time so we removed another bird and counted together that we had five birds, five weeks left.

> Amy is trying to make sense of her world. We imagine that there are a lot of pieces she's having trouble putting together. We think of the tentativeness of the gluing in contrast to her confident drawing. Is she beginning to expose a more real lack of self-assurance? we wondered. There's something about having a safe place. It feels like a very young and profound interaction where need and unknowing do exist. It feels tragic to us that there is no idea of an inner holding person, only of an external presence you must not lose control of. This is a very small infant psychically, not in any way able to tolerate a degree of letting go that one can expect from a preschooler. We wondered, Are the needy parents needy children themselves? Are some mothers having child after child to fill their own emptiness?

Amy, Session 4

I go outside into the playground to fetch Amy and she comes toward me as soon as she sees me. As we enter the building she takes my hand and says "Come with me!" She walks quickly, taking me, almost running, the long way around two tables and we both laugh.

"I've got an idea, I wanna do some of that one! I want water—I want this color, green or purple!" She asks me, "This color, or this color or that color? I want that color. Move that away. C'mon, sit down," she says, as she indicates she is going to be a teacher. "Actually I want green, d'you like green?" "Yeah," I say. She passes me paper, offers me two sheets of green. "Now you'll get a color and I'll get a color, now pink! Lift that up, hold that, actually, good idea, I'll get a piece of paper, just hold it like that." "Like that?" "No'oh! Just have to get water." She's ruffling the paper as it is selected and placed and rearranged. She sneezes twice. "Bless you! Bless you!" she says, "You know I had a boyfriend?" "You have a boyfriend?" I say. "You know, what's his name? What's his name? Ah uh uh ehh! Grahame's my boyfriend's name. Grahame? Do you like his name?" "I like his name, yes."

"Ohh, fucking dog! I know how to swear. I don't care about my mum, what my mum says." (Before I have a chance to respond she changes the subject.) "Who did you come with?" The therapist answers, "I came on my own." (I realized, as I typed these notes, that I repeat every question before answering it!) "Don't you care about what your mum says?" "No'oh, not talking to you! I'm talking to myself. Put that back" (she sounds angry). Am I getting too close to the hurting inside her? It feels like a show of bravado, not caring! "Move now, I'm goin'. Put that back. C'mon lets go. We'll come back." (She goes around to the naughty corner section with me in tow.) "Out the back. C'mon."

"Get the glue. Good idea. No I got it! Ah look at this here, sit down. Cut the little piece off" (she wants to cut a small piece of white paper) "so you can dip it in the water. I'll hold it, OK, go."

"You're a big noter," she says. "I'm a big noter?" "Yes, cause you've hurt someone." "Did I hurt someone?" "Yes." "Who did I hurt?" "My friends." "Your friends? What did I do to them?" I ask. "You hit them, you're a naughty girl." "I don't hit my friends," I say. "Yes you do, at your school. Yeh, you hit my friends at your school" (here she is returning to what she really wants to say). "When you're at my school you hit me and you hit my friends."

"I wouldn't want to hit you," I tell her.

"Sometimes I smack people. Sometimes some people be naughty and I smack 'em."

"You smack 'em?" I ask.

"Right, get out in the naughty corner now. Cause you're naughty, you won't listen to me. What I say. Cause you're naughty, you won't listen to me all the time." (I feel the weight of being silenced, the weight of not knowing why.) "Keep being naughty. Fuck you . . .? Do you want me to punch your face? Put glue in here."

I say "Mm'mm."

"Don't talk!" she yells out, cross. "I told you, no talking!" She talks to herself quietly (fiddling with the paper bits and the glue from memory, sort of organizing or packing up). "Leaving it here when I come back to school." Then there's a pause.

"Why you saying my name all the time? What, why you saying my name all the time? Wait there, nearly finished, then we go" (she returns to a more normal, upbeat voice). "Jenny, the schoolteacher. Her's a fuckhead. Her's a lazy. Her's a lazy dog. No, her's a lazy lady."

The manic flurry of activity stands out most in this session. The use of the therapist as an object rather than a person, the disorganized play and moving from one thing to another, the constant swearing in the effort to express anger and act strong and unafraid. She must not pause. She must not stop. If you stop you think, you feel you are in pain. The manic doing is a kind of crazy way of holding herself together so that she does not disintegrate. We are aware of a frenzy.

Amy, Session 5

Amy was away at the time scheduled for this session, but the narrative flow was not broken by the interruption.

Amy, Session 6

I go into the playground to collect Amy. She is standing on top of gym equipment and immediately turns to me when she spots me and asks me to "carry her down." I put my arms up and she puts her arms around my neck as I lift her down. (It reminds me of a much younger child, it is trusting and therefore touches me.) She takes my hand and we walk together to the art therapy room.

Once we are alone, the tone changes. In an angry voice she commands "Pass me the glue!" A moment later she asks "You wanna do one or what?" and I tell her that I would like to. We select some paper. "Don't touch it! Leave it!" she tells me, and then "Wait, show me your hand, its dirty," and I realize there are a couple of green streaks on the palm of my hand from opening paint jars.

She tells me "You shut up, or you'll be sent in the naughty corner now." (I have heard this so many times, it's almost as though she needs to say it, rather than have me do it.) I reach over to roll her sleeves up as she is draping them over the palette filled to the brim with paint, and she tells me to leave them down. I show her how my own sleeves are above my elbow and manage to roll hers up. She then she asks me to wipe a bit of paint that she has spotted on one of her sleeves.

She mumbles softly to herself that she "doesn't want to come to school anymore." She tells me that it is because she hates me. "I hate you singing out my name, I hate you singing out my name, I hate you singing out my name, I hate you singing out my name!" Then "No!" she says, "Call every people." (I later realize she is telling me that she does not want to be singled out and would like me to "call" others, but did not realize this at the time.) I continue, "You just want to be left alone and not be bothered." "I want to play," she says. I reply "Yes, you want to play" and she adds "Let me play around" and I add, "Yes, and it's no fun if somebody keeps interrupting." "Don't talk! I hate talking!" she warns, and then suddenly decides that she needs to go to the toilet. She asks in a soft voice "Can you carry me?" tucking her chin into her chest and looking at me shyly. (I am not certain that I have the strength to carry her but feel it is important to respond to her reaching out to me.) I tell her that I will carry her a little bit of the way. She gets up onto a chair so that I can pick her up more easily. I carry her to the top of the stairs and tell her I can't carry her down the stairs and she says, "Yes you can." I carry her to the bottom of the stairs and then set her down gently and she takes my hand. (Here there's a sense of her reaching out, and accepting my responding, as opposed to the shutting-down times.)

She reaches the toilet area, which opens out onto the main part of the preschool. I stand a few feet from her looking into the preschool area to give her some privacy. She talks the whole time and shows me the places for different children's things. She takes my hand again, and we return to the art therapy room.

She starts to wash her paintbrush and I think she is packing up, but no, she wants more paint and tells me to sit down so that she can paint another bracelet. "Sit down, fuckin, so I can reach!" I agree to sit "just for one second." (This is feeling now as though it is going too far, allowing this manner of speaking to me.) She paints again. I then say that when she has finished we have to count the birds. I ask her if she can remember how many sessions we have had and how many we have left.

I tell her again that the session is over and she tries again to get me to sit down. I attempt to distract her with counting the number of birds. "Blue, blue, blue lid, blue lid," she calls out. I try to pack up the paints and she starts to whine and I say again "I know, it's so hard to stop isn't it" (and I feel genuinely sorry for her—she really does not want the session to end). She climbs onto the chair to remove a bird, but then wants me to pick her up and lift her up higher, which I do. She removes a bird.

> Amy is losing control of the session. What will happen if you lose control? What happens if you cease to dominate the other? What kind of abandonment ensues? The movement has little goal in it, the goal is the moving. It has the quality of a masturbatory activity of sustaining excitation and aliveness as a defense against deadness. Then comes the anger. The hatred of needing the other. It is need that is the problem; if you can defend against need then you will not be hurt. No one can or will hurt you. You are omnipotent. Her infant dependency is beginning to expose itself, her need of a mother. This is terrifying, since the one you love will and can and does abandon you. The holding-

together defense is not working properly anymore. The therapist becomes the symbol of a much earlier infant–mother relationship. Love is the problem. It exposes neediness and the pain of loss. The idea of an ending cannot be conceived it is so painful. Easier to cut it off and end it yourself. Here we enter the central drama in the trauma.

Amy, Session 7

I go out into the playground today to collect Amy. She is sitting under the awning and as I approach I look at her and say "Hello Amy! Coming to do some painting with me?" and she replies "No." "Oh!" I say, surprised, and I sit down beside her, but her response remains firm. A teacher says "What's the matter, Amy, don't want to do painting today?" Amy then looks at me and says "Don't poose me." The teacher and I are puzzled. "Don't poose me!" she says again. "Don't choose me?" I say, and she says "Yes, don't poose me. Poose someone else." And she suggests the children Judy is meeting with.

Amy moves away to play over on the far side of the playground. I am uncertain as to what to do. I sit there for a while longer with various children milling around.

I wait until the time the end of the session is reached. I remove a seventh bird from the branch and go out to find Amy. She is sitting on her own at a table coloring in a Christmas drawing in orange and green. I tell her that our time is over and that I will see her again next week. I get up and move away and hear her say something softly under breath which sounds very much like "Go away!!"

As I wait I mull over what happened during our last session, with her reaching her arms out to me when I arrived, and how difficult it was at the end of the session when she really wanted it to continue. However, I also recall her clearly telling me soon into the session about not wanting me to call her name out, which at the time I thought was about her not wanting me to interrupt her, and then even telling me she hated me. I remember feeling at the time that something from her world was being enacted in our time together, a pattern of both approaching and rejecting.

Group discussion: We discuss this. We feel the pain of this child. One of the workers calls me the next day and says that she feels traumatized by the child's pain. We should not have begun something we cannot end. We think about the possibility of ongoing therapy for such deprived children and the difficulty if the therapist becomes the real love object. It is impossible. There is no union that does not have a frustration, a loss. The problem for such a child as Amy is that the initial loss was too much, too soon, and too out of her control. Such a child dreams of everlasting union as a real possibility. Not a union that slowly ends in a separateness. The discussion creates quite a feeling of distress. The end of the therapy is at first a no-end. Amy has terminated, aborted it.

Amy, Session 8 (final session)

The therapist reports: I went out into the playground today feeling somewhat nervous, not sure what her response would be, after her refusing last week's session by telling me not to choose her but to choose someone else. Her response today was the same. She told me very clearly that she did not want to do any painting with me. I said that was OK but that I would be around for our time together if she changed her mind. We had discussed in supervision about being somewhere that she could see me, so that if she decided that she did want to "do some painting" I would be accessible and able to take her around to the art therapy room.

Amy played around with the other children as if I wasn't there.

Amy assembled some blocks in the shape of a gun and pretended to shoot me. She then raced off with a couple of boys who were playing a shooting game, returning shortly afterward to make certain she'd "finished me off." She held the gun up to my face with the "barrel" pointing dead center between my eyes, from about 6 or 8 inches away, and then raced off again. All I could manage was "Oh, you're shooting me!" (really feeling the significance of this gesture). Amy went off and played in a place in the playground away from me.

At about the time for the end of the session Amy came up to me. She wanted to count the birds and asked me to take her into the room and then lift her up. There was a chair close by, so I suggested she step up onto that and I pulled it over for her. She began to count "One, two" for the sessions left. She wanted to remove both birds. I told her we usually remove a bird when the session is over (thinking still about next week, not realizing, as she already had, that this *was* our last session). She said "But I don't want to do any more painting," sounding very young, and with her feelings of not wanting to in her voice, not strident or angry, but real. I answered her gently that "Its OK, you don't have to," wanting her to know that I was hearing not only her words but, more crucially, her feelings.

I stood up to leave the center a little later, and as I did so Amy took both my hands in hers and said she wanted to do some painting. I looked at Amy and said I would love to do some painting with her but I couldn't, everything was already packed up, but that she had the bird which she could take home with her. I left with such a mixture of sadness and other hard-to-name feelings, many of which I still cannot sort out and am left with.

Then, right at the very end, just as I am finishing a session with another child, Amy comes to me and puts her arms around me. In that moment is a possibility of a spark of love that survives the hatred of loss. I leave in some degree of pain myself, but there has been one sweet parting moment between us.

We speak of teachers important to us in our childhood and how they shine within us as beacons on the darkest nights, how they have affected our lives. Of how much trauma is eased, relieved by the capacity to mourn loss. Actually this was difficult for us, discussing this ending or any of the cases, because the therapist could not be present. We too had lost her and been left alone. I later asked if she minded if I could use her sessions. She said she was grateful and would be really pleased if I did. When she read this write-up she said the reason she had left the group was that she herself could not cope with the pain at that time, or since. We were to continue with that preschool, but Amy never saw the therapist again.

Why is the memory of this work so alive in my mind eighteen months later? Why did the student interviewing the carer in her last supervision session with me share her own childhood traumas? Why did it feel like some kind of parting gift? She wanted me to know, she did not need me to do anything about it, just to know. How does the trauma of another become a trauma for the one receiving it, or awaken traumatic parts of the one receiving it? I am not sure I know the answer to this.

ATTACHMENT GONE WRONG

None of the disciplines that deal with infant development are any longer in doubt that the most crucial element of all is attachment by the infant to a singular safe caregiver, and that bonding by the mother or caretaker ensures this. From Amy we saw that the frustration of not being able to take one's love objects for granted is enormous and can only be observed as a massive trauma. It meant that children like Amy would close down in despair, seeking this bonding everywhere without discrimination, or maybe just doing what the adults wish as a matter of survival.

The issue of attachment is particularly relevant to the Aboriginal community. The disturbance of this attachment through loss of land, family, children, community, and culture has created a disorientation, an emotional confusion, made worse and further deepened by what occurred in what is known as the Stolen Generation. This core loss of individual attachment, obvious in Amy, means the child's entire secure base is undermined. In wider society this can create some serious problems with regard to mental health or addictions in early and later adulthood. In a culture already in disarray, the addition of another culture through an intercourse, whether willing or unwilling, does not give security.

The Child Care Center is the perfect place to correct this. We know that the life a child has with his or her mother in the beginning and onward for the whole of his or her life is made up of negotiated moments. We know these negotiated moments also make up the whole of our interaction with the children at the Child Care Centre.

THE TRAUMA OF ABSENCE

Here I would like to bring in the meaning of absence. For Bion, the unconscious cannot conceive of an absence. It conceives instead of a paranoid persecutory *presence* so that the pain of not having is converted into internal images of persecution; the child is not just hungry, a monstrous persecutory internal presence creates the bodily and psychic pain of want. If the wanting is greater than the images one holds of receiving and of having that want relieved, then the system breaks down. Balance or equilibrium is lost, and lost with it is the meaning of being able to construct ourselves in a way that can take basic living experiences for granted. Home is safe, dinner will be served, my mother and father do love me. Where the negative is more powerful than the positive experiences, the little child's being becomes preoccupied with defending against that negative terror experience. At the deepest level, the pain and suffering caused by loss—if it cannot be suffered—is cut off, as one of our earliest defenses occurs. This may be the psyche's way of protecting us so that we do not die of the pain. However, the cure may be worse than the illness, since then we cannot feel, either for ourselves or for others. The internal caring mother, the foundational brick of selfhood, is gone. The deadening leaves an empty, autistic-like space that has no life in it. Bion spoke of it being like a devastating explosion, with nothing left but ruins and total emptiness that kills anything that tries to enter it. The work to open up this space is long and deep and difficult. It has to be accomplished in small, tolerable doses; it has to happen at the right psychic times so that the vulnerable person can tolerate it at that time.

PARENTS

The parents give their best to their children, but sometimes a traumatized infancy has left them with a best that is not good enough. The mother, try as she might, has been given no real models on which to base parental behavior; the parents have no road map from their mothers. Amy's mother constantly turns up. She simply cannot defeat her own addictions. Tragically, the loss she has experienced we see repeated in her child, with devastating results. Amy clings to her when she turns up at the preschool. "You will come and get me after school?" The mother says, "Yes!" knowing she will not come but unable to cope with handling the pain of her child's need for her. What it means for Amy is an increasing sense of betrayal and mistrust.

This concept was put into words for me by psychoanalyst Jeff Eaton. "There is a 'shape,' a particular state of mind . . . that is very complex, involving horror, dread, violence, intrusion, humiliation, which can be experienced *but not thought about*. This may link to the worker's sense of fragmentation and dissociation. It is a chilling 'place' and it can be symbolized in the form of nightmares and waking panics" (Jeff Eaton, private communication, 2010). I am sure this is the experience I am attempting to write about in this chapter. We become trapped in this mind state. Our own traumas may be involved in this, and we may meet with such a collision, such an impact, that no space is available in the mind for processing or neutralizing or thinking about it. "So the analyst, in the midst of the noise of distress . . . still needs to be able to hear the sound of this terror which indicates the position of the person beginning to hope that he might be rescued" (Bion, 2005, p. 21).

BELONGING AND NOT BELONGING AS CENTRAL TO TRAUMA

For the Aboriginal people and their sense of oneness with the earth, this country was their womb. The Aboriginal people see colonization as being prematurely thrown out of this womb space. In discussion with Graham Toomey, our Aboriginal artist, I was shocked into the reality of what this meant for Aboriginal people. "Norma for you others, you care and tend the land, you own the land, you might even love the land. Norma, for us it is different. We Aboriginal people—*we are the land*!" The safe space is part of us, we are it; it is us. For these people, in losing this space their core existence is lost. If you are not in the womb you die. Belonging and not belonging is a theme throughout this book, a theme that creates tensions between First People and the new arrivals. It is true that no one really belongs, but it is a very serious matter when that illusion is ruptured prematurely and permanently; then the loss has very serious consequences.

For us health workers, for the preschool staff too, herein lies a paradox. Sometimes when we think we have arrived at a place of despair it may well be the beginning of hope. It may be we have truly heard the despairing voices of our children. Is there hope in this? We have allowed their despair into our being. Is this Dadirri way the healing?

The cost of this work is enormous. So too are the rewards.

NOTES

1. The Healing Foundation is a special funding set up after Sorry Day on February 14, 2008. On this historical occasion the Australian Prime Minister Kevin Rudd publicly in Parliament apologized to the Aboriginal people of Australia for all the wrongs perpetrated on them by white people since the colonial settlement of Australia. At that time the government, as part of the atonement, set up this special foundation funding to be used to work at understanding the nature of Aboriginal transgenerational trauma and how it impacted on present-day lives. It was the receiving of that fund, together with funding from VFFF (Vincent Fairfax Family Foundation) and The Trust that allowed this project to proceed.

2. I would like to thank Josephine Pretorius for granting me permission to use her sensitive work with this child and some of the material from that work in this chapter. I would also like to thank Diana Covic, who gave me permission to include her work with the child's carer. The

preschool has become an important center for Gunawirra, and at present six children there are in long-term psychotherapy with no time limit set, so that the work can continue for as long as it is needed. For his supervision of our work there we thank Jeff Eaton.

REFERENCES

Bion, W. R. (1970). *Attention and interpretation*. London: Tavistock. Also in *Seven Servants*, book 4, 1–128. New York: Aronson, 1977.

Bion, W. R. (2005). Seminar 2: Rome, 9 July 1977. In *The Italian Seminars*, 15–26. London: Karnac.

Creative Spirits. (2013). Australian prison rates. In www.creativespirits.info/aboriginalculture/law/aboriginal-prison-rates#ixzz2u0xTXKDA (accessed 2-19-14). Information drawn from the article, Australia, the mother of all jailers of Aboriginal people. *The Stringer* 11-22-2013.

Farrelly, E. (2003). *Dadirri: The spring within: The spiritual art of the Aboriginal people from Australia's Daly River region*. Darwin, NT: Terry Knight and Associates.

Grotstein, J. S., ed. (1981). Who is the dreamer who dreams the dream and who is the dreamer who understands it? In *Do I Dare Disturb the Universe: A Memorial to Wilfred R. Bion*, 357–417. Beverly Hills, CA: Caesura Press. Reprinted London: Maresfield Reprints, 1983; London: Karnac, 1990.

LaMothe, R. (2006). Constructing infants: Anthropological realities and analytic horizons. *The Psychoanalytic Review* 93(3): 437–462.

Schore, A. N., ed. (2003). *Affect regulation and the repair of the self.* New York: Norton.

Trevarthen, C., and K. J. Aitken. (2001). Infant intersubjectivity: Research, theory, and clinical applications. *Journal of Child Psychology and Psychiatry* 42(1): 3–48.

Ungunmerr, M-R. (2002). Dadirri: A reflection. Nauiyu, Daly River, NT: Emmaus Productions.

Ungunmerr-Baumann, M-R. (1993). Dadirri: Listening to one another. In J. Hendricks and G. Hefferan, eds., *A spirituality of Catholic Aboriginals and the struggle for justice*, 34–37. Kangaroo Point, Brisbane: Aboriginal and Torres Strait Islander Apostolate.

Chapter Five

The Neurobiological Basis of Trauma in Early Childhood

Shiri Hergass

This chapter explores the effects of early childhood trauma on the neurobiological development and structure of the brain. We place a particular focus on trauma experienced in the Australian Aboriginal culture, including transgenerational trauma, in order to support our work with preschool children and staff in Aboriginal areas. We aim to gain a better understanding of the causes and effects of trauma in order to provide more effective and timely therapeutic interventions.

For the benefit of a foundational understanding to our work we will define exactly what stress and trauma are, the trauma caused by colonization and transgenerational trauma, and how these affect early brain development. We will also discuss the importance of healthy relationships and attachments in the early years; the impact of trauma and stress on a child's well-being from a physiological, psychological, and social perspective; and, finally, interventions for helping to heal this trauma.

As child therapists, art therapists, social workers, psychotherapists, and preschool teachers, we understand the devastating effects trauma experienced in childhood can have on the development of any child. But what these children are experiencing is perhaps even more acute and devastating given the vast change in their social structure in such a very short period of time, and the chaos this has caused to their communities, family groups, and identities.

A GLIMPSE AT THE AUSTRALIAN ABORIGINAL CONTEXT

Before colonization, Aboriginal society provided optimal conditions for the health and well-being of families and children through its collective nature. Multiple mothering was common, men played a significant role, and elders and other members of extended families provided important support and nurturing to children. The current high levels of child abuse and neglect in Aboriginal communities reflect the deterioration of traditional nurturing practices since colonization, as well as the impact of transgenerational trauma on caregivers' abilities to successfully nurture children.

Children of the Stolen Generations were separated from their families, institutionalized, physically and sexually abused, and psychologically mistreated. Anger, substance abuse, ill health, self-harm, suicide, and post-traumatic stress disorder (PTSD) are some of the many consequences of this trauma. Moreover, these children missed out on the formation or continuation of a holding relationship, a traditional Aboriginal expression of attachment and bonding, thus eroding the opportunity for healthy and secure parent–caregiver experiences.

Indigenous Australians currently experience higher levels of illness and premature death than non-indigenous Australians. Aboriginal life expectancy is up to twenty years lower than that of the total population. Noncommunicable and largely preventable diseases account for 70 percent of this difference.

THE DEVELOPMENTAL IMPORTANCE OF CHILDHOOD

The first years of an infant's life are critical for brain, social, and emotional development. During early childhood (birth to age 4), brain development peaks, and its growth is then faster than at any other developmental stage. The size of a 4-year-old's brain is 90 percent the size of an adult's brain (Pally and David, 2000). Trauma experienced during early childhood may also alter the brain's biology and functions, and have long-term negative consequences.

For similar reasons, a child's emotional environment and caregiver experiences in early childhood are developmentally important. A safe environment with loving caregivers is important to support a child's developing sense of safety and trust in the larger world. A secure attachment to one or more caregivers in one's early years can affect behavior and relationships into adulthood (Perry, 2001). Stressors and traumatic experiences in children's early years may affect not only their physiology and physical health, but also their emotional and psychological development, and social and coping skills.

Fortunately, therapeutic interventions and nurturing relationships can help ameliorate the impact of early childhood trauma. Preschools with caring teachers who see the child often and are able to look after his or her physical and emotional needs can be the one profound catalyst in helping to heal trauma. Art therapy is another promising intervention, because it engages the brain in ways that enhance healing and promote positive coping skills. Art therapy also creates a safe space where children can explore their emotions, and provides an opportunity for children to form healthy relationships with adults. At the level of the body, both of these approaches create neuropeptides and dopamine in the prefrontal cortex of the brain, supporting the growth of new tissue and the rebuilding of neural pathways that have become inhibited by the effect of trauma.

WHAT ARE STRESS AND TRAUMA?

Stress is a state of high arousal that is difficult to manage. When experiences are too challenging, the body's stress response takes over and produces the stress hormone *cortisol*. The presence of a certain amount of cortisol is important, as it helps teach children what is unacceptable or dangerous. However, cortisol production during periods of long-term stress can undermine health.

Stress is generated by the unpredictable and uncontrollable. With support, stress may be manageable, particularly if strong social bonds are present. For example, one study found that children with secure attachments do not release high levels of cortisol under stress, whereas insecure children do (Gunnar and Nelson, 1994).

Trauma is any experience that threatens a person's life, or causes intentional harm (American Psychiatric Association, 2009). Experts have found that it is traumatic even to witness trauma toward someone else; it is also traumatic to be the perpetrator of harm or death to another person. Many of the Aboriginal children we work with have witnessed serious domestic violence and life within constantly chaotic surroundings.

Trauma invokes a feeling of helplessness and can be damaging or disabling to the body or mind. According to Kalsched (1996), "Any experience that causes unbearable psychic pain or anxiety" is considered traumatic (p. 1). An experience is considered unbearable "if it overwhelms the usual defensive measures (p. 1). There are two types of trauma: (1) a single, unexpected stressor, such as a school shooting or natural disaster (e.g., a hurricane); and (2) a long-standing ordeal, such as abuse or neglect extending over years. Verbal abuse, such as being called "stupid" or "worthless," can also be very traumatic for children, as can being left unattended or alone.

COLONIZATION AS TRAUMA

The traumatic effects of colonization on the Australian Aboriginal people have made it extremely difficult for them to maintain their traditional ways of caring for their children. One of the most profound traumas has been the forcible removal of Aboriginal children from their families. Most indigenous families have experienced removal of children or displacement of entire families into reserves, missions, or other institutions, and most families have been affected over one or more generations.

Children who were separated from their families were institutionalized, physically and sexually abused, psychologically mistreated, and had less exposure to cultural and spiritual knowledge and identity. Anger, substance abuse, physical ill health, self-harm, and psychological distress are some of the many consequences of such extreme traumatic experiences. These layers of violence and abuse have created what Atkinson (2002) calls "trans-generational trauma."

Transgenerational Trauma

Historical or *transgenerational trauma* is defined as the subjective experiencing and remembering of events, whether in the mind of an individual or the life of a community, that are passed from adults to children in cyclic processes as "collective emotional and psychological injury, over the life span and across generations" (Muid, 2006). Duran and Duran (1995) say that historical trauma becomes embedded in the culture memory of a people and is passed on by the same mechanisms through which culture is generally transmitted, and therefore becomes "normalized" within that culture.

Australian Aboriginal children continue to be exposed to the cycle of damage resulting from transgenerational trauma today, as indicated in the Western Australian Study of Aboriginal Child Health (Zubrick, Lawrence, Silburn et al., 2004), where 35 percent of Aboriginal children were reported to be living in households where a caregiver or caregiver's parents had been forcibly separated from their family, and 24 percent were living in families affected by forced relocation from their country.

Effects of Transgenerational Trauma

The transgenerational effects of trauma occur through a variety of mechanisms, including the impact on the child's attachment relationship with caregivers, the impact on parenting and family functioning, the effects of violence across generations, the association with parental physical and mental illness, and the disconnection and alienation from extended family, culture, and society. It is also now being discovered that transgenerational trauma has an impact on people's brain development.

ATTACHMENT, BONDING, AND CULTURAL VALUES

Attachment is as a bond that provides an enduring emotional relationship with a particular person, providing safety, comfort, soothing, and pleasure (Perry, 2001). The loss of this relationship may cause severe distress. The basic attachment relationship has been generally viewed as the mother–child relationship.

When Aboriginal children were forcibly removed from their homes, this bond (mother–child)—along with bonds between the child and other caregivers, which are common in Aboriginal culture—was destroyed. According to attachment theory, the absence of an important primary caregiver relationship can lead to emotional and behavioral problems throughout one's life and can affect a person's ability to form healthy relationships with others (Fiona, 2011).

For Aboriginal participants in Yeo's (2003) study, the values of interdependence, group cohesion, spiritual connectedness, traditional links to the land, community loyalty, and inter-assistance were common indicators of social and emotional competence. With children being removed from their families, and the subsequent negative effects of transgenerational trauma, Aboriginal children and families lost opportunities for practicing these important values. In essence, they lost the very important cultural and family values that were intricately tied to social and emotional competence.

The removal of generations of Aboriginal children from families and communities denied these separated children the opportunity to bond with parents and to experience their love and acceptance, and has additionally damaged the confidence of indigenous adults in their ability to parent their own children (Atkinson and Swain, 1999). Despite the fact that these children were in close proximity to their community, they still missed out on the continuation of a traditional "holding" relationship and the chance to bond with other caregivers and elders in the community. It was not possible for the traditional cultural values to be exercised, expressed, or experienced as the children grew up, and this eroded the opportunity for a secure attachment and nurturance (Yeo, 2003). It separated the children from the values and knowledge that are critical for developing social and psychological health, and it destroyed their belief in the safety of their world.

EARLY SOCIAL ENVIRONMENT AND NEUROBIOLOGY

The genetically timed emergence of brain circuits during infancy means it is especially important to experience healthy relationships and attachments then in order for the brain to develop normally (Pally and David, 2000; Schore, 2003). Birth to age 2 is a crucial time for emotional development. The basic systems that manage emotions, our stress-response systems, the responsiveness of our neurotransmitters, and other brain processes (e.g., the neural pathways that encode our implicit understanding of how relationships work) develop during this time.

The psychological and physiological coping strategies established in infancy and toddlerhood tend to persist through life. Both are developed in response to our earliest relationships. These earliest relationships shape our nervous systems, which influence future emotional well-being and the way we respond to stress.

Many aspects of our physiology and emotional behaviors are shaped by our social interactions. The brain itself has been called a "social organ." Our minds and our emotions become organized through engaging with other minds. Our emotional responses do not solely stem from biology, but also from our emotional experiences with other people (Gerhardt, 2004).

Early experiences have a great impact on a baby's physiological systems because these are then so unformed and easily influenced. Stress responses, emotional systems, and even the growth of the brain itself may not progress adequately if the baby doesn't have the necessary environmental and social conditions.

Research shows that genes provide the raw physical ingredients for our minds, but also documents the fact that relationships in infancy are what create our tendencies and personalities. These early relationships help shape the developing nervous system, as well as one's capacity to respond to future stress. This is because these early experiences create physiological expectations as to what are "normal" levels of bio-chemicals, such as serotonin, cortisol, and norepinephrine.

Parents and other caregivers provide meaning for infants both by leading and responding to play and communication of verbal and nonverbal interactions. Touch and physical holding are important (Kaufman and Zigler, 1993). Young children who are not handled or rocked have a reduced production of thyroid hormones, resulting in high levels of stress in the brain. This in turn gives the child an increased feeling of fear and a heightened adrenalin response (Teicher, 2000).

In the early months of life, infants establish what a normal state of arousal looks and feels like. When things drop below or rise above the normal range of arousal, the body's systems go into action to recover the normal state. This kind of norm establishment is a social process that babies do with the people around them.

Positive looks are the most vital stimulus for the growth of the social brain. When a baby looks at his parent smile, or reads her dilated pupils as information that her sympathetic nervous system is aroused, he is pleasurably aroused and his heart rate increases. Neuropeptides and dopamine are released and reach the prefrontal cortex, helping new tissue to grow in the prefrontal brain (Gerhardt, 2004).

Early positive experiences with other people produce brains with more neuronal connections—that is, more richly networked brains. More connections mean better brain performance. During the first year of life, connections are made at a rapid rate. By 18 months, our brain helps us navigate our environment, providing expectations of likely outcomes.

A negative look is remembered and can trigger a biochemical response, just like a positive one. A parent's disapproving face can trigger stress hormones such as cortisol, which stop endorphins and dopamine neurons and the pleasurable feeling they generate. Thus, a young child is highly dependent on the parent for regulation of her emotions. This is especially relevant for children of transgenerational trauma. For example, today Aboriginal children are more likely to be cared for by mothers who are anxious and stressed as the result of transgenerational trauma. Lacking support from the traditional ways of life, including the network of social support, and other caregivers for her children, both the mother and her children suffer the negative consequences.

EFFECTS OF TRAUMA ON EARLY BRAIN DEVELOPMENT

The majority of the brain's neurobiological processes begin early in life. These processes help us function and adapt to society. If these processes are disrupted by trauma, abnormal behavior and cognition may occur. Children, whose brains and body systems are still in the process of development, are especially vulnerable to trauma.

Traumatic memories activate the emotional right brain but decrease activity in the verbal left brain, as if the two were failing to connect. The right brain becomes highly aroused, while the left frontal brain is unable to make sense of the experience and to verbalize it. Without the verbalizing activities of the left frontal brain, in Broca's area and the hippocampus, it's difficult to process and evaluate feelings. These left-brain activities normally put experiences into a context and sequence. Without them, one cannot get into the past and therefore has no ability to let go of the traumatic experience and its memories. Instead these leap into the present as flashbacks.

Recovery may depend on activating the appropriate parts of the left brain to enable it to put the traumatic experience into context and heal (Pennebaker, 1993). However this is not an option for the small child, as the hippocampus is not fully functional until age 3. Without a fully developed prefrontal cortex, there is little chance of overriding the subcortical system with the orbitofrontal cortex, and therefore a child under age 3 who experiences trauma may get stuck in a state constantly appraised as threatening.

When previously traumatized patients were exposed to reexperiencing their trauma using their imagination, one study found that there was heightened activity only in the right hemisphere—the area responsible for most emotional arousal. This state of heightened arousal hinders healthy brain development. Moreover, the part of the left hemisphere called the Broca's area, which is responsible for making experience known as language, was "turned off," a state that is exemplified by the frozen watchfulness often observed in traumatized children (van der Kolk and McFarlane, 1996).

Because of the impact of these fundamental physiological processes, the post-colonization fragmenting of the Australian Aboriginal people's social, familial, communal, and cultural values is impacting the brain development of Aboriginal children. The effects of transgenerational trauma are literally creating changes in the neural pathways of these children's brains (Perry, 2001).

THE INTERPLAY OF TRAUMA, STRESS, AND PHYSIOLOGY

Human babies are born with the expectation of having stress managed for them. As long as a caring adult maintains an infant's equilibrium through touch, stroking, feeding, and rocking, the child tends to have low levels of cortisol (Levine, 2001). Alternatively, children's immature systems are very unstable and reactive, and can react with very high cortisol levels if no one responds to them (Gunnar and Donzella, 2002). By 6 months of age, the normal rhythm of cortisol levels is established, but it takes up to age 4 to establish an adult pattern of cortisol rhythm.

The normal response to traumatic experience is to be afraid. In the brain, the amygdala will initiate a fight or flight response. The sympathetic nervous system will release adrenaline, the heart rate and blood pressure will go up, and cortisol will be produced. These things usually return to normal after a few hours, but when trauma is extreme or chronic that might not happen and it may take up to a year or more to recover.

We know that there are strong links between high cortisol and many emotional dysfunctions such as depression, anxiety, and suicidal tendencies in adulthood, as well as eating disorders, alcoholism, obesity, and sexual abuse (Colomina, Albina, Domingo, and Corbella, 1997). Too much fear can damage the hippocampus and its capacity to retrieve information, as well as affect the ability of the prefrontal cortex to think and manage behavior (Schulkin and Rosen, 1998). High cortisol levels also compromise the body's immune responses, making the individual vulnerable to infection, and can even lead to a decrease in muscle mass and osteoporosis. They may in addition play a part in diabetes and hypertension through responses that increase blood glucose and insulin levels.

Cortisol also interferes with one's capacity to learn, and ability to relax. This response can be useful as a short-term mobilizer to support the fight or flight reflex, as cortisol breaks down fat and protein to generate extra energy. When the stressful situation is over, the body returns to normal. However, if stress persists and high levels of cortisol remain in the body over longer periods of time, other parts of the body can be damaged. Cortisol can then affect the lymphocytes of the immune system, and result in neuron loss in the hippocampus. If this persists, it can lead to forgetfulness in the child, as the hippocampus is central to learning and memory.

If a child experiences continuously high cortisol for a prolonged period, his or her body will eventually react by closing down its cortisol receptors. This is the body's attempt at disengagement from painful feelings through avoidance, withdrawal, and denial of painful experiences (Masone et al., 2001). Children in this state can fall into a pattern of passive coping, which can make them less able to respond when they need to. They may be less responsive to happy stimuli as well.

Alternatively, the brain system that responds to stress may cause children who experience trauma to be impulsive and on constant high alert, and may cause a decline in their overall health. Serious and long-term psychiatric damage, with its risks not only in the present but persisting into adulthood may then occur, which in turn can cause damage to future health and vulnerability to stress throughout life (Felitti et al., 1998; Pynoos et al., 1996).

Strong links exist between high cortisol levels and many emotional dysfunctions in adulthood, such as depression, anxiety, suicidal tendencies, eating disorders, alcoholism, obesity, and sexual abuse (Colomina et al., 1997). As Schulkin and Rosen (1998) point out, too much fear is metabolically costly. It can damage the hippocampus and the capacity to retrieve information, as well as affect the ability of the prefrontal cortex to think and manage behavior. It compromises the body's immune responses, making the individual vulnerable to infection. It can even lead to a decrease in the person's ability to think and manage behavior.

EFFECTS OF EARLY TRAUMA ON PSYCHOLOGICAL AND SOCIAL WELL-BEING

A child's secure attachment to its caregivers has a profound effect on the healthy development of the brain, and ultimately on the personality and future health of the individual. Distress in infants affects their future relationships (Bowlby, 1979), and what happens between the child and his or her primary caregiver is stored as a pattern for future experiences and relationships (Schore, 1994).

Traumatic experiences can cause damage to the brain's right hemisphere. In the first years of life, the right hemisphere is most dominant for processing, expressing, and regulating emotions, and in understanding social interactions (Schore, 1994). Psychological trauma can break down these coping skills and defenses. Children who have been traumatized may later develop such serious conditions as depression, borderline personality, or PTSD. Damage to the right hemisphere occurring through early trauma is also associated with later difficulties in establishing love relationships (Mollon, 1993).

In the early months of life infants establish, along with the people around them, what a normal state of arousal feels like. Babies of depressed mothers adjust to low stimulation and get used to a lack of positive feelings. Babies of agitated mothers, a situation that is common in Aboriginal populations as a result of transgenerational trauma, may stay overly aroused and have a sense that feelings are explosive and can't be controlled. In contrast, well-managed babies come to expect a world that is responsive to their feelings and that helps bring intense states back to comfortable levels.

Socially, children react to stress in one of two ways after trauma: either in a hyperresponsive mode with uncontrolled anxiety and hyper-reactivity; or a diminished or hyporesponsive mode and withdrawal, both socially and emotionally. Traumatized children show a heightened sense of vulnerability and sensitivity to environmental threat; thus they tend to reexperience the events emotionally, both from reminders of the event and from intrusive thoughts of images of the event (Armsworth and Holady, 1993). Traumatized children have also shown feelings of apathy, withdrawal, and a decreased motivation (Armsworth and Holady, 1993).

One response to trauma is dissociation. *Dissociation* is a process in which external and internal stimuli are stopped as a result of the child becoming overwhelmed by a traumatic experience. Infants respond to stress with intense startle, crying and screaming, and high levels of hormones are released into the brain (Schore, 2001a, 2001b, 2003). Mothers are ideally able to soothe infants with face-to-face looking and rocking; however, if no emotional comfort or regulation is available, the highly aroused state will eventually cease, and in its place the infant will quieten, become immobile, avoid contact, become compliant, and restrict output—responses characteristic of dissociation.

This sequence can become a familiar one when hyperarousal is followed by dissociation that is accompanied by a rise in pain-numbing endorphins and high hormone levels. This psychic deadening defense is eventually entered into for long periods, as its function is to numb the pain and chaos of the body. Repeated experiences of insensitive attachment or abuse cause such distress in infants that they learn to stop feeling. The child can never find a coping strategy when their parent is the abuser, because they need to seek both proximity and avoidance at the same time. Input from external stimuli then becomes unbearable, which prevents emotional learning, reduces the possibility of development, and makes attachment and understanding impossible.

The full range of symptoms associated with PTSD can be experienced by traumatized and abused children (Pynoos et al., 1996; Teicher, 2000), including sexual abuse (Aldridge and Hastilow, 2001). PTSD is an emotional disorder that may be caused by a one-time traumatic event or by repeated traumatic experiences such as physical abuse, community violence, or maltreatment. Startlingly similar connections have been found between abuse of all kinds and permanent, debilitating changes in the brain that lead to psychiatric problems, including MSD or Multisomatoform Disorders (Teicher, 2000). Attention Deficit Hyperactivity Disorder (ADHD) is often present with PTSD in traumatized children (van der Kolk and McFarlane, 1996).

Infants and toddlers who witness violence in their homes or communities show increased irritability, immature behavior, sleep disturbances, emotional distress and crying, fears of being alone, and loss of skills (such as regression in toileting and language). Young children who have either witnessed or experienced a traumatic event usually appear very serious and even spacey, or disorganized, and they smile very little (Appleyard and Osofsky, 2003).

When traumatized children are emotionally stimulated, they lose the capacity to make sense of their feelings, or to use them as a guide in assessing situations. Instead they go directly from stimulus to response, unable to use the thought process in between. This results in aggression or numbing of feelings and becomes a pattern of behavior (Schore, 2001a; van der Kolk and McFarlane, 1996). Negative outcomes in both children and adolescents can also include disruptiveness, impulsivity, inattentiveness, poor socialisation, and low academic achievement.

EFFECTS OF EARLY TRAUMA ON COGNITIVE DEVELOPMENT AND PHYSICAL HEALTH

Exposure to extreme violence may interfere with a child's developmental processes, affecting memory, cognition, and learning (Alvarez, 1992; Pynoos et al., 1996). The years of language acquisition—between ages 2 and 10—are a period when children are especially vulnerable to the effects of early maltreatment.

Normal development enables children to organize a story into a continuous narrative that has a beginning, middle, and end. Alternatively, chaotic narrative construction results from traumatic experiences and adversely impacts reading, writing, and communication skills. In addition early childhood trauma causes permanent alteration in the development of the left hippocampus, resulting in problems with processing memory and dissociative symptoms that persist into adulthood (Teicher, 2000).

Neuroimaging studies of traumatized patients show that dissociation occurs when patients are asked to remember their traumatic experiences. The left frontal cortex, and particularly the Broca's area, remains inactive. At the same time, the right hemisphere, particularly the area around the amygdala, which is associated with emotional and automatic arousal, lights up (Bremner et al., 1992; Rauch, van der Kolk, Fisler, Alpert et al., 1996). When reliving traumatic experiences, a traumatized person's frontal lobes become impaired and they have trouble thinking and speaking (van der Kolk, 2003). They are no longer capable of communicating either to themselves or to others (Wylie, 2004).

Trauma sufferers process their trauma from the bottom up, body to mind—and not top down, mind to body (Ogden and Minton, 2000; van der Kolk, 2002). Thus, in order to treat trauma effectively therapists must move beyond words and language in order to integrate the person's cognitive, emotional, and affective memory.

Traumatic experiences may cause physiological damage in vital organs such as the heart and lungs. People with developmental trauma often have heart disease, diabetes, and asthma, as well as weakened immune systems, conditions that can account for early deaths. Infants and toddlers who witness violence in their homes or communities often have physical complaints (Appleyard and Osofsky, 2003).

HEALING TRAUMA WITH INTERVENTION

Many psychologists have found the most important determinant in recovering from trauma is the presence of loving and attentive people (Werner, 2004), including family and community members, teachers, therapists, elders, and neighbors. This support network provides a relational milieu that has a positive neurological influence on the brain. It is these people, and the presence of their personal, relational contacts—smile, touch, tone of voice, and even literally being able to see them—that calms the stress-response situation and allows for healing (Perry, 1997).

To counteract the effects of trauma on infants, Aboriginal and Maori healers use traditional healing techniques that involve repetitive, rhythmic patterns such as drumming, singing, and touch. These are powerful and direct ways to reach and seep into the area of the brain affected by trauma. Severely traumatized children require interventions that address both low and high brain functions affected by trauma. The use of art in healing helps rebuild the emotional brain as it forms new connections between the prefrontal cortex and other parts of the body's emotional systems (Perry, 1997).

The therapist–child or teacher–child relationship is also important to healing because it serves as a safe and a positive relationship for the child. It creates a safe space where the child can explore his or her emotions. It helps the child build social and relationship skills outside of therapy. It may also help rebuild trust in others, since experiencing trauma at the hands of another person can decrease trust in other people.

Similarly, this is why the preschool space is so important. In the very chaotic world of these children, preschools allow a space where connections can be made, relationships formed, and where children can be seen and heard. In this safe space children can begin to express themselves and find a place where their physical needs are met. Support of this kind helps to build connections between the prefrontal cortex and the amygdala (Perry, 2001; Schore, 1994). These connections linking the prefrontal cortex to the amygdala enable children to exercise a conscious control over the anxiety that may be caused by a traumatic event.

Finally, art is a way to express oneself. Having the chance to express oneself through art—and particularly ideas or emotions that may be difficult to express with words—can be a safe and very therapeutic method for healing. It offers a way to release energy related to trauma that may have been held in or repressed for years. Humans often feel the need to tell their story, to vent, and to be heard upon experiencing something traumatic. Simply being able to have an audience, such as a therapist or caregiver, and to feel heard or cared for can go a long way to healing traumatic wounds.

REFERENCES

Aldridge, F., and S. Hastilow. (2001). *Multiple family therapy: The Marlborough model and its wider implications*. London: Tavistock.

Alvarez, A. (1992). *Live company: Psychoanalytic psychotherapy with autistic, borderline, deprived, and abused children*. London: Tavistock/Routledge.

American Psychiatric Association. (2009). Diagnostic and Statistical Manual of Mental Disorders: DSM-IV-TR. 4th ed., text rev. Washington, DC: American Psychiatric Association and the American Psychiatric Task Force on DSM-IV.

Appleyard, K., and J. D. Osofsky. (2003). Parenting after trauma: Supporting parents and caregivers in the treatment of children impacted by violence. *Infant Mental Health Journal* 24(2): 111–125.

Armsworth, M. W., and M. Holaday. (1993). The effects of psychological trauma on children and adolescents. *Journal of Counseling and Development* 72: 49–56.

Atkinson, J. (2002). *Trauma trails; Recreating song lines: The transgenerational effects of trauma in Indigenous Australia*. North Melbourne, Australia: Spinifex Press.

Atkinson, S., and S. Swain. (1999). A network of support: Mothering across the Koorie community in Victoria, Australia. *Women's History Review* 8(2): 219–230.

Bowlby, J. (1979). *The making and breaking of affectional bonds*. London: Tavistock/Routledge, 1992.

Bremner, J. D., S. Southwick, E. Brett, A. Fontana, R. Rosenheck, and D. Charney. (1992). Dissociation and posttraumatic stress disorder in Vietnam combat veterans. *American Journal of Psychiatry* 149(3): 328–332.

Colomina, M. T., M. L. Albina, J. L. Domingo, and J. Corbella. (1997). Influence of maternal stress on the effects of prenatal exposure to methylmercury and arsenic on postnatal development and behavior in mice: A preliminary evaluation. *Physiology & Behavior* 61(3): 455–459.

Duran, E., and B. Duran. (1995). *Native American post-colonial psychology*. Albany, NY: State University of New York Press.

Felitti, V. J., R. F. Anda, D. Nordenberg, D. F. Williamson, A. M. Spitz, V. Edwards, M. P. Koss, and J. S. Marks. (1998). Relationship of childhood abuse and household dysfunction to many of the leading causes of death in adults: The adverse childhood experiences (ACE) study. *American Journal of Preventive Medicine* 14(4): 245–258.

Fiona, R. (2011). Kanyininpa (holding): A way of nurturing children in Aboriginal Australia. *Australian Social Work* 64(2): 183–197.

Gerhardt, S. (2004). *Why love matters: How affection shapes a baby's brain*. New York: Brunner/Routledge.

Gunnar, M. R., and B. Donzella, B. (2002). Social regulation of the cortisol levels in early human development. *Psychoneuroendocrinology* 27(1-2): 199–220.

Gunnar, M. R., and C. A. Nelson. (1994). Event-related potentials in year-old infants: Relations with emotionality and cortisol. *Child Development* 65(1): 80–94.

Kalsched, D. (1996). *The inner world of trauma: Archetypal defenses of the personal spirit*. London: Routledge.

Kaufman, J., and E. Zigler (1993). The intergenerational transmission of violence is overstated. In R. J. Gelles and D. R. Loseke, eds., *Current controversies on family violence*, 167–196. Newbury Park, CA: Sage.

Levine, S. (2001). Primary social relationships influence the development of the HPA axis in the rat. *Physiology and Behavior* 73(3): 255–260.

Masone, J., S. Wang, R. Yehuda, S. Riney, D. Charney, and S. Southwick. (2001). Psychogenic lowering of urinary cortisol levels linked to increased emotional numbing and a shame-depressive syndrome in combat-related posttraumatic stress disorder. *Psychosomatic Medicine* 63(3): 387–401.

Mollon, P. (1993). *The fragile self*. London: Whurr. Reprinted 2003.

Muid, O. (2006). Then I lost my spirit: An analytical essay on transgeneration theory and its application to oppressed people of color nations. Ann Arbor, MI: UMI dissertation Services/ProQuest.

Ogden, P., and K. Minton. (2000). Sensorimotor psychotherapy: One method for processing traumatic memory. *Traumatology* 6(3): 1–20.

Pally, R., and O. David. (2000). *The mind-brain relationship*. London: Karnac.

Pennebaker, J. (1993). Putting stress into words. *Behaviour Research and Therapy* 31(6): 539–548.

Perry, B. (1997). Incubated in terror: Neurodevelopmental factors in the "cycle of violence." In J. Osofsky, ed., *Children in a violent society*, 124–149. New York: Guilford.

Perry, B. D. (2001). The neurodevelopmental impact of violence in childhood. In D. Schetky and E. P. Benedek, eds., *Textbook of child and adolescent forensic psychiatry*, 221–238. Washington, DC: American Psychiatric Press.

Pynoos, R. S., R. F. Ritzmann, A. M. Steinberg, A. Goenjian, and I. Prisecaru. (1996). A behavioral animal model of PTSD featuring repeated exposure to situational reminders. *Biological Psychiatry* 39: 129–134.

Rauch, S. L, B. A. van der Kolk, R. E. Fisler, N. M. Alpert, et al. (1996). A symptom provocation study of posttraumatic stress disorder using positron emission tomography and script-driven imagery. *Archives of General Psychiatry* 53: 380–387.

Schore, A. N. (1994) *Affect regulation and the origin of the self.* Hillsdale, NJ: Lawrence Erlbaum.

Schore, A. N. (2001a). The effects of a secure attachment relationship on right brain development, affect regulation, and infant mental health. *Infant Mental Health Journal* 22: 7–66.

Schore, A. N. (2001b). The effects of relational trauma on right brain development, affect regulation, and infant mental health. *Infant Mental Health Journal* 22: 201–269.

Schore, A. N. (2003). *Affect dysregulation and disorders of the self.* New York: Norton.

Schulkin, J., and J. Rosen. (1998). From normal fear to pathological anxiety. In D. M. Hann, L. C. Huffmann, et al., eds., *Advancing research on developmental plasticity*, chapter 8. Washington, DC: National Institutes of Health.

Teicher, M. D. (2000). Wounds that time won't heal: The neurobiology of child abuse. *Cerebrum: The Dana Forum on brain science* 2(4), 50–67.

van der Kolk, B. A. (2002). Beyond the talking cure: Somatic experience and subcortical imprints in the treatment of trauma. In F. Schapiro, ed., *EMDR: Promises for a paradigm shift*, 57–83. New York: APA Press.

van der Kolk, B. A. (2003). The neurobiology of childhood trauma and abuse. *Child and Adolescent Psychiatric Clinics of North America* 12(2): 293–317.

van der Kolk, B. A., and A. McFarlane. (1996). The black hole of trauma. In B. A. van der Kolk, A. C. McFarlane, and L. Weisaeth, eds., *Traumatic stress: The effects of overwhelming experience on mind, body, and society*, 5–23. New York: Guilford.

van der Kolk, B. A, O. van der Hart, and C. R. Marmar. (1996). Dissociation and information processing in posttraumatic stress disorder. In B. A. van der Kolk, A. C. McFarlane, and L. Weisaeth, eds., *Traumatic stress: The effects of overwhelming experience on mind, body, and society*, 303–327. New York: Guilford.

Werner, P. (2004). Reasoned action and planned behavior. In S. J. Peterson and T. S. Bredow, eds., *Middle range theories: Application to nursing research*, 125–147. Philadeliphia, PA: Lippincott, Williams & Wilkins.

Wylie, M. S. (2004). The limits of talk: Bessel van der Kolk wants to transform the treatment of trauma. *Psychotherapy Networker* 28(1): 30–41.

Yeo, S. (2003). Bonding and attachment of Australian Aboriginal children. *Child Abuse Review* 12(5): 292–304.

Zubrick S., D. Lawrence, S. Silburn, E. Blair, H. Milroy, T. Wilkes, T. Eades, S. et al (2004). *The Western Australian Aboriginal Child Health survey: The health of Aboriginal children and young people.* Subiaco, Perth, Western Australia: Telethon Institute for Child Health Research.

Chapter Six

Trauma, Childhood, and Emotional Resilience

Marilyn Charles

We are are born into the world incompletely formed, dependent on caregivers for survival. In the early months and years of life, we hope to build the type of solid foundation that will be crucial for later resilience. Because there is always more perceptual data than we can possibly take in or make sense of, learning depends on our ability to selectively attend to and manage the "too-much" of daily existence. Familiarity builds a sense of comfort so that over time what once might have caused startle in the infant is either not noticed or else noticed with whatever pleasure or discomfort has been linked with the event. These repeated moments of pleasure and displeasure, novelty and familiarity, begin to organize meanings in the world (Beebe, Rustin, Sorter, and Knoblauch, 2003).

Early experiences with caretakers build resilience by first protecting the child from distress and then soothing her when distress occurs. This type of *empathic attunement* (Stern, 1985) tells the child that her distress is recognized, cared about, and endurable. Too much emotion is itself experienced as traumatic, and the child shuts down. Trauma thus not only cuts us off from what is happening in the moment but also from the very self-regulatory capacities that might help us to cope. Our capacity for dissociation, to distance from self and experience, can help us to survive a difficult moment. That protective distance, however, impedes integration and repair, and interferes with obtaining the type of mastery that builds self-esteem. We are then further impeded by shame, which interferes with the optimism and interest so crucial for new learning.

We learn through our experience. We begin life as sensory beings, taking in the world through taste, touch, sound, and smell. These early experiences form a template against which all later experience is tested and understood. Over time, words are attached to those experiences and become a useful shorthand for indexing and talking with one another about them. Language helps us to sort our experiences into categories, organizing the complexities of daily life. While some of this knowledge remains conscious, many of our activities are driven by the implicit *procedural* knowledge that guides routinized activities, such as riding a bicycle or driving a car. The implicit memory system depends on our ability to recognize patterns that provide cues to help us to navigate the complexity of signals coming our way. These patterns can be seen as nonverbal units of meaning that are "read" intuitively without necessarily invoking conscious attention (Charles, 2002). Emotions, for example, are highly patterned, allowing us to recognize their imprint in a person's face or by tone or gesture.

The nonverbal, implicit memory system functions most efficiently in moments of relative inattention. At times of disequilibrium or startle, when our expectancies do not match our experience, we are drawn to more focused attention, which can be useful in a crisis but constrains our ability to attend to other data. Being able to make sense of our experience is inherently soothing, whereas unpredictable environments leave us in a state of distress and disease. Factors that inhibit active engagement, such as stress and trauma, constrain our attention and disrupt the fluid interplay of explicit and implicit understandings, interfering with our ability to make sense of self and world. At the extreme, the novelty that should invite curiosity and exploration instead invites fear and vigilance. Because it disrupts our ability to be present in the moment, trauma interferes with the integration and consolidation of memories and the development of a coherent worldview.

Psychoanalytic theory has long recognized the importance of early relationships in building resilience and facilitating normal development. Empirical evidence shows how early experiences shape the organization of our brains, particularly those functions that affect nonverbal learning (Schore, 2003). Increasingly, neuroscience affirms many of the suppositions underlying psychoanalytic treatment. Research into mirror neurons, for example, illuminates some of the dilemmas encountered by the child who does not receive sufficient or adequate mirroring (Gallese, 2009). *Mirroring* refers to the experience of being able to find oneself in the eyes, and therefore the mind, of another person. We experience this type of recognition when our feelings are acknowledged. Data on mirror neurons show that much of our recognition of and responsiveness to the human face is hardwired. For example, one can watch an infant begin to initiate smiling in the presence of other people, and see the delight that occurs when the smile is returned. We can also observe a child playing with her tongue in response to the "la, la, la" being crooned by the mother.

These identification processes are strong and far-reaching. An MRI study assessing responses to one's own and others' facial affect, for example, suggests that mirror neurons aid in empathic engagement at the level of the brain through mimicry of the emotion on the face of the other (Schulte-Rüther, Markowitsch et al., 2007). At a very primary level, we seem to be hardwired to generalize, across modalities, visual or other sensory data into visceral and motoric sensations and sequences (Gallese, Eagle, and Migone, 2007). The mirror neuron system depends on our ability to adequately take in data that are consistent with experience. For example, studies show that when individuals are offered discrepant data, they can become confused as to the contours and limits of their own bodies (Petkova and Ehrsson, 2008). In families preoccupied with trauma, there can be mixed messages that make it difficult for the child to make sense of their experience, and therefore also to be able to generalize intention in accordance with categories of experience (Knox, 2009). In this way, trauma can interfere with the development of the capacities for abstraction and generalization that facilitate learning.

Primary sensory experiences become integrated as models that guide and constrain all later understandings. The attachment literature offers useful metaphors through which to understand how these experiences are taken in and communicated nonverbally. For example, Stern (1985) and Beebe and Lachmann (1988, 1994, 1998) describe an innate facility for *intramodal processing*, in which information taken in through one sensory modality is then recommunicated through another modality, retaining the primary pattern of the information. Implicit communications form the basis for these patterned understandings that, over time, themselves evoke responsiveness and also provide criteria regarding what is to be perceived as useful information and what is to be warded off as "noise" or "threat."

Intramodal processing is perhaps best illustrated by looking at affect, which functions at a presymbolic level and is linked across different domains of sensory experience (Bucci, 1997, 2001). Affect is to some extent separate from and more impactful than cognitive memory, influencing our thinking even when the affect is not conscious (Krystal, 1988). We recognize affect intuitively through its patterns, in terms of both our internal experience and our ability to perceive its traces on faces or in body position or gesture (Ekman, 1982). Affect can be recognized across cultures by reference to its prosody (the patterned form) and intensity (Tomkins, 1982). Optimally, we learn to read affect like a signal and to notice those signals at relatively low levels, so that we can respond accordingly and generally keep our affect within tolerable limits. From this state of relative equilibrium, spikes of affect are useful signals telling us that something is wrong that needs our attention. This signaling system can be extremely valuable, helping to mark pleasurable and unpleasurable experiences, and to organize our ideas about how to encourage or avoid them.

Experiences stored within the body provide a complex coding system, enabling us to respond affectively to meanings we may not consciously recognize. Our capacity for affective resonance helps us to communicate without conscious awareness or verbal language. Affective resonance includes all aspects of experience associated with those states, and may best be conceptualized in terms of *contours* of feeling, in which the form and pattern come to have both evocative and symbolic functions (Stern, 1985). We can watch the transfer of these contours in the interactions between parent and child and also in our own interactions, in the impact we have on one another. For example, we can notice how the mother's regulatory function is internalized, as when the child comforts herself through a doll, using the mother's soothing tone to say, "It's *all right*. Mama will be *right* back."

Tone comes to carry meaning beyond—and often in disjunction to—the words expressed. There are many times when our words are eclipsed by the tone, which conveys important elements of meaning, rather like the child who complains about being "yelled at" when there has been no increase in volume but rather some note of disapproval in the tone. With children, the nonverbal meanings tend to carry more weight than the words themselves. Denial of these noverbal elements of meanings can be literally crazy-making, whereas acknowledgment can provide opportunities for the child to recognize the validity and potential value of his perceptions and thereby to make sense of contradictions when they occur (Bowen, 1978).

AFFECT REGULATION AND TRAUMA

Deficits in the capacity for affect regulation put us at risk. Survival has depended on our ability to respond quickly and efficiently to the signal qualities of affect, which are integrated far more rapidly than conscious, verbal awareness. In the moment, the prosody of affective patterns provides important cues as to one's relative safety and the likely trajectory of a given interaction. Overstimulation disrupts this feedback system, encouraging a shutting down when disregulation occurs rather than the fine-tuning of emotion that might take place with sufficient resilience. Experiences of overwhelming affect, unmoderated, can themselves be experienced as traumatic, interfering with our ability to make sense of and organize our experience (Krystal, 1988; LeDoux, 1999; Schore, 1994). Trauma interferes with the signal functions of affect, blurring the features by which the signal might be recognized. In the extreme case, affect itself can become a signal for avoidance, further impeding our ability to encounter and use affective signals. This dilemma is amplified in fear reactions, which tend to be extremely entrenched and are particularly difficult to overcome because of their inherent survival functions (LeDoux, 2002). Similarly, shame can also be highly resistant to change because of its virulence and avoidant properties.

Infants are active learners who are not merely responsive to and imitative of the gestures of others but also come to anticipate and invite a continued exchange. Nagy and Molnár (2004) found that "newborns spontaneously produced previously imitated gestures while waiting for the experimenter's response" (p. 54), a capacity they termed *provocation*. Such observations show the significance of the developing child's ability to elicit responses from the parent in ongoing exchanges of meaning making. These findings also stress the intersubjective rhythmicity or musicality that is at the heart of the intermodal processing through which meanings are exchanged with the preverbal child (Trevarthen, 2005). Trauma interferes with this dyadic communication system and also interferes with the parent's ability to respond empathically and effectively to inevitable moments of misattunement. Such moments of rupture and repair are considered to be crucial to the development of resilience in the child, a repair process that is hindered when the parent is too preoccupied with his own distress to effectively turn his attention to the needs and feelings of the child (Beebe and Lachman, 1994).

Trauma also tends to disrupt narrative coherence, which is especially problematic when parental incoherence interferes with the development of a secure self in the child (van Ijzendoorn, Schuengel, and Bakermans-Kranenburg, 1999). Unresolved trauma or loss can make the parent unavailable in those very moments of distress when the child needs to be able to approach the parent as a secure base. Even with otherwise caring and attentive parents, disjunctive behaviors are frightening and can lead to the type of disorganized attachment described by Main and Hesse (1990), characterized by a breakdown in a more generally organized and consistent strategy of affective regulation. Even children who function relatively effectively under normal conditions can become disorganized and lose their self-regulatory capacities under strain.

Pushing past mourning rather than facing it takes a toll that haunts successive generations. The parent who cannot face her own traumatic past turns that same blind eye to the difficulties faced by the child as well. In turn, the child registers the difficulty but, without the words to speak about it, the unrecognized knowledge often lodges in the body itself, through physical symptoms, disorganization, or heightened distress (Liotti, 2004; McDougall, 1985). Communal trauma takes an even larger toll on children because there are fewer resources within the extended family and community to help attenuate the difficulties encountered with parents. The parent caught up in unmourned losses can be profoundly inaccessible to the child (Field, 1992). Because of the importance of imitation and interaction in the early months and years, the failure to engage the parent has signficant consequences for the child's social and emotional development (Tronick and Reck, 2009).

Self-knowledge is built on interactions with others, so that the child who cannot elicit responsiveness from the parent tends to become preoccupied with the environment at the expense of self-knowledge, and with self-soothing at the expense of interpersonal engagement (Tronick, 1989; Winnicott, 1971). As such, the fundamental disciminations between self and other that are a precondition for self-knowledge are impeded, and the intramodal processing through which we make meaning of such interactions is disrupted.

Together, these data highlight the debilitating effects of trauma, disruption, and neglect on the developing child in terms of both identity and interpersonal relatedness (Schore and Schore, 2008). Too much exposure to stress and distress interferes with the child's affective and cognitive development and the failure of the parent to soothe the infant adds to the distress (Fonagy, Gergely et al., 2002). These developmental failures inhibit learning, decrease resilience, and thereby increase the negative impact of later traumatic or disruptive events. Development is further impeded when children are exposed to frightening or overwhelming experiences with caregivers. Such experiences are associated with a disorganized attachment style that is characterized by dissociative behavior and a tendency to freeze and be unable to manage challenges as they arise (Lyons-Ruth, 2003; Main and Hesse, 1990).

As noted, one consequence of such disruption is that it makes it more difficult for the person to recognize or make adaptive use of the internal signals and external cues that otherwise might guide behavior rather than merely inhibiting or provoking it. Interventions that invite us to encounter and reflect on these internal and external cues help to develop resilience by building the metacognitive capacities that provide a stronger foundation through which to encounter the world. Psychoanalytically informed therapies, for example, have as a major goal the development of insight: the ability to take oneself, one's feelings, thoughts, and desires seriously. This intention takes a stand against hierarchical models in which one might turn to an authority to obtain received knowledge. Rather, this is a model that contends that we can learn to be more resilient and to make more adaptive choices to the extent that we are aware of our feelings, desires, and motivations. For those who have been severely traumatized, coming to the point of thinking of oneself as the primary frame of reference can demand a fundamental shift from avoiding the aggressor (or searching for a savior) to respecting one's vulnerability as well as one's strengths. For the child, this shift can only occur within the context of a relationship that is safe enough to risk allowing oneself and one's struggles to be known.

Available and empathic caregiving helps to moderate stress for the child, whereas children whose parents are either unavailable or not empathically responsive to the child's needs and feelings show elevated levels of stress (Gunnar and Fisher, 2006). Notably, there is evidence that deficits in caregiving have an impact on *executive function*, the child's ability to organize and effectively manage his activities and behavior (Curtis and Cicchetti, 2003). Executive function can be seen as a marker for the metacognitive capacities that are so crucial in making one's way in the world. The ability to reflect on one's own thoughts and feelings in relation to the thoughts and feelings of others is integral to both self-esteem and healthy relationships.

The tendency to freeze and dissociate that is linked to severe abuse and neglect interferes with the ability to be aware of one's own perceptions, feelings, and thoughts. Interventions that recognize the primary importance of affect and the relative inaccessibility of trauma to verbal language are much more likely to be successful. In recognizing the fundamental link between a child's cognitive capacities and his ability to self-regulate his emotions, one useful adjunct is to work with parents to help them to be more sensitive and responsive to the child's needs and feelings, as well (Dozier, 2003). It is also important to do reparative work with the children, using play as a means to replay difficult experiences and thereby afford the possibility of greater mastery.

Play offers an opportunity to show where the trouble lies. Recalling that implicit knowledge is defined as knowledge that is not easily recognized or communicated in verbal terms, in work with traumatized children we need to be able to hear the story being told through the play, and to witness and recognize important aspects of those stories. In this way, the child is not left so alone with his trouble. Moreover, the child who is experiencing trauma at home likely knows that it is dangerous to speak of such things. For abused children, the injunction not to tell can be utterly immobilizing. Being able to act out the problems in play without further disrupting the household can be crucial, particularly in the initial stages of building trust.

Through play, we hope to allow thoughts and feelings that may be largely unconscious to express themselves. In trying to create an environment in which the child can develop her capacity to play, we must recognize that rigidity and constraint may be defenses against precisely the type of playful engagement so essential to working toward adaptive engagement with challenges. In engaging our less-conscious resources, play helps us to work through implicitly what cannot be fathomed or effectively addressed explicitly. Children cope with trauma by putting it out of their minds, at times dissociating as a way of not-knowing what is too terrible to bear (Terr, 1994). This capacity for dissociation, to enter another plane of consciousness, is adaptive in the moment but over time can obstruct working through. It can also, however, offer the child the opportunity to act out, in the displacement, whatever cannot be spoken about more directly. In this way, through her play, the child can communicate to the attentive and attuned adult some of what she is struggling with. Being able to hold these communications in our minds without necessarily imposing our understanding on the child can help to titrate the distress and build a "holding environment" of greater safety for the child (Winnicott, 1971).

One of the difficulties in dealing with trauma is that it is by definition overwhelming, making it challenging to work with those who have experienced trauma, particularly to allow ourselves to be deeply empathically present with their distress. The research that shows how responsive our brains are to one another, and how tied we are to one another emotionally, highlights the dilemma of therapists and teachers who work with traumatized individuals (Gallese, Eagle, and Migone, 2007). It is relatively easy to share the other's joy and empathize with their distress, but it is hard to sit with terrible pain. At such times, we may want to soothe the other person, in part so that we don't have to be so painfully aware of their distress. It is therefore important for caregivers to try to ease the child's distress enough so that they can share it with us, while also holding in mind the hazard of perhaps giving her the message that she should just make the pain go away.

There is a power to having one's trauma be witnessed by another. Psychoanalytically informed work involves a titration process, so that, in Bion's (1977) terms, the intolerable experience can be broken into tolerable and meaningful chunks that then can be further elaborated and integrated. Over time, what is internalized is the process itself, so that the individual can begin to titrate and better manage his own thoughts and feelings and the experiences they are linked to. In part, this process is effected nonverbally, as we sit together in empathic recognition of the extent of the distress. That being-with provides a holding environment through which primary experience can be transformed into symbolic forms, whether through words or some other type of communication, as in art. With children, in particular, being able to enact the experience through play, or to depict it through pictures or other creative products, can allow something that did not yet have words to be given a greater, more highly elaborated form. These forms then become symbols that help us to play with aspects of experience that are not accessible to conscious thought, including whatever might be too terrifying if it were to be perceived as too real (Charles, 2002, 2004).

The reversal of this integrative process is the dissociative *unlinking* of associations described by Bion (1967) in terms of factors that inhibit creative thinking. Denial of meaning can be an important safeguard against the traumatic onslaught of overwhelming affect that may occur when we are faced with things that seem too terrible to think about. Many primary experiences have never been encoded into verbal memory, but rather become part of the nonverbal, implicit system, the background knowledge through which we make sense of self and world. Some of these experiences occurred before language was acquired, whereas some were too traumatic to be integrated. These unmetabolized experiences become sensory memories that can only become conscious by being transformed in some fashion. Memories of this sort tend to be experienced as truth, without inviting reflection. It can be important to recognize the fundamental truth carried by such experience but also to be able to disrupt some of the certainty that can lead us to avoid, ignore, or dissociate thoughts and feelings associated with the trauma. Certainty of that type can be a block against the pain of knowing more, which in turn also blocks the potentially healing functions of knowing more. Those who work with traumatized children are charged with being the "good enough" parent who can track the child's experience and keep it within manageable limits, while also challenging the child enough to allow for growth.

When working in this strange realm of trauma and nonverbal experience, the therapist is often reframing a story that is only partly told, trying to recognize the realities at play while also trying to shift those realities toward a story that might be more easily known and worked with. With adults, when the trauma is far enough past, we can get a bit of distance and point to the person's survival. With a child, however, for whom the trauma may be ongoing, there is still the open *question* of her survival, and the need to recognize the part of her that is working hard to effect that survival. To aid in this survival process, we try to reframe the difficulties in ways that recognize the adaptive aspects of the person and also encourage further growth.

Growth depends on our ability to be interested in the challenges we encounter so that we can look beyond the surface, deconstruct, recontextualize, and reconsider meanings. Whereas experiences of mastery enhance those capacities, fear inhibits curiosity, closing down the potential for new learning. To learn, we must be able to take apart the picture as we have known it and allow some fragmentation so that integration might occur at a higher level. This is the essential dialectic between fragmentation and integration that Winnicott (1971) points to in his idea of the "use of an object." According to this formulation, in order to be able to interact with another person as a separate and sentient being, we must learn that the other can survive our attempts to differentiate ourselves, even if these feel destructive. We need to be able to bump into one another and leave an imprint, and then back away and try to get some perspective on the encounter. Perception may be better defined as *apperception* because our lenses are inevitably colored by our experiences (Grotstein, 2000). From that perspective, it is our *myths* about one another that are being destroyed. Traumatization invites heightened sensitivity, which makes it difficult to think clearly and to look beyond the myth when emotions are high.

Entrenched family and cultural myths are particularly difficult to dislodge, but if we can see our ideas as myths or *theories* about the nature of reality rather than reality as such, we are in a better position to learn. We tend to organize our theories in line with what Bion (1977) calls the "selected facts" we have learned to steer by. Our field of vision shifts along with our presumptions, requiring us to alter our focus periodically in order to see what we might be missing. The therapist's capacity to alter her focus in line with that of the child helps her to recognize ways in which that child *assigns* values and meanings. There is no substitute for learning the "code book"—the idiosyncratic ways in which meanings are assigned, and the symbols that carry intense, condensed, and important meanings for that individual. We can only learn these meanings through taking in the story as the person tells it. Our ability to register these meanings depends on our ability to participate deeply, so that we can register the affective melodies along with the narrative as it is being told. Often, it is the pattern of an experience or interchange that draws us in and marks meanings, through both rhythmicity and anomaly. Through our implicit understanding, we often bump into an important fact that may be offered symbolically or may, in contrast, be offered *by omission*, as we begin to recognize a gap in the story being told (Charles, 2012).

When working with traumatic experience, real engagement requires recognizing the uncanny ways in which meaning can be both known and unknown at the same time. This tension between the known and the unknown—the visible and the invisible—gives rise to psychoanalytic metaphors that mark the recursive nature of growth. Metaphors such as Bion's (1977) *container and contained* and Klein's (1946, 1952) *paranoid-schizoid* and *depressive* positions mark the relativity of meaning as well as the way growth occurs as meanings become fragmented and assimilated, leading to increasingly more complex integrations of experience. All learning needs to be able to break apart to make room for further learning. The breaking apart can be particularly treacherous when we are dealing with trauma, and when what is broken into is protective armor. With such individuals, it is crucial to recognize the fragility that hides behind the armor so that we can help to build the resilience that makes the armor less necessary rather than abruptly trying to tear it away.

Psychoanalytically informed work recognizes an essential dialectic between the desire and the fear of knowing self, particularly the parts of self that have been affected by trauma or shame. One complicating factor in trauma is that it is inherently shameful because we encounter our limits so painfully and are faced so vividly with our inability to effectively manage life's challenges. The protective world of childhood usually shields us from such painful realities, and having that protection broken into is itself traumatic. Shame is particularly insidious because it breaks the social bond, making it difficult to even look another person in the eye. This turning away makes repair difficult, inviting the feeling that we are deficient in relation to those who would judge us harshly, rather than safe in the presence of those who might offer assistance. The therapist, then, must try to develop a relationship that is experienced as respectfully supportive so that the shame can be relieved sufficiently to make new learning more possible.

Relational metaphors have evolved as we recognize parallels between the roles of therapist and parent. The *holding* metaphor recognizes the symbiotic entanglement of self and other so crucial to early attunement processes. This metaphor also recognizes the importance of the encounter with otherness that enables the child to begin to develop a sense of self. The good parent frustrates the child just enough to promote development while protecting against excessive extremes of emotion. This balance helps the child to develop his own internal self-regulatory functions. As Winnicott (1971) notes, it is fundamentally important for the child to be able to push against the parent and learn that both can survive the encounter.

Trauma can interfere with the ability to successfully test one's own potency, particularly if the self or other is experienced as too fragile. When trauma is passed along the generations without being successfully worked through, the child learns to protect the parent over and above himself because of his dependency (Charles, 2005). This blurring of boundaries between self and other is a terrible price to pay for safety because it interferes with the development of a healthy self. Rather, vigilance for the affect of others tends to take the place of learning to effectively attend to and regulate one's own affect, thereby destabilizing and crippling self-development. In such cases, therapeutic interventions must pull toward helping the child to take his or her rightful place as the focus of attention and control. Such containment helps to build the capacity for affect regulation that enables us to tolerate the excitement of moving out into the unknown.

A RELATIONAL MODEL FOR INTERVENTION

The literature on early child development shows how this containment is built when there is sufficient balance between attunement and autonomy in caretaking relationships. That containment provides the safety necessary to enable the infant to tolerate the disorganization that accompanies growth. Included in this developmental challenge is tolerance of the loss entailed in experiencing an evolving relational matrix in which one must stand increasingly alone. Relational models that point to the essential and evolving interplay between self and other in intimate relationships have profound relevance to the challenges we face in work with traumatized children. Such models invite us to consider more deeply the subtleties involved in the analytic task of entering into the world of the other person sufficiently to be able to accurately read idiosyncratic meanings and nuance, while also standing as a separate, differentiated person in counterpoint. It is only in our deep and continuing encounters with similarity and difference that we can build a world based on shared meanings.

The literature detailing nonverbal communications highlights the importance of attending to the extent of fragmentation in a given moment so that we can better track the extent to which learning might occur. Sensitivity to levels of tension is particularly important with those who experience difficulties in affect self-regulation, who may need us to titrate affect sufficiently that they can begin to develop this function themselves. Our attunement to nonverbal elements helps us to attend to the emotions at play, which may provide our best cues regarding how to proceed. An appreciation of the richness and diversity of communication processes helps us to recognize the symbols and metaphors that are embedded in the child's own system of meanings. In this way, we offer the type of deep, respectful recognition that is so crucial to the sense of interpersonal safety that is essential for any real work to be done. Without that safety, behavior is more likely to be merely compliant or defiant rather than growth-enhancing. In this work, the greater our appreciation for the subtleties and nuance of nonverbal interchanges, the more we can fine-tune our moment-by-moment understandings of what is being taken in by self and other, and consider what we might usefully offer.

When working with children, play is both the theater in which the plot, settings, and characters are introduced (McDougall, 1985), and also the canvas on which meanings are painted. In such work, we are always at the edge of the intersections of diverse and often elusive meanings being communicated in ways that may evoke intense emotional resonance without necessarily providing sufficient anchors by which to name the experience. As such, it is often the form or pattern of the depiction that carries the meaning, a situation that highlights the importance of our ability to resonate to and explicitly attend to the patterns, the primary units of meaning that we recognize at a fundamental level. With trauma, in particular, sensory memories, the *language of the body*, may be where the story is held (Charles, 2002). The language of the body is built on the patternings of elements that undergird what Bollas (1987) terms the *unthought known*, aspects of awareness that are so integral to our sense of self and world that they remain unnoticed. Over time, our sensations are organized into complex narratives of self, other, and world, mediated by the rules of language (Solms, 1996). In decoding these meanings as they manifest in the art and play of the child, the attentive therapist provides the recognition that is so crucial to allowing the story to unfold.

Work with children requires our attention to the ways in which these resonances play out through the exchange of patterned movements of interaction (Charles, 2002), as, for example, in the child who plays with covering and uncovering her own hands with paint and then sees whether the therapist is willing to be covered with paint as well, first with a brush, and then with the imprint of the child's hands upon her own. At other times, these movements may take the form of autosensuous shapes (shapes traced by the hands or movements of the body) that provide self-soothing and also carry meanings through their forms. In art therapy, these patterns can be recognized in the child's productions and also in her ways of approaching the materials. Presuming meaning helps us to recognize these emergent shapes and forms as presymbolic movements that can become symbolized through our engagements with one another (Charles, 2002).

These presymbolic bits are often pieces of experience that could not be assimilated. Through the therapist's willingness to experience these bits and to turn our attention to them, we begin to metabolize the bits. In this process, we affirm our faith that one might come to know impossible things and survive the encounter (Charles, 2003). As can be seen in the case to follow, reciprocal patternings of body and gesture can at times become a means for aligning with another person and forming identifications. These embodied simulations provide crucial information. When the internalization of self-regulatory functions has been disrupted, the ability to moderate affect through identifications with the therapist's tone and body language can aid in the transition toward greater self-regulation and mutual meaning making.

APPLYING THE MODEL

At Gunawirra, a not-for-profit, member-based organization in Australia, Aboriginal and non-Aboriginal professionals work together to provide innovative and transformational programming with the aim of preventing and reducing harm to Aboriginal and Torres Strait Island children, families, and communities. Interventions are directed toward breaking the intergenerational cycle of poverty and violence by providing emotional and social support, developing positive role models, and providing training and education in culturally sensitive ways. The goal is to empower parents and children to become more resilient, productive members of society. The working assumption is that these parents want the best for their children but are impeded by a cycle of suffering caused by the combined losses of community, culture, family, and country.

The programs devised by Gunawirra tend to be grass-root efforts that include self-help, professional support, and intense evaluation in a service area that includes thirty-five Aboriginal community preschools across New South Wales and in two Sydney locations. I was invited to provide support to the Gunawirra team, and consultation on an art therapy intervention and research project at two preschools with some of the lowest socioeconomic demographics in the country, including low rates of child literacy and health, and high rates of poverty, domestic violence, and alcohol abuse. Working from the premise that trauma interferes with mentalization, impeding learning and imagination, this project focused on using art therapy as a means for building communication, self-expression, and personal growth.

At Gunawirra, there is a recognition of the trauma embedded in the history of the imposition of an alien culture upon the Aboriginal people. Affirming the importance of community and tradition, this project had a particular focus on including Aboriginal preschool teachers and community elders to help reinforce their sense of value to the community. Training was offered to teachers regarding the impact of present-day and intergenerational trauma, and the value of art therapy as a means for expressing and healing trauma. Attention was given to the social contexts in which these children were living, both in terms of hazards and of potential resources on which to build.

Art therapy is a particularly useful medium for working with young children, who are still developing their verbal capacities. Art affords opportunities to immerse oneself in the play and to express oneself without having to worry about what is being said or how it might be interpreted. From a psychodynamic perspective, this is called *working in the displacement*. In this way, play affords opportunities for self-expression, in the positive sense, and also to show where the troubles lie—without the type of explicit self-focus that can make the child self-conscious and inhibited. Both aspects of self-expression were apparent in the detailed write-ups made by the art therapists in this project.

Writing detailed notes that include the process as it happened between child and therapist, along with salient aspects of the therapist's experience, is an important part of psychodynamic learning. Such *process notes* afford the therapist an opportunity to reflect more deeply on the work being done and on possible meanings that might be attributed to the work. In this project, psychodynamic supervisors were relied on to encourage the therapists not only to process their experiences, but also to value and make use of those experiences as they tried to understand what was happening in the sessions. Aware of the potential for vicarious trauma, project developers gave particular attention to the roles of affect, countertransference, and the construction of meaning in the work, and also to the importance of supporting empathic engagement with the art therapists. Group consultation afforded opportunities to recognize and manage distress, and to receive empathic engagement and assistance from others. This focus on affect also helped the therapists to consider ways in which the feelings they experienced in their work with the children might reflect the child's experience as well. Such consideration of *countertransference* as an important informational tool is particularly useful when working with anyone who has been traumatized and who may not be able to put their experience into words.

Because play invites an immersion into the experience, the child's ways of engaging with the tools as well as with the therapist afforded important clues regarding the child's character and the troubles she carries. The holding environment created for the therapists through Gunawirra's system of intensive training, supervision, and consultation helped them to sustain this difficult work and also to gain from it, and to recognize that their work was, indeed, meaningful in spite of the extent of the difficulties facing these children and families. Group supervision helped to untangle some of the threads present in the child's play and also helped the therapists to tolerate what might otherwise have seemed chaotic, turbulent, or disorganized. Group experiences afforded opportunities for direct-care workers to describe and share their work, which helped to attenuate their distress and thereby to reduce the impact of trauma and the likelihood of burnout. Such reparative group experiences helped to encourage resilience and to develop a sense of mastery in the therapist along with an enhanced sense of community, thereby furthering the cycle of healing (Charles, in press).

Particularly important to the art therapy project was for the therapists to have reasonable expectations of what they might and might not be able to expect or accomplish in their work with the children. Given the short-term nature of the intervention and the extent of the trauma many had endured, providing a space in which a relationship could be built while also acknowledging that it would end was a paramount element. One difficulty in working with traumatized children is that our attempts to be supportive and caring may be experienced quite differently than we intend. Optimally, the human face and gaze become associated with signals of presence, of soothing and "feeling held" (Stern, 1985), but when a child has been confronted with frightening or confusing parental behaviors (including a lack of responsiveness or contingency in interactions), the human face can be a danger signal. When relying on others has been disappointing, empathy may be distressing rather than soothing, and warmth and care may invite the child to let down his guard in a way that feels dangerous. This situation can be heightened when the caregiver is part of the dominant majority, and power imbalances and historical differences in worldview complicate the picture. Recognizing discrepancies between our worldviews helps us to be respectful of the child's perspective.

With children who have experienced insufficient parental attunement, it is crucial for potential caregivers to be acutely attuned to the child's affect in the moment, *not* in order to avoid conflict but rather to play out patterns of disruption and repair in ways that provide the child with assurance that repair is possible (Lachmann and Beebe, 1996). Because models of relationship are idiosyncratic, we must be able to focus on actual responses rather than generic ideas as to how things *should* feel, and recognize when attempts at care feel intrusive, frightening, or seductive. For those who have felt abandoned or overly disappointed, longings for closeness can make the intimacy of working together both tantalizing and terrifying, at times resulting in the type of chaotic engagement we see in the case of Annie, which follows. Although the child's history can offer information about her relational world, it is really only in our moment-by-moment interactions that we obtain a more palpable sense of the emotional realities of that world. Our attunement provides us with data regarding the feelings experienced and meanings construed by the child in a given interaction. Checking back in with the child on these then helps her to play her part in the building of shared meanings together.

Our ability to attend to differences between us helps us to make decisions about what might be too much or not enough, and to thereby titrate affect in line with the child's needs and limits. Much as the parent registers the child's communication, takes it in, and then optimally feeds back to the child a metabolized version of the communication, so too the therapist can play an important role in the internalization of self-regulatory processes. This metabolization process serves many functions. At one level, it is a direct interchange regarding the lived experience of the moment, so that what is taken in through these exchanges is a *process* by which meanings can be exchanged and refined (Gallese, 2009). At another level, this interchange serves as a metacommunication regarding the nature of the world and of the possibilities inherent in a relationship in which one person assumes some responsibility in relation to the other.

The therapist's ability to tolerate the child's distress communicates that distress can be tolerated and meaning can be made. This is a very different universe than one in which the child's distress is either ignored, punished, or taken on by the parent in ways that amplify the distress. As we demonstrate that we can recognize distress and care about it without becoming undone by it, the child is afforded greater safety to offer information that helps to build shared meaning and metaphors. As we will see in the case vignette to follow, these shared symbols become points of reference we can refer back to and build on. In this way, rather than merely recapitulating traumatic experiences, we build both resilience and understanding.

As we focus on the nonverbal aspects of our interchanges, we can learn a great deal about patterns and meanings in the child's world. These patterns lend not only coloration and tone, but also include judgments as to what one can know about oneself and the world. Devalued aspects of self may be profoundly difficult to recognize or know anything about. Breaking up areas of humanness into good and bad parts in this way is a relatively primitive defense mechanism. The therapist's willingness to recognize and accept all aspects of self makes a contrasting statement about what it means to be human. In this way, she provides an opportunity to integrate rejected aspects of self, so that the child is better able to confront difficulties as they arise rather than merely stumbling into them once again in ways that feel defeating and demoralizing.

CASE ILLUSTRATION

When we look at the child's play for a better understanding of ways in which trauma reveals itself, we can recognize many of the hallmarks of the *disorganized attachment style* as described by Main and Hesse (1990). The girl we are calling Annie, for example, presented as shy, with large, anxious eyes that avoided contact. Easily startled, she initially painted in total silence, using her brush systematically, obsessively and deliberately filling in the spaces with care and concern and little mess. This type of inhibition is common in traumatized attachment, as is the ease with which Annie is startled by unexpected noise or movement. The therapist takes her cue and is quiet, as well, while attentive to Annie's movements and behavior. She asks Annie what her preferences are without presuming, and keeps her comments concrete, directed toward Annie's play as it unfolds.

From the first session, we see that the therapist has a good sense of what it means to be with a traumatized child. Rather than insisting on speech or some other form of direct contact, she respectfully recognizes the child's silence and inquires into it by making a sound with the paper, inviting the child to do the same. This shared noise-making allows sound to come into the room without insisting that something be said. By the end of this session, the therapist reports that the tension has eased gradually, and that Annie was able to smile and wave good-bye as she departed.

Over time, Annie develops a habit of startling her therapist by surprising her and saying "Boo" as they make their way to the therapy room. When she repeats this behavior on the way to their next-to-last session, she succeeds in indeed startling the therapist. In this way, we see her playing out the type of disjunction that is a hallmark of disorganized attachment, thereby providing the opportunity for rupture and repair. During this session, Annie works intently and, unlike her behavior in earlier sessions, is not disrupted by external noises from people walking by. Rather, she is able to sustain her concentration and is also able to be playful, squishing the paint with her hands and laughing together with the therapist. In stark contrast to her silence in the first session, by this time Annie is talkative and engaged, commenting on her own play and also inviting the therapist into the conversation. Although Annie participates in the cleaning up at the end of the session, the therapist is pleased to note that her participation is less obsessive. In her notes, the therapist writes of her pleasure that "the sessions are moving toward the play increasing in importance and the tidying and cleaning being less significant."

The therapist notes a repetitive theme of play that focuses on seeing one another. In the next-to-last session, for example, Annie asks the therapist to say her name and then says, "I've seen you," to which the therapist replies, "You have seen me and I have seen you." The therapist describes this repeated exchange regarding recognition of one another "as a gaze that mirrors and reflects," quite unlike the frightening, absent gaze noted in the literature on disorganized attachment. We can trace, as we follow these sessions, the developing shift in this young child from the type of inhibited, frozen, rigid and routinized behavior so typical of disorganized attachment to the greater playfulness, engagement, and verbal communicative capacity associated with greater resilience in young children.

On their last day together, the therapist notes aloud that this will be their last day together and Annie responds, in words the therapist cannot quite decipher, something about the last bird sitting on the branch. The birds on the branch have been their way of keeping track of their sessions along the way, and recognizing the limits of their time together with one another. Annie paints a vertical strip and a reverse number seven, and asks the therapist what it is. The therapist is initially anxious, not knowing what the correct answer will be. We can wonder if this is a countertransference enactment of the dynamics at play when they first began, when Annie was the one who was likely anxious, not knowing what the correct behaviors might be, and who then had to learn to relax and engage in the play. In this session, in contrast, it is the therapist who anxiously comes up with a wrong answer and asks for the right one. But Annie is playing. She "wants a guess, not an answer, so it is a game, not a test. What matters is that I am 'playing,' not whether I get it right or wrong." Annie adds some lines to her drawing and says that it is a window, which strikes the therapist as "a powerful metaphor, looking in, looking out, internal world, external world." This metaphor evokes a recurring theme in their play together, beginning with the first image Annie created in their work.

During this last session, Annie asks if one of her classmates had taken one of the birds that they have used to mark the weeks as they go by. The therapist intuits that Annie is afraid to ask what she really wants to ask: whether she might take this last bird home. The therapist asks Annie if she would like to have the bird, and tells her she can take it home at the end of their session. Annie clutches the bird, saying "He loves me." She finds a box for the bird and then dips the bird in red water and covers it with cloth. She pours some red paint on top of the cloth that covers the container and then places another cloth on top. Red paint begins to ooze up and "she lifts both cloths up and carefully lifts underneath, thinking out loud that perhaps the bird has 'died.' But no, its still 'alive.'" Annie then spends most of the rest of the session covering and uncovering the bird, and tending to it when it gets "hurt." At one point, she decides to leave the bird in the art therapy room and to come to collect it at the end of the day. She then says that when she returns, the "little bird will die for me." The therapist is "puzzled, and she repeats it, making it sound like something good by the tone of her voice." Later, "in supervision we talk about how the session will be dead by the time she returns."

We see the difficulty Annie faces in coming to the end of a relationship that has had value for her. In the next-to-last session, she works at recognizing and being recognized by the person with whom she has developed trust. In the last session, she struggles with what can be taken and what must be left, taking with her the little bird as a transitional object through which she carries with her a representation of the therapist and the time they have spent together. Notably, Annie also tried to talk the therapist into giving away her wristwatch, a representation both of the therapist and explicitly of time and the time they have spent together. Ultimately, however, she cannot take away more than she has internalized of this relationship. She plays with that dilemma throughout the last session, as she covers, uncovers, kills, maims, and brings back to life the bird that has become the representation of what can be taken away. In these efforts, we recognize the traumatized child who is struggling with issues of life, death, and impermanence, a child who will likely go back to facing difficult realities but who also seems to have internalized greater capacities for self-regulation and adaptive coping than when the sessions began.

CONCLUSION

Engagement in play helps the child to learn to attend to subtleties and nuances of experience that may have previously eluded or overwhelmed her. This heightened engagement affords greater vitality. From the realm of play, change feels more possible. For a child whose interpersonal experience has largely been one of misrecognition, disappointment, and despair, encounters with others are fraught with peril, making the play space an important transitional space within which to play with dangers that otherwise might seem too real to negotiate. For the therapist, this play space affords us opportunities to be actively engaged in the prevailing emotional truth, which may provide our only marker regarding the extent to which we are moving in the direction of greater understanding or evasion (Bion, 1977), whether we are perpetrating further traumatization or facilitating constructive working through. Trusting our emotional experience and being willing to be as present as we can helps to invoke greater presence and greater trust in the child as well.

One of the difficulties often encountered by the new therapist is how difficult it can be to tolerate being with someone who is in distress. And yet "feeling bad" is often *not* the problem, but rather can be a marker for the dilemma the child is trying to resolve. The overwhelming intensity of the child's affect may be both a demonstration of the magnitude of the trouble and also an obstacle to overcome. As affective intensity increases, it becomes more difficult to distinguish differences between similar objects or events (Matte-Blanco, 1975). At a certain level of intensity, I am not merely *like* the hateful mother, I *am* the hateful mother. Although that type of equivalence can be problematic, it also provides useful opportunities to work out relational difficulties in the displacement, through the play. In such cases, our acknowledgment and affirmation of the child's reality as she experiences it can provide some containing relief, helping the child to begin to tolerate her distress rather than either being overwhelmed by it or relieving ours at her own expense.

It is often the assurance that we understand what is at stake, and can keep this in mind, that relieves the distress sufficiently that we can be more present with one another. Noting and naming patterns can help to provide some relief, as we recognize and give words to meanings that the child may not have known how to name or perhaps did not dare to. Such recognition also helps to relieve the affective intensity, thereby facilitating further and perhaps deeper play. Much as has been described in the mentalization literature, being able to soothe ourselves well enough to begin thinking again helps to reduce the overall emotional intensity in the room, thereby making it easier for the other person to begin thinking more clearly as well. Types of interventions like this can make a difference in these young children's lives, as they learn to calm and soothe themselves more effectively. Data that shows the importance of early relationships in building resilience, also shows that *early deficits can be moderated* with sufficient attention (Mayes, Fonagy, and Target, 2007; Schwandt et al., 2010).

As we can see in the case of Annie, play can at times feel either inhibited and foreclosed or aggressive, hostile, chaotic, and even violent. It is important to have sufficient boundaries to make the play space safe, but with sufficient room that the child can express difficult feelings. In the moment, the art therapist must be able to distinguish between a safe and a dangerous expression of emotion, and to recognize the importance of being able to survive the child's attacks, not just control or manage them. In Winnicott's (1971) terms, the child needs to be able to destroy those on whom they depend, and have them survive the attack, in order to begin to be able to be more playfully creative and engaged with others and with the materials.

In such interchanges, we begin to build a universe in which alternative realities can be encountered and considered without their needing to annihilate one another. In the case of Annie, we see the importance of the therapist's ability to withstand her assaults without retaliating and to tolerate the chaos without overly managing it. Our willingness to consider the child's frame of reference opens up possibilities and allows further engagement in ways that also help to further development and solidify identity. Developing the ability to engage more fully in relationships helps to build sufficient sense of self and resilience to provide the solid foundation needed for building the important metacognitive capacities that are crucial in mentalization, developing an effective theory of mind, and building healthy relationships

(Dimaggio and Lysaker, 2010). The work with Annie shows that important scaffolding for enhanced metacognitive capacities can be built even in a short-term intervention, when the therapist recognizes the opportunities available through engagement with the child in play.

REFERENCES

Beebe, B., and F. M. Lachmann. (1988). The contributions of mother–infant mutual influence to the origins of self and object representations. *Psychoanalytic Psychology* 5: 305–337.

Beebe, B., and F. M. Lachmann. (1994). Representation and internalization in infancy: Three principles of salience. *Psychoanalytic Psychology* 11: 127–165.

Beebe, B., and F. M. Lachmann. (1998). Co-constructing inner and relational processes: Self and mutual regulation in infant research and adult treatment. *Psychoanalytic Psychology* 15: 480–516.

Beebe, B., J. Rustin, D. Sorter, and S. Knoblauch. (2003). An expanded view of intersubjectivity in infancy and its application to psychoanalysis. *Psychoanalytic Dialogues* 13: 805–841.

Bion, W. R. (1967). *Second thoughts: Selected papers on psychoanalysis*. Northvale, NJ: Jason Aronson.

Bion, W. R. (1977). *Seven servants*. New York: Jason Aronson.

Bollas, C. (1987). *The shadow of the object: Psychoanalysis of the unthought known*. London: Free Association Books.

Bowen, M. (1978). *Family therapy in clinical practice*. New York: Jason Aronson.

Bucci, W. (1997). Symptoms and symbols: A multiple code theory of somatization. *Psychoanalytic Inquiry* 2: 151–172.

Bucci, W. (2001). Pathways of emotional communication. *Psychoanalytic Inquiry* 21: 40–70.

Charles, M. (2002). *Patterns: Building blocks of experience*. Hillsdale, NJ: The Analytic Press.

Charles, M. (2003). Faith, hope, and possibility. *Journal of the American Academy of Psychoanalysis and Dynamic Psychiatry* 31: 687–704.

Charles, M. (2004). *Learning from experience: A guidebook for clinicians*. Hillsdale, NJ: The Analytic Press.

Charles, M. (2005). The intergenerational transmission of unresolved mourning: Personal, familial, and cultural factors. *SAMĪKṢĀ: Journal of the Indian Psychoanalytical Society* 54: 65–80.

Charles, M. (2012). *Working with trauma: Lessons from Bion and Lacan*. Lanham, MD: Jason Aronson.

Charles, M. (in press). Caring for the caregivers: Consulting with therapists in the trenches. Special Issue: M. Akhtar, Guest Editor, *Psychoanalytic Inquiry*.

Curtis, W. J., and D. Cicchetti. (2003). Moving research on resilience into the 21st century: Theoretical and methodological considerations in examining the biological contributors to resilience. *Development and Psychopathology* 15: 773–810.

Dimaggio, G., and P. H. Lysaker. (2010). *Metacognition and severe adult mental disorders: From research to treatment*. New York: Routledge.

Dozier, M. (2003). Attachment-based treatment for vulnerable children. *Attachment and Human Development* 5: 253–257.

Ekman, P. (1982). *Emotion in the human face*. Cambridge, UK: Cambridge University Press.

Field, T. (1992). Infants of depressed mothers. *Development and Psychopathology* 4: 49–66.

Fonagy, P., G. Gergely, E. L. Jurist, and M. Target. (2002). *Affect regulation, mentalization, and the development of the self*. New York: Other Press.

Gallese, V. (2009). Mirror neurons, embodied simulation, and the neural basis of social identification. *Psychoanalytic Dialogues* 19: 519–536.

Gallese, V., M. N. Eagle, and P. Migone. (2007). Intentional attunement: Mirror neurons and the neural underpinnings of interpersonal relations. *Journal of the American Psychoanalytic Association* 55: 131–175.

Grotstein, J. S. (2000). *Who is the dreamer who dreams the dream? A study of psychic presences*. Hillsdale, NJ: The Analytic Press.
Gunnar, M. R., and P. A. Fisher. (2006). Bringing basic research on early experience and stress neurobiology to bear on preventive interventions for neglected and maltreated children. *Development and Psychopathology* 18: 651–677.
Klein, M. (1946). Notes on some schizoid mechanisms. In *Envy and gratitude and other works, 1946–1963*, 1–24. New York: Delacorte Press, 1975.
Klein, M. (1952). Some theoretical conclusions regarding the emotional life of the infant. In *Envy and gratitude and other works, 1946–1963*, 61–93. London: Hogarth Press, 1975.
Knox, J. (2009). Mirror neurons and embodied stimulation in the development of archetypes and self-agency. *Journal of Analytical Psychology* 54: 307–323.
Krystal, H. (1988). *Integration and self-healing: Affect, trauma, alexithymia*. Hillsdale, NJ: The Analytic Press.
Lachmann, F. M., and B. A. Beebe. (1996). Three principles of salience in the organization of the patient–analyst interaction. *Psychoanalytic Psychology* 13: 1–22.
LeDoux, J. E. (1999). Psychoanalytic theory: Clues from the brain. *Neuro-Psychoanalysis* 1: 44–49.
LeDoux, J. E. (2002). Discussion: Trauma, dissociation and conflict: The space where neuroscience, cognitive science, and psychoanalysis overlap. Presented at annual meeting of Division 39 (Psychoanalysis) of the American Psychological Association, New York City.
Liotti, G. (2004). Trauma, dissociation, and disorganized attachment: Three strands of a single braid. *Psychotherapy: Theory, Research, Practice, Training* 41: 472–486.
Lyons-Ruth, K. (2003. Dissociation and the infant-parent dialogue: A longitudinal perspective from attachment research. *Journal of the American Psychoanalytic Association* 51: 883–911.
Main, M., and E. Hesse. (1990). Parents' unresolved traumatic experiences are related to infant disorganized/disoriented attachment status: Is frightened and/or frightening parental behavior the linking mechanism? In M. Greenberg, D. Cicchetti, and E. M. Cummings, eds., *Attachment in the preschool years: Theory, research, and intervention*, 161–182. Chicago: University of Chicago Press.
Matte-Blanco, I. (1975). *The Unconscious as infinite sets: An essay in bi-logic*. London: Duckworth.
Mayes, L., P. Fonagy, and M. Target. (2007). *Developmental science and psychoanalysis: Integration and innovation: Developments in psychoanalysis*. London: Karnac.
McDougall, J. (1985). *Theaters of the mind*. New York: Basic Books.
Nagy, E., and P. Molnár. (2004). *Homo imitans* or *Homo provocans*? Human imprinting model of neonatal imitation. *Infant Behaviour and Development* 27: 54–63.
Petkova, V. I., and H. H. Ehrsson. (2008). If I were you: Perceptual illusion of body swapping. PLoS ONE 3(12): e3832. doi:10.1371/journal.pone.0003832
Schore, A. N. (1994). *Affect regulation and the origin of the self: The neurobiology of emotional development*. Hillsdale, NJ: Lawrence Erlbaum.
Schore, A. N. (2003). *Affect regulation and the repair of the self*. New York: Norton.
Schore, J. R., and A. N. Schore. (2008). Modern attachment theory: The central role of affect regulation in development and treatment. *Clinical Social Work Journal* 36: 9–20.
Schulte-Rüther, M., H. J. Markowitsch, G. R. Fink, and M. Piefke. (2007). Magnetic resonance imaging approach to empathy. *Journal of Cognitive Neuroscience* 19: 1354–1372.
Schwandt, M. L., S. G. Lindell, R. L. Sjöberg, K. L. Chisholm, J. D. Higley, S. J. Suomi, M. Heilig, and C. S. Barr. (2010). Gene-environment interactions and response to social intrusion in male and female rhesus macaques. *Biological Psychiatry* 67: 323–330.
Solms, M. (1996). Towards an anatomy of the unconscious. *Journal of Clinical Psychoanalysis* 5: 331–367.
Stern, D. N. (1985). *The interpersonal world of the infant: A view from psychoanalysis and developmental psychology*. New York: Basic Books.
Terr, L. C. (1994). *Unchained memories: True stories of traumatic memories lost and found*. New York: Basic Books.

Tomkins, S. S. (1982). Affect theory. In P. Ekman, ed., *Emotion in the human face*, 353–395 Cambridge, UK: Cambridge University Press.

Trevarthen, C. (2005). First things first: Infants make good use of the sympathetic rhythm of imitation, without reason or language. *Journal of Child Psychotherapy* 31: 91–113.

Tronick, E. (1989). Emotions and emotional communication in infants. *American Psychologist* 44: 112–119.

Tronick, E., and C. Reck. (2009). Infants of depressed mothers. *Harvard Review of Psychiatry* 17: 147–156.

van Ijzendoorn, M. H., C. Schuengel, and M. J. Bakermans-Kranenburg. (1999). Disorganized attachment in early childhood: Meta-analysis of precursors, concomitants, and sequelae. *Development and Psychopathology* 11: 225–249.

Winnicott, D. W. (1971). *Playing and reality*. New York: Basic Books.

Chapter Seven

The Intergenerational Transmission of Trauma

Effects on Identity Development in Aboriginal People

Marilyn Charles

Identity begins to develop very early on, with children being able to differentiate between self and other during the second year of life. As early as age 3, a shift occurs in the form of a qualitative change in which memories begin to be organized around a relatively stable psychological sense of self (Welch-Ross, 1995). As described in chapter 6, children learn best in environments in which caregivers are attuned to the child's needs and feelings, and are appropriately responsive to those needs and feelings. Such environments help children learn to effectively regulate their emotions, which also makes them better able to negotiate the tasks of learning, as well as developmental challenges as they arise.

Optimally, caregivers are able to attend to their own needs and feelings sufficiently to be available to their children. Children whose parents are not emotionally and empathically available tend to have higher stress levels, which interferes with their capacity to freely explore the environment and to learn from those explorations (Gunnar and Fisher, 2006). Unresolved grief has been found to be a key factor that impedes the child's development. Even otherwise attuned and responsive parents with unresolved grief issues are less accessible as resources to their children and may even impede development through disorganized or disregulated behaviors that are frightening to the child (Main and Hesse, 1990).

Although identity becomes further consolidated in adolescence and young adulthood, the underpinnings of identity development are built upon early relationships with caregivers. As detailed in chapter 6, the early engagements between parent and child form the bedrock of all later development. Receptive, responsive engagement with the child tells him that he is valued and valuable, worth paying attention to. One of the important constituents of this receptive, reflective engagement is that the child's experience is recognized and elaborated on, first in nonverbal and then in verbal forms. Such verbal elaboration appears to be critical in the development of autobographical memory, a fundamental aspect of identity (Fivush, Habermas, Waters, and Zaman, 2011). The development of a coherent, elaborated sense of self is profoundly and integrally linked to the co-construction of narratives between parent and child (Fivush, 2007). The ability to discuss difficult or negative emotional experiences and also to recognize positive aspects of those events appears to be particularly important, enhancing understanding of self and relationships.

Cultural differences do emerge in the ways in which autobiographical narratives are constructed between parent and child (Fivush et al., 2011). It is likely that these cultural differences point to the values and skills required for adaptation within that cultural milieu. This variability can cause difficulties for the individual caught between two disparate cultures. Gender differences also emerge, with girls' stories focusing more on relational themes and boys' stories on autonomy-related themes. Such differences highlight the importance of teachers' and therapists' sensitivity to individual ways in which the child constructs his or her inner world and relationships.

TRAUMA AND IDENTITY

As mentioned, identity development can be complicated for those who are caught between cultures, particularly for those whose cultural ties have been disrupted (Charles, 2010). Difficulties associated with disrupted mourning are compounded in cultures in which individuals have lost touch with the cultural legacies that facilitated mourning in previous generations. The history of Australia is marked by trauma and disruption, both for the Aboriginal people and also for the settlers who left family and home to come to a new country. Although loss and disruption tend to be denied in the white culture, all Australians have in common a heritage of loss, disruption, and rupture in relation to their own particular ancestral histories (Schmidt Neven, 2005). For all Australians, there is a complicated legacy of cultural burdens that have been compounded by denial, disruption, and silence. For the Aboriginal people, in particular, there are cultural burdens of rejection, denigration, and persecution that make it even more difficult to develop a healthy, resilient sense of self.

Because the problems associated with trauma, ethnic tensions, and loss have been so entrenched in Australian history, they also permeate the social systems, even those that intend to ameliorate them. Garvey (2008) notes three major issues that have negatively impacted the social and emotional well-being of indigenous Australian people: "the denial of humanity, the denial of existence and the denial of identity" (p. 789). The losses, in terms of cultural and spiritual heritage and of family and community connections, have been massive. "For many indigenous people, the destruction of areas and objects of sacred and spiritual significance (or uncertainty as to their fate) remains a source of unrelenting turmoil and sadness" (Garvey, p. 789).[1]

Many of the difficulties associated with massive cultural losses can be traced in part to the virulent shame that results from being discriminated against, devalued, and depicted in negative terms without recourse to the collective social knowledge, lore, and practices that might have moderated or attenuated these destructive forces (Atkinson, 2002; Charles, 2000). These difficulties are further exacerbated when identity needs associated with one's ethnic identity are at odds with those of the majority culture (Akhtar, 1995). Children growing up under such conditions can feel torn between two worlds, neither of which entirely fits, making it difficult to develop a healthy identity that integrates aspects of each culture (Charles, 2010).

Cultures develop *master narratives* "that contain abstracted information about the cultural standards that individuals should follow and use to position themselves while constructing/sharing an autobiographical narrative" (Fivush et al., 2011, p. 334). A shared traumatic past disrupts the transmission of the master narratives that might engender pride in one's ethnic identity. Studies have shown that a strong ethnic identity is associated with higher self esteem when the individual also has a positive identification with the majority culture (Phinney, 1991). Findings in a study applying Phinney's model with Australian youth, however, showed that model to be effective in predicting racial but not cultural identification (Germain, 2004). In the Australian study, visible ethnicity had profound effects on cultural identification. Children who reported looking white were more likely to identify as Australian, whereas "visibly ethnic respondents were more likely to report bi-culturality rather than the original culture identification" (p. 140). In these findings, we can see the young peoples' attempts to be part of the larger social matrix in which they are embedded.

In part, these latter findings may be a function of the age of the respondents. Cultural identity may become more important than peer group identity with increasing age. In a study with young adults in the United States, findings showed that engagement with indigenous identity was linked with psychological well-being, measured both conventionally and in terms of community efficacy (Adams, Fryberg, Garcia, and Delgado-Torres, 2006). Findings with younger children are more equivocal. A study looking at self-esteem and perceptions of cultural group in Aboriginal and Anglo-Australian 6 to 12 year olds, for example, showed no differences between groups on self-esteem. Subtle but important distinctions do emerge on closer scrutiny, however, with Anglo children showing strong in-group preference, in contrast to Aboriginal children, who did not show a strong preference for their own group (Pedersen and Walker, 2000).

In addition to the cultural factors that can impede ethnic pride and interfere with the ability to mourn and effectively work through traumatic experiences, familial factors also come into play (Charles, 2000). Families pass along both strengths and deficits to their children, directly and indirectly. Through a process called *social referencing*, infants develop the capacity to learn about the objects around them by recognizing the adult's emotional reactions, whether positive or negative (Flavell, 2004). As noted in chapter 6, nonverbal elements of communication are taken in directly from parent to child, including the attendant affect and the associated meanings implied by that affect. In this way, aversions or inhibitions of the parent may be passed along directly to the child without inviting reflection, instead being experienced as "truth."

The intergenerational transmission of risk in children of Aboriginal heritage not only creates social disadvantage but also jeopardizes the development of self-esteem by inhibiting experiences of mastery that might enable a child to more effectively engage with challenges and overcome them (Benzies, Tough, Edwards et al., 2011). Experiences of mastery elicit pride, whereas failure elicits shame. According to Tomkins (1982), shame is evoked when our interest, concern, or curiosity is broken into suddenly or disappointed. Shame not only casts down our eyes, it also amplifies emotion, leading to the development of *scripts*, ideas about how the world works that are so powerful that they can preclude reflection or integration of new experience (Tomkins, 1979). When our natural curiosity has been punished, it is easier to turn away rather than to face a challenge. Shame amplifies affect, making it difficult to sustain curiosity in the face of novelty. We need our curiosity in order to take the types of risks required for new learning to occur and, in turn, to acquire the experiences of mastery that build positive self-regard and help to develop our metacognitive capacities (Fonagy, Gergely, Jurist, and Target, 2002; Lysaker, Erickson, Buck et al., 2010; Lysaker, Erikson, Ringer et al., 2011). Shame also interferes with the development of healthy social relationships, so crucial to the development of self-esteem in childhood, by inhibiting our ability to look outward. Looking outward helps us to obtain sufficient perspective to make sense of ourselves in relation to others, the very perspective that is essential for metacognition and reflective function.

Negative effects of colonization persist across the generations and create shame on both sides, making it difficult to work through these tensions and to overcome their effects. Complicating these difficulties, in Australia (as also occurred in North America) there were social practices that directly disrupted the transmission of culture in Native and First Nations individuals. In relation to the First Nations people in Canada, Ball (2008) writes: "Most children in residential schools were forced to stop speaking their language [and to] repudiate their culture and spiritual beliefs" (p. 7). This disruption of familial and cultural ties, as happened also in Australia with the Stolen Generation, was profound. Perhaps most problematic was the disruption of the social interactions that are the "primary means of instilling self-esteem, a positive cultural identity, empathy, language development and curiosity about the world" (p. 7) so essential to healthy development. In this way, also impeded was the ability to pass along those essential capacities to the next generation. For a culture in which kinship ties are such an important aspect of identity, the effects of the disruption of these ties has been particularly devastating (Bishop, Colquhoun, and Johnson, 2006; Clark, 2000).

INTERVENTION

If part of the journey into adulthood is to slay whatever "beast" stands in the path of self-knowledge (Campbell, 1949), those who carry a burden of self-denigration have a particularly difficult path. We all must be wary of our willingness to yield to the authority of others if we are to encounter ourselves in ways that invite enrichment of our innate capacities rather than the sense that we must be other than ourselves in order to be valued. Particularly for those who have been neglected or maltreated and are hyperresponsive to threat, treatments that focus primarily on behavior change may encourage compliance rather than resilience (Gunnar and Fisher, 2006). More effective are treatments that recognize that "development, in itself, contains the power for growth and change" and so attempt to harness the particular force of the developmental thrust present during early childhood and adolescence in order to facilitate development that has gone awry (Schmidt Neven, 2005, p. 190).

Compliance keeps the focus on others, thereby lodging knowledge and the power to change outside of oneself. Such a position encourages dependency on others rather than learning to more effectively recognize and respond to internal cues. Maintaining contact with one's own perceptions, thoughts, and feelings can be a particular challenge for traumatized individuals, who are more likely than others to dissociate under pressure and lose touch with their experience. In our work with children, in particular, it is important to appreciate how fundamentally their cognitive capacities are tied to the self-regulation of emotions that allows them to stay present in their experience and work through challenges as they arise. It is therefore crucial to devise interventions that help the child to gain greater access to and recognition of his or her own internal experience, and sufficient sense of safety to do so. For children, the primary "work" is being able to play at the challenges facing them in daily life. Interventions that encourage free play are most likely to open up opportunities that can show receptive adults where the trouble lies and, in that way, to take a stand against the bonds of secrecy that further entrench both the difficulty and the attendant shame. Playing out problematic experiences also affords opportunities to explore and work them through in the safety of a containing environment in which there is a reliable adult present. The adult is charged with keeping the play within manageable limits so that the distress does not exceed the child's capacity to manage it, and so that moments of disregulation can be soothed, softened, and met with repair.

Interventions with children are only successful to the extent that the family environonment can support or sustain whatever gains are made. Therefore, perhaps the most important element in devising interventions for children with trauma histories and disrupted attachments is to provide training for caregivers that helps them to develop more secure and supportive attachment relationships between parent and child. Such interventions help to moderate the ongoing difficulties in the home that the child is likely to encounter. Training parents to more effectively read the child's signals and to respond appropriately and supportively to the child's needs has been found to reduce stress sensitivity and to improve outcomes (Dozier, 2003). Schmidt Neven (2005) suggests that one primary responsibility of the child therapist is to promote insight in the parent so as to help the parent better understand the needs and feelings of the child and, in this way, to be more attuned to the child in interactions. That greater attunement opposes the destructive tendency for preoccupied caregivers to behave in confusing, noncontingent ways that leave the child unable to develop reasonable expectations through which to govern his or her own behavior (Beebe, Lachman, Markese et al., 2012). Being able to more effectively evaluate risk helps to soften the certainty of the negative scripts that can preclude reflective thought and thereby lead to dissociation under stress.

Such parental training not only helps to empower parents to be more competent and effective in caring for their children but also empowers the child to be more competent. In cultures where a group has been disempowered, it is crucial to have in mind the importance of empowerment in any intervention (Garvey, 2008). Interventions that are sensitive to the complex effects of the intergenerational transmission of trauma are more likely to be effective by recognizing and supporting the cultural traditions that are protective for social and emotional well-being, while also helping to develop and build other resources that might be useful to the parents. A case in point is the Boomerang Parenting Program, which adopts the Circle of Security Program and the Marte Meo Program to improve parents' caregiving capacities and develop parental skills through a twenty-session camp program for mothers with preschool children (Lee, Griffiths, Glossop, and Eapen, 2010). Sharing our knowledge in ways that are user friendly and accessible, so that they can be integrated and applied, invites the experiences of mastery so crucial for inviting further learning and development.

Early-intervention programs that recognize the particular needs of Aboriginal children have been found to be effective in increasing both academic proficiency and cultural competence (Ball, 2008), as well as greater social competence (Benzies et al., 2011). Although explicit parenting training is also important, the persistence of the effects of the intergenerational transmission of trauma suggests that interventions for caregivers should focus on spiritual and emotional healing as well as on learning more effective parenting skills (Benzies et al., 2011). In addition, focusing on training Aboriginal people so that they can be active in providing services in such programs is an integral aspect of building opportunities for identification with positive role models for children and parents alike.

Given the extent of the trauma that has followed colonization, interventions that focus on ameliorating the distress of Aboriginal children and building healthier self-esteem should include Aboriginal individuals not only in the interventions but also in planning policies (Bessarab and Crawford, 2010). This type of active collaboration recognizes and includes the knowledge and values held by the caregiving professionals and the people being served. Such a collaborative model also recognizes the importance of sharing knowledge so that work with Aboriginal people is increasingly informed by indigenous traditions and values, and is increasingly provided by the Aboriginal people themselves. Respectful engagement between Aboriginal and non-indigenous practitioners helps to build greater understanding and more effective interventions for all, as we become more knowledgable of and sensitive to the values, needs, and feelings of one another.

The issue of helping to build positive self-identities in Aboriginal children is particularly complicated given that clinical practice has, itself, evolved as a white, majority-culture enterprise. Attempts to recognize and ameliorate these complications do exist at the social and political levels. As noted previously, Aboriginal history is complicated by the disruption of culture and community that occurred with the British invasion. The policies instituted by the British did not value traditional systems and, in fact, interfered with the transmission of indigenous culture and traditions. In 2002, the Australian Association of Social Workers included in their code of ethics a mandate for cultural awareness and sensitivity. This move marks an increasing awareness of the importance of developing models that oppose the denigration of indigenous values by explicitly basing themselves on "indigenous knowledge that encompasses Aboriginal philosophical and healing methods that can be incorporated into contemporary social work approaches to wellness" (Sinclair, 2004, p. 58).

Acknowledging the involvement of social work in unjust, racist, and patronizing practices, Green and Baldry (2008) seek to build an integrative model that is attentive to the values of Aboriginal people. This integrative model of health care incorporates indigenous values along with social work values of social justice, anti-oppressive practice, emancipation, and self-determination. Crucial, they contend, is a recognition of the importance of decolonization as a way of building a healthier self-identity. In part, decolonization involves a recognition that many of the social and emotional problems faced by Aboriginal people are a product of the disruption of the traditions that had stabilized Aboriginal society before colonization occurred. It also implies supporting the reinstitution of indigenous healers and elders to help guide successive generations. Given the extent of the disruption of cultural traditions and values, such reinstitution must be effected through mindful efforts at remediation and repair that highlight the present and future value of reclaiming what has been lost.

Complicating the transmission of a positive sense of identity is the high incidence of neglect and maltreatment in Aboriginal children, which cannot be understood outside of the social and cultural conditions in which it occurs (Hunter, 2008). Poverty and the disruption of the cultural traditions that kept children safe in precolonial times have had a devastating impact at the individual, familial, community, and cultural levels. Increasingly, there is a recognition that family violence reflects a breakdown in community, and is best addressed within the communities in which it occurs. There is also a recognition of the importance of supporting, sustaining, and developing personal resources so that each individual might be better empowered for effective action. Healthy self-esteem is a crucial mitigating factor that helps to stabilize the individual during times of stress and thereby leads to more reflective and adaptive action.

In cultural contexts in which loss and strain are prominent features, the child will be faced with noncontingencies that impede meaning-making and effective action. An important source of intervention, therefore, lies in assisting the child to better negotiate difficulties and to make better sense of the contingencies faced in his or her environment. Recalling that implicit knowledge is precisely defined as knowledge that is not easily recognized or communicated in words, it is important for those who work with traumatized children to be able to hear the story being told through the play, and to witness and recognize important aspects of those stories. In this way, the child is not left so alone with his or her trouble, and the experiences that have been left unsymbolized can be brought into words. Actively seeking out the potential for engagement and communication is particularly important for children whose lives have been affected by loss, given that the debilitating effects of trauma can otherwise be mistaken for incapacities in the child.

When symptoms are misconstrued as deficits, a terrible injustice is done to the child that further impedes learning and healthy identity development.

Potential caregivers should also be cautioned to be attentive to the importance of the primary bonds between parent and child, and to recognize the hazards of interfering with those bonds. The attentive caregiver of neglected or traumatized children should have in mind the child's need to be part of the family system, so that reparative work can be done without further damaging the attachment bonds. Having in mind that parents have good intentions, without necessarily being able to effectively act on them, can help the therapist or teacher to hear the child's story and recognize her distress without disrespecting the parents. Crucial here is the capacity to hold a person responsible for their behaviors without denigrating them. For children for whom shame is part of the struggle, this distinction is critically important. We must remember that the child inevitably will—and also needs to be able to—identify with each parent. Being able to find the good along with the bad in caregivers is essential to the child's well-being.

In providing opportunities for the child to play, we hope to allow thoughts and feelings that may be largely unconscious to express themselves. The attentive therapist will recognize that such safety depends on the ability to hold in mind the parents as people who are both good and bad, and also to be able to act out the good and bad aspects of self, including one's loving and hateful feelings toward important others. Being able to play relatively freely requires an awareness that play is reversible. We can build, destroy, and reconstruct. Such play shows the child that bad feelings can be expressed within the safety of the therapy space without necessarily having any further impact, and that having or expressing bad feelings does not mean that one is a bad person or that harm will come to those with whom we are angry.

The therapeutic play environment provides a context within which impediments to development may be encountered and worked with. With children whose development has been delayed or impeded, play is an important medium through which to repair and remediate some of the damage that has accrued (Alvarez, 2012). When working with children who have been neglected emotionally, there may be insufficient arousal in the face of novelty (Stern, 2010), so that, according to Panksepp (1988), "only the strongest emotional messages instigate behavior" (p. 144). It may be extremely difficult to invite these children into the world of play, so that "a more intensive, vitalizing insistence on meaning is required because it creates what some developmentalists call a 'heightened affective moment' (Beebe and Lachmann, 1994). The pulse and pitch of our voices change at such moments of urgency, where we 'reclaim' our patients into the world of meaning" (Alvarez, 2012, p. 183).

In being with the child who has given up due to trauma or neglect, we show that something more is possible. In this way, the therapist or teacher can be sensitive to the possibility that a seemingly apathetic or disenterested, disengaged child may need heightened engagement by adults. Such engagement could be a crucial factor in helping to regenerate the capacity for engagement, interest, and curiosity so important not only for learning more generally but also for the development of self-knowledge. As mentioned previously, factors that inhibit self-knowledge and self-regulation also inhibit identity development. Identity development, however, depends not only on interpersonal engagements with caretakers. It is also important to have in mind the various contexts in which that identity is embedded, and the values affirmed or denied in those contexts. Such knowledge requires both a general awareness of the cultures in which the child is living, and also the ability to learn from the child about her own idiosyncratic ways of making meaning within those cultures.

Children begin to develop ideas about what is to be valued or devalued very early on. Even at preschool age, children demonstrate a sensitivity to issues such as social structure, privilege, and status (Black-Gutman and Hickson, 1996). There is a long history of oppression in Australia, with Aboriginal people being denied even voting rights until 1967. This second-class status has an impact on children's racial attitudes. A recent study found that Euro-Australian children had more negative evaluations of Aborigines than of their own group (Black-Gutman and Hickson, 1996). The authors noted that "negative images of Aboriginal people are embedded in the majority culture's jokes, literature, and idiomatic expressions, making them easily accessible to children" (p. 455). What is likely most destructive is the impact of these representations of negative stereoptypes on Aboriginal children themselves, particularly in light of the evidence that exposure to racism exacerbates psychological trauma and increases the effects of PTSD (Ford, 2008).

Increasingly, there is recognition that colonization has resulted in a view of difference as equivalent to being deficient, which negatively affects self-esteem (Fryberg, D'Arrisso, Flores et al., 2013). Self-esteem itself may be thought of as a culturally loaded construction, given that in many parts of the world interdependent representations of self predominate. Identity is built upon "representations of self and other [that] are inevitably tied to the social context, which is grounded in historically, culturally, and socially derived philosophical, religious, political, and legal systems" (Fryberg and Markus, 2003, p. 326). We can recognize ways in which young people struggle to integrate and makes sense of disparate and at times conflicting aspects of cultural identifications. Although indigenous cultures tend to focus more on interdependence than autonomy, studies such as those conducted by Fryberg and Markus show an integration of Native and majority culture values by Native American adolescents, who described themselves in both independent and interdependent terms. Negative sterotypes were most apparent in these young people's depictions of feared possible selves.

Studies have found that strong engagement in traditional culture has a buffering effect for young people caught between conflicting cultural identities. As noted previously, strong identity development is built upon the early interactions with caregivers. When parents themselves have been traumatized, the effects of that trauma are passed along the generations unless they can be effectively mourned. Intergenerational transmission of trauma interferes with identity development in successive generations, in part because of the tendency for parents to dissociate or become proccupied in moments of high affective arousal, which can leave them unavailable to the child (Main and Hesse, 1990). The dissociative response to trauma is particularly toxic in the parent–child relationship. Whereas the preoccupied parent shifts the focus away from the child's needs and experiences toward those of the parent, the dissociated parent presents the child with a terrible absence that cannot be penetrated and is difficult to endure. "If the mother's face is unresponsive, then a mirror is a thing to be looked at but not to be looked into" (Winnicott, 1971, p. 113). This child does not so easily learn to attend to the parent to ensure his own survival but rather is pulled toward further emptying out when overloaded with emotion, making it even more difficult to develop and sustain consistent and organized strategies for affective self-regulation. In the absence of such strategies, environmental strains and pressures that otherwise might merely present bumps in the road can become calamities.

For the traumatized child, whose developmental capacities may have been impeded, art therapy provides an important means for finding a space of safety within which to begin to once again explore one's environment and oneself. The attentive and attuned therapist can orchestrate her own interactions in line with the child's nonverbal communications, and can check in verbally with the child to evaluate the extent to which she is getting or missing the child's meanings. As we will see in the case to follow, although the therapist may want to soothe and soften the child's distress, it is also important for the child to be able to lead the way and to show something of the chaos with which she is attempting to contend.

In the chaos, we can see a lack of contingency, the failure of the child to have an impact upon the other, and so to be unable to find self in the engagement. "The infant's perception of contingencies, in conjunction with an optimally contingent environment, organizes the infant's expectation that he can affect, and be affected by, the partner, a crucial origin of the experience of effectance" (Beebe, Rustin, Sorter, and Knoblauch, 2003, p. 826). Incoherent narratives can have far-reaching effects because disruptions in the experience of contingency are so profoundly disorganizing for both parent and child in ways that echo back and forth between them (Murray and Trevarthen, 1985).

Holes in the family story also make it difficult for parents to pass along to their children not only the particulars of their life story but, perhaps more importantly, the process of narration itself (Thorne, 2000).

CASE ILLUSTRATION

At age 4, the girl we are calling Emmy was initially very hesitant, and seemed quite small and frail. She startles at noises from the neighbourhood. The art therapist acknowledges her own strangeness to the young child, and shows deference to the fact that they are in *her* neighborhood. Through these interactions Emmy begins to relax. In her initial painting, she works in dots from the far corner of the page, announcing the name of her mother and then her sibling, asserting her family ties. In spite of her seemingly fragile presentation, she is direct and forthright, inquiring "Why do we come here?" as she mixes the colors. She then asserts "I'm Aboriginal. I do dots. You do dots when you're Aboriginal. You don't do dots when you're not Aboriginal." The therapist notes, "Her sense of identity appeared to be important and she repeated this a number of times to make sure I got it." Emmy seems preoccupied with mixing and separating the colors, asking for clean water so she could make another color. She then gives the therapist crayons to hold. She tries using one of the crayons over the paint but then quickly cleans it.

During this initial session, the therapist tries to stay close in, attentive to the child and overtly acknowledging her choices and actions. When Emmy paints over the dots, the therapist acknowledges this activity in words. After painting over the dots, Emmy then splashes water all over the painting. One might wonder to what extent she is rebelling against the scrutiny of such close attention, showing something and then covering it over. The therapist wonders to herself what Emmy was painting over, and whether she was, indeed, escaping scrutiny. This sensitivity to the child's possible experience of an offering that the therapist intended to be respectful shows a deeper respect for the possibility that Emmy's actual experience might not match the intention of the therapist's response.

When the therapist announces the end of the session, Emmy, in turn, announces where she lives, and that she lives with her mother and brother. She draws a figure but then when the therapist tries to name it, Emmy covers it over. The therapist wonders to herself whether these exchanges represent some negotiation over shared meanings across differences. Emmy has trouble finishing as the session comes to an end. She turns her back on the therapist and continues to paint. In these actions, we can see that Emmy is trying to use the space for her own benefit but is uncertain as to what extent this space can be shared with the therapist. In her initial assertions of difference, we can see not only an assertion but also an implicit question regarding what possibilities of relationship there might be between two people who begin in such different places and do not share a common heritage or history.

When the time comes for the second session a week later, however, Emmy is eager to begin. She notes that both she and the therapist are wearing thong shoes and seems happy at this identification. She clearly wants to paint but is also curious about and attentive to the space. "Why is that door open?" she asks, as a noisy car goes by, and the therapist is able to ascertain that Emmy would prefer to have it closed. Between the two of them, they are creating a shared space that feels safer, more comfortable when it is contained, the outside world set apart. Emmy paints a face, reporting that she "made the man," and then pours the paint, seeming to enjoy the excess. "It's a really, really, really lot," she says, and then "this looks like a number," referring to the compartment into which she had been pouring the paint. The therapist inquires about the number and Emmy responds "seven." The therapist acknowledges that she had not been able to see the number and thanks Emmy for pointing it out, saying "sometimes you look at something and you don't see it." We can see in this statement both a recognition of human fallibility and also a recognition of mutual interdependence. It is a statement that refers not to deficit but rather to what might be gained from one another. In retrospect, we can imagine that this statement answers an unanswered question regarding the extent to which Emmy can be respected for her uniqueness as an individual and as an Aboriginal. Later, the therapist realizes that this was also the number of sessions remaining as well as the number of birds pointed out earlier that marked that number.

Emmy places pink tissue paper on top of the blue face, layering this over with glue water she had made, then further layering with successive colors of paint, applied meticulously and intentionally, almost as though she were icing a cake. On top of these layers, she lays down damp cloth that she had cut with help. When she removes the cloth, the man shows through. "That's a ripped one now," she says, and then moves on to the next project. Emmy makes it clear that she prefers to do things on her own. "I'm a big girl," she says proudly. "I draw a happy, happy man." At that point, she is willing to allow the therapist to clean all of the paint spots off her face. "This was an intimate sharing," wrote the therapist later. "We were very close. She held my gaze and seemed to enjoy my cleaning her face."

Emmy then puts her hands into the paint and swirls them onto the man from side to side. The therapist recalls Emmy's reference to the dots the previous week and "how handprints are often seen in rock paintings, from historical Aboriginal rock paintings." In that moment, the therapist is particularly "struck by her strong associations with her Aboriginal identity." The therapist attempts to preserve the wet and heavy painting by flipping it over, which allows the face of the man to emerge once again, and leads the therapist to wonder about her own need to preserve the work and "needing the man to get out."

By the third week, Emmy is looking forward to her session, asking her teacher repeatedly "When is my painting time?" The therapist mistakes Emmy's proferred jar as a request to hold it rather than to open it and, in that moment, is aware of her own desire to hold Emmy in the space. Emmy opens each jar in turn until there are only two left. The therapist's desire keeps her from being in touch with Emmy and her questions are at odds with the child's focus of attention. "I wonder who the man is," says the therapist, and then "I wonder how he feels?" "He feels happy in this," responds the child, but then she proceeds to cover him up. The relationship that is developing between the two shows through, however, as she begins to use the therapist as an extension of the table to hold some of her materials. At that point, the therapist's experience is of having finally arrived into a real and engaged relationship so that "I was in her world."

We see Emmy engaging quite directly with the therapist, pushing the edges to see how she will respond. At one point, near the end of the third session, Emmy looks up expectantly at the therapist before plunging her hands into the paint on the paper. "He loves having my fingers," she says. Emmy continues testing the limits, taking one of the birds and putting it into the paint and then into the dirty water. As noted, the birds represent limits and ending. Emmy takes one down and then replaces it, acknowledging the relationship to ending by relating the bird to the time "for me to come." She then begins smearing the paint again and covering over the man with more paint and paper, accompanied by a song. Emmy then makes it clear that she wants to put her handprint on the wall, to "make her mark," but settles for splashing paint on the floor.

After the fourth session, the therapist writes that "I wondered about the fact that she continues to choose this fragile tissue paper that won't survive." Later, in supervision, the group wonders "whether this particular choice of materials is based about whether she can survive, this fragility, whether things can survive for her." The therapist is aware of the contrast between the quiet of the shared space inside and the noises from the housing project outside. Emmy spends a great deal of this session immersing her hands and arms in painting and then cleaning them off. "I felt that the cleaning was more important than the painting." Again, Emmy seems to be testing the limits. Wanting to put paint on the walls, being told not to, she then puts her soapy hands on the bricks, seeming to want to make her mark.

With Emmy, the themes of identity and Aboriginality come forward from the very beginning, as she very explicitly defines lines between self and other, the Aboriginal child who "makes dots" and the white therapist who does not. Another theme that is prevalent in the work with Emmy is the issue of leaving one's imprint. She plays with leaving an imprint on the paper, on the walls, and also on the therapist's hands, taking her hands that are black with paint and leaving their imprint on the hands of the therapist. "As she pressed her hands on mine I was impressed at the impression her prints had made on my palms. The symbolism of her small hands imprinted on mine was not lost. I would not forget this little troubled girl."

Later in the same session, Emmy continues to paint and clean her hands, finally painting various colors on her hands until they drip onto the table. "This time she slowly and carefully placed her hands on to the table, deliberately leaving her handprint. 'That's my big hand,' she informed me. 'You want to leave your mark,' I said. Again she asked to put her painted hands onto the wall. Again I explained why not. She then started to only use the tip of her finger to 'do dots,' she told me," hereby reminding the therapist of the assertion she had made in the first session: "I'm Aboriginal, I do dots, you can't you're not Aboriginal."

Pushing the edges and leaving her mark seem to be Emmy's way of making room for herself. Much as we find in Winnicott's (1971) descriptions of the "use of an object," we see Emmy playing with being able to join in and also to reject, to be able to say goodbye and also hello. Her preoccupation with limits and time come forward, for example, in her repetitive question "Can we go now?" yet not wanting to leave. In this question, we can see her anxiety over intimacy, relying on another, and also, perhaps, over transgression. The therapist later wonders about "the frequency of the 'how comes?' I wondered about whether it was a matter of 'How come you're here for me?' I also wondered about the quality of the questioning; on reflection I felt it was unnatural and almost pressured. There appears to be so much anxiety for this little girl that it is almost like a pressure cooker and a release of emotions."

In session five, Emmy continues with her theme of covering the birds (who she unilaterally calls Mr. Carrots) with paint and then immersing them in water. "I'm putting him underneath," she says. "Stay underneath." The therapist wonders to herself "what was being buried down there and felt that whatever it was needed to come up." In a squeaky voice, the therapist says, "I don't want to be down here, I don't want to be in the dark." Immediately after, Emmy lets the bird come to the surface and, looking up at the therapist says "There," in a quiet voice. "There was relief in her face that was apparent in her handling of the bird."

The therapist experiences the sixth and next to last (but what in actuality will be the final) session as strikingly different. Emmy fills only one compartment in the palette rather than overfilling the entire palette, as she has done before. She then makes handprints on the paper, painting her hands very deliberately and then placing them on the tissue paper she had laid out. She goes on to immerse her hands in white paint and then cleans them off, a familiar process. "She alternated between squeezing the brush and stroking softly on her hand and arm." The therapist notes that after painting her own face, "her eyes . . . totally fixed on mine, . . . she grabbed the paintbrush and painted on her arm and then onto my arm. As in previous sessions, I had noted that she sometimes did not differentiate between the edge of the paper and the table. So I now felt that my arm and hers were together in the way she painted on them both, although they were not right next to each other, they were close."

The issues of covering and uncovering are salient in the work, as Emmy piles layers of paint, paper, and cloth on top of one another. "Turning back toward the table, she started to slowly peel the two towels from on top of her artwork. As she slowly peeled them back, I said, 'I wonder what they were covering up?' 'Look what happened,' she proudly said, as the sodden image appeared. She was showing me what had been covered over for some time. There was relevance in the reveal, I felt, a trusting in allowing me that." At the end of this session, Emmy again wants to make her mark on the wall. In spite of the therapist's refusal, Emmy hesitantly lays a finger on the brick, and says "You can't clean it off," and then "Ta Dah" "as she pulled her hand back from the wall. She curled her hand so that the tips of her fingers made little pale pink dots on the wall." Although Emmy missed her final session, she was able to come in later to say goodbye and to choose a "Mr. Carrots" for a memento.

DISCUSSION

In this case illustration, we can see how a child who is both fragile and vulnerable can also have a strong sense of identification with her ethnic heritage and can draw on that heritage as a way of defining self versus other. As Emmy manages to assert her individuality, she seems better able to engage with the therapist as someone who is different but also in some ways similar. Throughout the sessions, she works at at defining herself. We see her struggling with questions regarding what might be shown, and how, as she works at covering and uncovering, painting and cleaning, and, in her own way and time, revealing that which had been covered.

In the act of asserting her Aboriginal identity in contrast to the white therapist, Emmy both takes a stand and asks a question regarding to what extent this difference can be recognized and valued. We see a child who, in spite of whatever trauma she has endured, specifically locates herself in her own lineage. She makes a demand on the therapist to recognize ways in which her creations are embedded in a specific cultural history with its own legacy and ways of marking meanings. In spite of the difficulties she has endured, we see a child who is determined to find herself within her own cultural heritage and to be recognized and respected as such.

In her play, we also see Emmy struggling with questions about how to make sense of and locate herself in relation to this woman who offers herself up as a resource but who is part of a group that has overridden the needs, feelings, and values of Emmy's own people. After asserting difference verbally, Emmy plays at mixing the colors and then cleaning the brushes, at some level working at issues regarding what it means to be separate and whether one can mix with others and maintain one's own identity. Given the legacy of the Stolen Generation and the terrible losses that were endured, this is a question she cannot rely on the white therapist to answer. In some moments, Emmy employs the therapist almost as an appendage or an object, a thing to be used rather than a person to be engaged with.

These questions regarding relationships are also played out in the surprise and startle sequence. "Can you tolerate my separateness, can you tolerate being discomforted by me?" she seems to be asking. The therapist's willingness to be used and bumped into, while also setting limits, along with her continued interest in what Emmy might be feeling or communicating, helps to confirm that this is, indeed, a person with whom one might engage with some safety. At a certain point, however, the therapist's willingness to accommodate to Emmy seems to invite anxiety, and we see the child pushing the limits, looking, we might imagine, for the firm boundary required in order to keep the play space safe.

Painting and then cleaning one another provides an opportunity for reciprocal closeness, whereas Emmy's black handprints on the white hands of her therapist make a statement regarding the separateness that allows sufficient differentiation so that each can truly "leave her mark" upon the other. This engagement seems to make room for the chaotic and violent play that ensues, as Emmy comes up hard against the inevitability of limits. As the reality of ending comes forward, she struggles, in her play, with the birds that represent the end of their time together. In this poignant sequence, we can recognize the previous theme of the "happy, happy man," who keeps peeking through in spite of all her efforts to cover him over. In similar fashion, the birds, who represent time and ending but also, inevitably, the relationship itself, are drowned and rescued, maimed and killed, while, throughout it all, declarations of love are maintained.

In the interplay between child and therapist, we see the struggle between what Emmy seems to want to cover over and what the therapist would like to open up. Two worldviews collide, raising questions regarding what it means to be buried and what it means to be open to the light. In what is to become the last session, we hear that Emmy's movements are deliberate. She immerses her hands in white paint and then cleans them off. She then shifts from painting her own arm to the arm of the therapist. There is a seamlessness in this move from one arm to the other, the dark to the light, such that the therapist feels the closeness, even though their arms are not touching.

Later in the session, as Emmy uncovers her artwork, the therapist experiences this "reveal" as an expression of trust. Emmy then leaves her mark on the wall, the handprint that the therapist has linked to Emmy's heritage in the Aboriginal culture, along with a splatter of the dots in which Emmy's declaration of self-identity was initially embedded. We sense that these two souls have made their mark on one another, and that what Emmy has been able to show and to reveal, through her play, in making its mark within the therapeutic environment, facilitated greater affective self-regulation in this young child, which in addition has helped her to further consolidate her identity.

NOTES

1. For some interesting perspectives that expand and inform the concepts of therapy and healing and that may be useful in the ongoing journey of bringing traditional Western concepts together with ancient cultural ones, both describing where they overlap and where they may differ, see *Traditional Healers of Central Australia: Ngangkari* (Alice Springs, NT, Australia: Magabala Books and the Ngaanyatjarra Pitjantjatjara Yankunytjatjara Women's Council Aboriginal Corporation, 2003, ISBN 978-192-124882-5).

REFERENCES

Adams, G., S. A. Fryberg, D. M. Garcia, and E. U Delgado-Torres. (2006). The psychology of engagement with indigenous identities: A cultural perspective. *Cultural Diversity and Ethnic Minority Psychology* 12: 493–508.

Akhtar, S. (1995). A third individuation: Immigration, identity, and the psychoanalytic process. *Journal of the American Psychoanalytic Association*, 43:1051–1084.

Alvarez, A. (2012). *The thinking heart: Three levels of psychoanalytic therapy with disturbed children*. London: Routledge.

Atkinson, J. (2002). *Trauma trails; Recreating song lines: The transgenerational effects of trauma in Indigenous Australia.* North Melbourne: Spinifex Press.

Ball, J. (2008). Promoting equity and dignity for Aboriginal children in Canada. *IRPP Choices* 14: 1–27.

Beebe, B., and F. M. Lachmann. (1994). Representation and internalization in infancy: Three principles of salience. *Psychoanalytic Psychology* 11: 127–165.

Beebe, B., F. M. Lachman, S. Markese, K. A. Buck, L. E. Bahrick, and H. Chen. (2012). On the origins of disorganized attachment and internal working models: Paper II. An empirical microanalysis of 4-month mother-infant interaction. *Psychoanalytic Dialogues* 22: 352–374.

Beebe, B., J. Rustin, D. Sorter, and S. Knoblauch. (2003). An expanded view of intersubjectivity in infancy and its application to psychoanalysis. *Psychoanalytic Dialogues* 13: 805–841.

Benzies, K., S. Tough, N. Edwards, R. Mychasiuk, and C. Donnelly. (2011). Aboriginal children and their caregivers living with low income: Outcomes from a two-generation preschool program. *Journal of Child and Family Studies* 20: 311–318.

Bessarab, D., and F. Crawford. (2010). Aboriginal practitioners speak out: Contextualising child protection services. *Australian Social Work* 63: 179–193.

Black-Gutman, D., and F. Hickson. (1996). Attachment and reflective function. *Developmental Psychology* 32: 448–456.

Bishop, B., S. Colquhoun, and G. Johnson. (2006). Psychological sense of community: An Australian Aboriginal experience. *Journal of Community Psychology* 34: 1–7.

Campbell, J. (1949). *The hero with a thousand faces*. Princeton, NJ: Princeton University Press.

Charles, M. (2000). The intergenerational transmission of unresolved mourning: Personal, familial, and cultural factors. *SAMĪKṢĀ: Journal of the Indian Psychoanalytical Society* 54: 65–80.

Charles, M. (2010). When cultures collide: Myth, meaning, and configural space. *Modern Psychoanalysis* 34: 26–47.

Clark, Y. (2000). The construction of Aboriginal identity in people separated from their families, community, and culture: Pieces of a jigsaw. *Australian Psychologist* 35: 150–157.

Dozier, M. (2003). Attachment-based treatment for vulnerable children. *Attachment and Human Development* 5: 253–257.

Fivush, R. (2007). Maternal reminiscing style and children's developing understanding of self and emotion. *Clinical Social Work Journal* 35: 37–46.

Fivush, R., and T. Habermas, T. E. A. Waters, and W. Zaman, W. (2011). The making of autobiographical memory: Intersections of culture, narratives and identity. *International Journal of Psychology* 46: 321–345.

Flavell, J. H. (2004). Theory-of-Mind development: Retrospect and prospect. *Merrill-Palmer Quarterly* 50: 274–290.

Fonagy, P., G. Gergely, E. L. Jurist, and M. Target. (2002). *Affect regulation, mentalization, and the development of the self.* New York: Other Press.

Ford, J. D. (2008). Trauma, Posttraumatic Stress Disorder, and ethnoracial minorities: Toward diversity and cultural competence in principles and practices. *Clinical Psychology: Science and Practice* 15: 62–67.

Fryberg, S. A., A. D'Arrisso, H. Flores, V. Ponizovskiy, T. Mandour, et al. (2013). Cultural mismatch and the education of Aboriginal youths: The interplay of cultural identities and teacher ratings. *Developmental Psychology* 49: 72–79.

Fryberg, S. A., and H. R. Markus. (2003). On being American Indian: Current and possible selves. *Self and Identity* 2: 325–344.

Garvey, D. (2008). *Review of the social and emotional wellbeing of Indigenous Australian peoples – considerations, challenges and opportunities.* From www.healthinfonet.ecu.ecu .edu.au/sewb_review (accessed 4-18-2013).

Germain, E. R. (2004). Culture or race? Phenotype and cultural identity development in minority Australian adolescents. *Australian Psychologist* 39: 134–142.

Green, S., and E. Baldry. (2008). Building Indigenous Australian social work. *Australian Social Work* 61: 389–402.

Gunnar, M. R., and P. A. Fisher. (2006). The Early Experience, Stress, and Prevention Network. Bringing basic research on early experience and stress neurobiology to bear on preventive interventions for neglected and maltreated children. *Development and Psychopathology* 18: 651–677.

Hunter, S. V. (2008). Child maltreatment in remote aboriginal communities and the Northen Territory Emergency Response: A complex issue. *Australian Social Work* 61: 372–388.

Lee, L., C. Griffiths, P. Glossop, and V. Eapen. (2010). The Boomerangs Parenting Program for Aboriginal parents and their young children. *Australasian Psychiatry* 18: 527–533.

Lysaker, P. H., M. Erickson, K. D. Buck, M. Procacci, G. Nicolò, and G. Dimaggio. (2010). Metacognition in schizophrenia spectrum disorders: Methods of assessment and associations with neurocognition and function. *European Journal of Psychiatry* 24: 220–226.

Lysaker, P. H., M. Erickson, J. Ringer, K. D. Buck, A. Semerari, A. Carcione, amd G. Dimaggio. (2011). Metacognition in schizophrenia: The relationship of mastery to coping, insight, self-esteem, social anxiety, and various facets of neurocognition. *British Journal of Clinical Psychology* 50:412–424.

Main, M., and E. Hesse. (1990). Parents' unresolved traumatic experiences are related to infant disorganized/disoriented attachment status: Is frightened and/or frightening parental behavior the linking mechanism? In M. Greenberg, D. Cicchetti, and E. M. Cummings, eds., *Attachment in the preschool years: Theory, research, and intervention*, 161–182. Chicago: University of Chicago Press.

Murray, L., and C. Trevarthen. (1985). Emotional regulation of interactions between two-month-olds and their mothers. In T. Field and N. Fox, eds., *Social perspectives in infants*, 177–197. Norwood, NJ: Alex.

Panksepp, J. (1988). *Affective neuroscience: The foundations of human and animal emotions.* Oxford, UK: Oxford University Press.

Pedersen, A., and I. Walker. (2000). Urban Aboriginal-Australian and Anglo-Australian children: In-group preference, self-concept, and teachers' academic evaluations. *Journal of Community and Applied Social Psychology* 10: 183–197.

Phinney, J. S. (1991). Ethnic identity and self-esteem: A review and integration. *Hispanic Journal of Behavioral Science* 13: 193–208.

Schmidt Neven, R. (2005). Under fives counselling: Opportunities for growth, change, and development for children and parents. *Journal of Child Psychotherapy* 31: 189–208.

Sinclair, R. (2004). Aboriginal social work in Canada: Decolonizing pedagogy for the seventh generation. *First Peoples Child and Family Review* 1: 49–61.

Stern, D. N. (2010). *Forms of vitality.* Oxford, UK: Oxford Uniersity Press.

Thorne, A. (2000). Personal memory telling and personality development. *Personality and Social Psychology Review* 4: 45–56.

Tomkins, S. S. (1979). Script theory: Differential magnification of affects. In H. E. Howe, Jr., and R. A. Dienstbier, eds., *Nebraska symposium on motivation.* Vol. 26, 201–236. Lincoln: University of Nebraska Press.

Tomkins, S. S. (1982). Affect theory. In P. Ekman, ed., *Emotion in the human face*, 353–395. Cambridge, UK: Cambridge University Press.

Traditional Healers of Central Australia: Ngangkari. Alice Springs, NT, Australia: Magabala Books and the Ngaanyatjarra Pitjantjatjara Yankunytjatjara Women's Council Aboriginal Corporation, 2003.

Welch-Ross, M. K. (1995). An integrative model of the development of autobiographical memory. *Developmental Review* 15: 338–365.

Winnicott, D. W. (1971). *Playing and reality.* New York: Basic Books.

Chapter Eight

The Importance of Being Contained

Kylie, for Whom Nothing Could Be Held

Celia Conolly and Judy King

> Kylie then took one of the tubs and poured water from the bucket onto the floor, retreating backwards as she did so. Once the pot was empty she ran back to the bucket and refilled it again, dribbling the water on the floor, farther and farther toward the door that led back to the Playroom. This she did four or five times, each time venturing a little farther from the bucket and closer to the door. As the rhythm of this became apparent I wondered out loud "I wonder why you're running the water back into the room." "Because I need to," she replied.

Containment is a vital part of being able to feel that I am "me." When I feel "contained and "held all together," my world feels like a safe place, and I know where I belong, and that it is okay for me to be there. Whatever happens, when things start to fall apart, I know there will be someone who will be able to help me "hold it together." This would be the experience of a child who has been fortunate enough to have a consistent, competent adult, who watches over him, making sure that he remains within safe limits, both physically and emotionally. For those children who have not been so fortunate, who have not had someone ready to step in to hold things together for them, the world can feel disorganized and unsafe, and they can feel they are "all over the place" on the inside.

Those who work with children see this being played out, literally, in the child's environment. Physically they are often on the move, from one place to another, unable to settle, and impulsively reactive to distractions. They are "all over the place" in the outside world because they feel "all over the place" on the inside. We can often see their feelings literally "thrown out" towards other people (even *into* other people), as they throw tantrums or become physically aggressive. This is a familiar enough scenario, and it makes sense to think about how these children are asking for containment—begging for limits—to make them feel safer.

There are other, less dramatic ways, however, in which children show that they do not have a strong enough sense of containment. Such children could more easily "fly under the radar." In the example at the beginning of the chapter, Kylie shows us her way of feeling uncontained: for her everything seems to spill out, to run over and run away. Within her art therapy sessions, she created situations over and over in which everything spilled, everything ran out and nothing was held because, as she tells her therapist so clearly, she "needs to." We can surmise that she is showing how things are inside of her. Nothing is held together on the inside, and she feels her emotions and her sense of self is spilling over, unable to be held.

In our society we often use the phrase that someone is "so together" to describe a person who is emotionally stable and able to cope with different life experiences in an appropriate way without losing control of themselves or their emotions. We might say they are "self-contained." Conversely we say that people can be "blown apart" or "lose it" when their emotions overtake them and they are unable to remain in control of themselves. We are trying to express something about the psychological concept of *integration*—the process through which a person can remain themselves, and in control of themselves, when under stress or in a difficult situation.

WHAT IS BEING INTEGRATED?

What is it exactly that is being integrated? Many psychological theories, including psychoanalytic theories, suggest that each of us is made up of different parts—that inside of us we have different aspects of ourselves which may or may not be "connected" to each other at any one time (Bromberg, 2008, p. 454). For example, there may be one part of myself which is generally quite strong and confident, but also another part which can feel vulnerable at times, and then yet another part of me which is quite frightened when particular circumstances arise. If all these parts are integrated, then when the frightened part is activated by particular circumstances, the strong part of me doesn't disappear—it can remain in some shape or form, and be called upon to help, and even if it is weakened somewhat it is still there, available for the rest of "me" to use. When a person says to themselves "It will be okay, just hang on for a minute, it will soon be over," for example, one part of the person is literally speaking to another part of themselves. The different parts of a person are connected to each other and can work together. Most of the time this happens automatically and we are not aware of it.

However, for those people whom we would not describe as "together," or who are easily blown apart, when the frightened part is activated it can seem as though the confident part has completely disappeared—as if it had been blown away with the wind. It is simply not there to be used, so the person crumbles, or explodes, because it feels as though only the weak, frightened part of the person is available, and so he can't cope.

How does a child develop the capacity to hold himself together? Bion (1962) describes the process of the parent containing the child—that is, becoming an emotional container for the child. The parent is like a bucket for all the emotions pouring or spurting out of the child, and the parent hangs onto the emotions in his or her mind, thinking about them and trying to understand them. For example, as the baby cries and the mother rocks her baby, the mother feels the baby's distress, wondering "Are you cold? Are you hungry? Are you frightened?" The mother rocks and calms the baby, talking about the feelings and making them manageable: "You're frightened. It's okay, Mummy's here. I know you're scared. Don't worry, Mummy will keep you safe." The act of thinking about the feelings, understanding them, and then communicating them back to the child (through words, through the tone of voice, and through the gentle rocking) makes the emotions manageable for the child. The parent fulfils the role of being a container for the child's overwhelming emotions. The container-parent "holds" the child's overwhelming thoughts and feelings, so the child doesn't become overwhelmed and blown apart by their intensity.

As this process occurs time after time after time, the child gradually comes to realize that when he is under stress, the parent will be there to hold him together, by talking to him, calming him down, providing safety, and generally making the stressful situation more manageable. Stern (1985) describes how frequently the holding happens literally, as the parent takes the child into his or her arms, making the child feel safe and held together. Gradually the child learns from the adult how to do this, and begins to be able to do some of these things for himself (it is as if he takes a little bit of the adult inside of himself), comforting himself, and looking for other ways to manage the stress.

While those who work with children, and those who study child development, have known and worked with these concepts for a long time, recent neuroscience research is now showing how this specific process occurs within the development of the brain, in the earliest years of life (Fonagy and Target, 2009; Mayes and Thomas, 2009, p. 232; Siegel and Hartzell, 2004). The brain develops the capacity for emotional self-regulation within the context of a safe, secure relationship.

Other children, though, are not so lucky. Not all parents have the capacity to provide a container for their child's emotions. If a mother has not had someone to contain her emotions, then she will not have developed her own coping mechanisms (Fraiberg, Adelson, and Shapiro, 1975, pp. 387, 454; Slade, Sadler, De Dios-Kenn et al., 2005). An adult mother who did not receive adequate containment as a child herself will struggle to contain her own emotions under stress. It follows therefore that it will be even harder for her to be a container for her child. (If nobody taught you to speak Japanese, then how can you teach your own children to speak Japanese?) A child's emotions can be very raw and very strong, as all parents know. A mother who has been emotionally contained as a child, and who has developed the necessary neurological pathways, will be able to sit with the child's raw, powerful feelings without being blown apart herself. She will find it distressing, but she won't be too frightened of what might happen, as she will know from experience that this onslaught can and will be survived. She then has a chance of containing her child's feelings. However, a mother who hasn't been contained, and so who doesn't have a well-developed capacity to contain herself, is unequipped to cope at all well with a child's intense feelings. The intensity may leave her feeling out of control herself, so that she might respond either with anger ("You pull yourself together!") or distress (perhaps going away in frustration and helplessness). Either way, the child is left feeling overwhelmed, rather than together. It would be virtually impossible for a child in this situation to be able to hold himself together by himself. In fact, by default he is being taught that his emotions are too much and can't be contained.

Many uncontained children show that they are, literally, "all over the place." Unable to sit still, getting up when they are meant to be sitting down, moving around constantly, calling out when they are meant to be quiet. In other words, on the outside we see that their actions are all over the place, showing that on the inside they feel uncontained and fragmented. This is a familiar scenario for anyone working with young children.

However, Kylie, the three-and-a-half-year-old who was described as spilling water in the opening scenario, uses a different way to show that she feels unheld. For her, *nothing* can be held. She tells her art therapist that she feels compelled to spill water all over the art therapy room not as a game, but because she "*needs to*." She is expressing something very important inside of her. Young children communicate their feelings through their actions. We can understand their internal state by very closely observing their actions and behaviors (Hodges, Steele, Kaniuk et al., 2009). When Kylie's art therapist watched her actions closely she gained a picture of a little girl for whom everything seemed to spill over.

> She then splashed me purposely with the painterly water, with the same excited squeak each time. I wondered at how much containment I could provide for her and quietly went on to say "But I don't want to get really, really wet" as I felt she needed a boundary somewhere, for her safety, as she continued to

> splash me with the uncomfortable squeak that signified that she "had to get something away from her." She then stopped splashing and poured the painterly water over the palette so that it ran over, soaking the paper, the table, and dripping over the side of the table. I said "Bye-bye water," which she repeated back in the same tone. "Does the water have to go spilling over the edge?" I asked. "It does," she replied. "That water's running away, it doesn't stay here," I said, and she nodded at this, her head down. (It seemed hard for her to hang on to anything.)

And then again, at another time:

> Kylie carefully rubbed her painterly hands together and then tipped the full palette tray into the bucket of water. She picked up the tub of water from the table and emptied that and proceeded to tap it on the bottom. As I sang "pat-pat" in time to the number of taps she laughed and became quite excited. The tapping got faster and my song got quicker, in time. She then seemed not to be able to stay with the strength of the emotion and stopped abruptly and threw the tub away off the table. "Throw away that pot" I said "Throw away that pot," she repeated "He couldn't hold anything because he's upside down" I said. She so quickly discarded it when she couldn't stay with the intensity of the emotion.

So much of her session time was spent spilling paint and water, tipping paint into already full pots or an already full palette, and watching the consequences of everything spilling over. She had to have lots of pots and containers for her artwork, gathering together as many tubs and containers as she could each session. It was as if she needed to collect containers because that's what she craved—something to hold her own spilling-over feelings and thoughts. Like the full palette that she tipped into the water, when she became too full with emotions during the activity she also became overwhelmed, and "threw the pot away." She was showing the world, and her art therapist, that she didn't have an emotional container inside her, at least not a useful one, which could actually hold her feelings and worries.

> She picked up the jar of green paint and poured it into the already full palette. She poured the green on top of the yellow so that again the jar was empty. As the paint plopped slowly out I made an onomatopoeic sound to accompany each plop. She giggled delightedly at this. I interrupted the flow of play a little to lift everything up and hurriedly put a tarpaulin down, anticipating the potential for more mess. (Again I wondered whether interrupting the "proceedings" for purely practical reasons such as the tarpaulin or replacing her apron was appropriate. Was I giving her further permission to make more mess, to allow more out? Did she think I expected that because I was putting a protective covering either on her or on the floor?)

The art therapist was concerned about the degree of uncontained behavior, but the child was not. Kylie needed to show just how uncontained her world is. The therapist was the one left holding all of the anxiety about the consequences of so many uncontained feelings (in the form of paint) spilling out all over the place. Hence the therapist rightly began the delicate moment-by-moment decision-making process of letting Kylie show exactly how she was feeling, and then beginning to contain her expression of feelings before too much damage occurred. It is important that there was some period of unfettered expression. If the therapist had been too concerned from the beginning about not making a mess, then Kylie would never have been given the opportunity to express just how uncontained she felt. The therapist was sensitive to the feeling of freedom that this expression seemed to give Kylie. It gave the therapist a chance to really understand just how uncontained life is in her world.

We can wonder if the therapist's anxiety to protect the premises was only partly due to a real-world understanding that the premises had to be returned to their original state for the next person to use them, and also partly due to her sensitivity to Kylie's feelings. She was carrying the anxiety that Kylie couldn't express: When our feelings spill over, with no container to hold onto them, then everything gets messy. Not just the floors and walls, but our lives also get messy when our feelings are allowed to spill over everywhere, without anyone to hold them. Kylie's play in these sessions enables us to guess at how little help Kylie had had in her life to hold onto her own spilling-over feelings.

While most other children painted on the paper provided, Kylie's world was so uncontained that her painting also spilled over onto herself, and her own body.

> She then started tentatively spooning the paint over her left hand and arm. I continued the "tap noise" each time she tapped on her arm and again she giggled. I sometimes anticipated the tap before the tap itself and she gasped and giggled. More and more paint got spooned on her hand and arm. She tried to catch the dropping paint globules with the spoon and layers of thick paint dropped onto her apron. She rubbed her hands together (much like you would rub hand cream on). I wondered out loud "You're putting more paint on your hand, I wonder if it can hold it?" She then said "I'm going to clean this" and immediately put more paint on her hand. She ventured farther and farther up both arms so that her T-shirt was sodden with paint, and the paint dripped on to her shoes. Again I said "It's hard to hold, isn't it?" as she covered every bit. She smeared the paint on the back of her hand and arm with the spoon. This spooning and smearing went on for quite some time. Finally I felt she had settled on one action and stayed with it for longer than a couple of minutes.

It seemed that she needed to show the therapist that she was flooded by her messy feelings, thoughts, and experiences. They covered her. Nothing was neat and thought-through, or ordered. Rather, she was overcome and overwhelmed, and anyone who looked at her covered in paint would be able to tell that no one had helped her to keep her feelings in their own pots. Her feelings were everywhere, including all over her. We say that some people "wear their feelings on their sleeves"—here, Kylie was wearing her feelings all over her, because they weren't held securely in place on the inside.

Through the therapy, the art therapist was sensitively attuned to Kylie's internal world, carefully observing her behavior and her emotional state. Occasionally she would make comments (as part of the activities) to show that she knew Kylie was overwhelmed by her feelings, and needed a container to hold them. Kylie seemed to respond to this attunement by showing that she felt held by the therapy, and the art therapist. Two examples from her sessions demonstrate her experience of being held: a drawing, and another piece of play with crayons that was very different from the pouring and spilling that constituted most of her artwork.

The drawing came at the end of her first session. The therapist had told her that there was only five minutes left. She immediately wanted each of them to draw a person on the same piece of paper, one on each side of the page. The therapist drew a person, according to the child's instructions. Kylie then drew her own person on her side of the paper.

> Kylie then became quite animated with the idea of her doing the eyes. She drew them in "side by side" she said, and then quickly wanted to "now do yours" following up with "I'm going to do yours" as she leaned over to my side of the page. Quickly she gave me the pink so I could "do the head" and then she started to draw the "legs" all the way down, saying "they're big legs." It was important that the legs reached all the way to the bottom of the page. She faltered with the line on the way down and determinedly restarted it so that it would get to the bottom (with a sigh of exertion), exclaiming "There!" when she had finished.
>
> I looked at the contrast between the legs that she had asked me to draw and hers, which came straight from the body, long and thin and fragile, almost as though they were not able to hold the head up.
>
> She then said, "and you want a face, a happy face" as she started to draw the mouth. She bent over the page so that her long blonde hair obscured my view. As she pulled back from drawing the square mouth she started explaining how the legs "went all the way up here" pointing to the head and then "they're always going to go down here" as she followed the line to the bottom of the page. She then put the two squares in the chest area and then quickly started to color in the chest of her figure, asking me "Can you color this in for me?" (There seemed an urgency about things, so much to squeeze in, in a short amount of time. I wondered whether the first painterly image and the overflowing had been almost a pressure valve.)

It seemed that even one session was enough for her to begin to hope that she could feel held. It was so important for her that, as the session neared its end, she drew the long legs all the way to the ground. Perhaps she could sense that this therapist, who was naming and giving space to her feelings, had her feet on solid ground. Perhaps she felt that there was a chance she could have her feet on solid ground, if someone could only notice her feelings, acknowledge them, and help her to find a way for them to be expressed. Then she might feel held.

In session three she picked up the crayons, and then was very concerned about how they fitted in their box. The therapist was aware that the box was very symbolic, as a container for the crayons, and wondered if Kylie wanted to have a crayon-box person to hold her feelings. Maybe the therapist provided a box for her feelings, by giving names to the feelings ("sometimes it feels scary," "now they feel safe"), and by being open to thinking about them with her.

> Her patting continued, this time on the table, in fact on top of the place where the crayon box was covered by the paper. As she tapped she seemed surprised that it had always been underneath. The shape of the box became apparent and I asked, "What's underneath the paper?" "Crayons," she informed me, and tore the paper back to reveal them. She continued to tear the white paper and threw the little pieces on to the floor. She then gave an excited sigh as she picked up the box of crayons. "You've found the box. The box holds the crayons," I said. At this she tipped the crayons out of the box onto the table "Ah now the crayons aren't in the box." She then slowly started putting them back without looking up. "Ah you're putting them back in the box, then they'll feel nice and safe" I continued, "Sometimes it feels scary being out of the box."
>
> Kylie then cut two small parts of the wet green paper and asked me to close my eyes. This I did and she placed one piece very gently with a little "there you are, ta-dah" sound into my two hands cupped together. She then gently placed a second piece there. (What importance did these pieces have for her? I wondered. Were they parts of her that she was entrusting to me or did these two pieces represent us two together?)
>
> She then started picking up the crayons individually using the scissors like forceps and adeptly placing different crayons into my cupped hands, on top of the two pieces of paper. The process continued until my hands were slowly filled with a small mountain of crayons. "I'm holding them all for you," I said, and she continued to fill up my hands. (I felt like she was trusting me with a lot at this moment.)
>
> "It's getting bigger and bigger," I said, as she finished collecting each crayon that had been on the table and not in it's "safe box." I described each color as it was dexterously maneuvered to my now very full hands. The last crayon was quite difficult to scoop up yet she persevered. It then rolled off the mountain in my hands and into the water in the bucket under the table. She scooped it out of the water and placed it on top of a tub that she had turned

> upside down previously, tapping it on top of the tub as she had earlier in the session.
>
> This crayon didn't stay there long and she moved "him" back into the box. "He feels safe back in the box," I said. "That's where he lives, that's his home." With this she started to lay the crayons ninety degrees around from how they would normally lie in the box informing me that that was "the roof." She slowly lined up more crayons from my hand for the roof across the bottom of the box, also ninety degrees around from how they would normally sit. There was a meditative quality to her movements. "It's good to be able to take them out and put them back in again, so that they are back feeling safe, isn't it?" "Now they feel safe," she replied.
>
> She then started to take the crayons out with the scissors and place them back on the painterly page. After a long time of maneuvering crayons with the scissors she decided to use her hands and grabbed seven or eight of them and placed them on the table. She then scooped them all up together, "in the box, in the box, in the box" as she sang their reentry to the box. "Do they like being out of the box?" I asked. "No, they don't like being out of the box," she said with authority. With this she laid them back in the "correct alignment" saying, "It's their home." "It's where they live," I continued, affirming her statement.

It was as if she were playing with the concept that her feelings could have a safe home here with her therapist. She asked the therapist to hold all of the paper and all of the crayons in her hands, and the therapist felt that Kylie was asking her to hold Kylie's thoughts and feelings, hopes and fears safely in her hands for her. It piled up, dangerously, because that is her experience—she doesn't have a neat little pile of unheld feelings, she has a huge big mountain of feelings that no one has helped her process, think about, or manage. But she did recognize that her therapist could hold them for her. She understood that this is her therapist's job, and that this is what the activities of her art therapy could do for her. The delicate maneuvering with the scissors, and her persistence at such a complex task, seemed to be her way of showing that this is no easy job—her feelings are very delicate and she is very vulnerable.

During this interaction, however, she found even this positive experience to be overwhelming. She was not used to having her emotions held, and eventually she showed her therapist her all too familiar experience—"nothing can hold all of me and all of my intense feelings." Prior to putting the crayons back into the box, her play reflected exactly this:

> She then dropped all of the crayons into the water from my hand, scooping them and delighting in their descent into the water. She then peeled the "present pieces of paper" from my hand and threw them into the water. The palette tray, the jars of paint. and everything else from the table was quickly dumped into the bucket of painterly water.
>
> She then moved to the basin of water to wash her hands, quickly upturned the basin, and emptied it all onto the floor. (This action surprised her and me. It seemed that it all had to be emptied, and not just in one spot, as the water

> flowed across the room.) She walked backward out of the room, tipping the water on the floor as she appeared to back out of the room, away from where we had spent so much time placing the individual crayons and where there had been some connection, some trust, some allowing of those inner emotions to come out, and even to be heard.

Her play showed that she had had some experience of being held by the therapy, but in the end the intensity of even her positive feelings overwhelmed her, and they too could not be held.

MIND AND BODY

For little children, as for adults, the body and the mind are intimately linked (McDougall, 1989). We see this in so many aspects of daily life, and it is reflected in many of our everyday comments, as for example, someone is a "pain in the neck"; I have a "broken heart"; you are "choking with anger." Feelings that are not held psychically (that is, in the mind) need to come out somewhere, and very often this is through the body. We are all aware of occasions when the tension of spending time with someone who makes us annoyed or irritated can literally "give us a headache," or when a very emotional experience leaves us feeling nauseous and unable to eat. The physicality of feelings is obvious when observing a tiny baby crying as his whole body "cries" (Stern, 1985). His face is screwed up, the tears flow, and arms and legs fly all over the place. Similarly, a 2-year-old overcome by emotion throws a tantrum not just by yelling, but his whole body is thrown to the ground and writhes in (emotional) pain.

If we receive adequate help to contain our emotions as we grow, we learn to express them in words and thoughts. Bion (1962) describes this as changing an unthought-experience (imagine the toddler's tantrum) into a thought (as the parent says, "You are upset that I won't let you have that toy"). A physically dominated experience of crying and yelling and throwing oneself around then becomes a verbalized thought. One of the valuable aspects of having someone help you with your feelings is that they can be held symbolically. Words are symbolic. Art, play, stories, and dance can fulfill the same valuable function. Symbolism enables a "circuit breaker" to stand between the strong feelings and their bodily or physical reactions. Preschool teachers and parents will often say to little children "Use your words," encouraging them to transform feelings into verbal symbols. When a feeling is expressed symbolically the child does not have to urgently discharge it; rather, the feeling can be expressed and yet still be held onto, explored, and thought about.

Kylie showed us through her bodily responses how she has not been helped to symbolize or hold onto her feelings. Even positive, happy feelings spilled over, in a very concrete way, as can be seen above. When she became excited it was as if she couldn't even hold the happy, excited feelings together. Without a circuit breaker of symbolism, when her mind was overwhelmed, so was her body (McDougall, 1989), and hence during the therapy itself she lost control of her bladder on a number of occasions, and her bowels once.

> She then started to rhythmically pour from the tub to the little tin and back from the tin to the tub. Sometimes she spilled over, and she appeared to enjoy this aspect. As the big tub poured into the little tin the water spilled over the edge. "The Little One's so full" I commented. (She was delighted with the "feel" of this play. By this point it became apparent to me that it was as if I was the big tub, and she the little tin. The Little One wanted to hold on so much but it couldn't.)
>
> As she poured from the Little One to the Big One, I said "The Big One wants to help, it wants to hold it for the Little One." She then emptied the tub and placed it over the top of the tin so that the tin was no longer visible. "Now you can't see the Little One" I said, as she tapped on the bottom of the upside-down tub. "Where's the Little One gone?" I asked. Slowly she lifted the tub so that the base of the tin could be seen. "Ah there's the Little One," I exclaimed, pleased to see the tin. She laughed excitedly and pulled the tub down so we could continue this game.
>
> As she slowly revealed the tin a few more times I exclaimed, "There she is." The game continued and sped up so that it turned into peek-a-boo with each lifting up. Her laughter got more excited and she jumped up and down on the spot.
>
> Kylie then announced that she was going to pour what was left of the water into the palette tray. She carefully poured into each of the little compartments. She then poured from the bowl into the tub and from the tub into the tin. She stopped midway through filling the Big One (the tub) as I felt she was conserving the water, and finished tipping the water into the little tin. "Ah, the Little Pot needs more, doesn't it?" "Yes," she replied, filling the Little Pot right up to the brim. "The Little Pot needs more than the Big Pot, the Big Pot only needs a little bit."
>
> She continued to pour from the Big Pot into the Little Pot. I then used a booming deep voice for the Big One (the tub) and a birdlike high voice for the Little One as the water flowed from one to the other. Her laughter was truly genuine and delightful and I laughed myself as I made their voices.
>
> This went on for quite some time until suddenly she said, "I've got to go to the toilet" and abruptly walked away from the table. (It had taken her by surprise, she couldn't hold on any more. She had allowed herself to become vulnerable and then she couldn't hold on to that emotion anymore.)

A similar situation occurred in session 1:

> Kylie put an empty tin on top of the jar of paint so that the jar was hidden (much like a magician does when swopping things under cups). She giggled as

> she pulled it back up to reveal the jar. This game went on for a little while with my commentary and my surprise at her being able to "hide" the jar and then to reveal it. She then scooped the tin into the water in the bucket and poured it into the tubs I had on the table for the paintbrushes. Water spilled and the table got wetter and wetter. As the water started to loudly drip over the side I said "All the water's going on the floor." She just looked at me for a moment and then returned to her "work" with the jars and tins.
>
> She stood up at the table to lean across. As she stood on the sodden floor I commented how her socks might get wet. As she stood she then said "I think I'm doing wee's." It seemed like we really were awash. I asked if she wanted to go to the toilet and she said "No" and then straightaway she said "yes." I noticed she had already wet her jeans and socks there and then. She then said "I'm doing a wee on the floor." (There was no distress in this comment; it was said with the same tone and delivery as comment about the puppy dog that she had noticed walking past outside.)

Her games explored the concept of having somebody hold her feelings (the Big Pot) and help her with them. She was showing the art therapist just how much she needs a "big pot"-person to hold her feelings, not only when she gets upset, but even when she is happy and excited (Siegel and Hartzell, 2004; Trevarthen and Aitken, 2001). Her excitement built up and she struggled to find a way to hold onto the excited feelings. They spilled over, and as she has no way to express her excitement symbolically, her body joined in and her wee spilled out too. In the following session a similar situation occurred with her bowels.

> When she poured the water from the bucket a seedpod from a banksia tree ("banksia man") fell onto the floor, much to her delight. The banksia man then became the vehicle as he was put into the different pots. She poured water on top of the banksia man and we laughed together.

With the fine covering of water on the tabletop some of the pots had appeared to aquaplane across the surface of their own accord. Again, the tin appeared to move, and I said, "You stay there, Mr. Tin," and she promptly pointed out "He can't talk." I smiled as I replied, "I was just pretending" as she placed the banksia man on top. Again the pot moved and she exclaimed, "You stay there, Mr. Tin" and looked at me for reassurance.

> She announced she was "going to wet him" and promptly poured water on top of the banksia man; this caused another pot to move with the water and she laughingly said, "You stay there, Mr. Pot." As the laughter increased she then stopped abruptly and quietly walked toward the door again. Over her shoulder she said, "I'm starting to do a poo" and walked away down the stairs. She had really got in contact with some strong feelings, and it seemed so hard for her to hang on.

CONTINUITY: CAN THINGS STAY TOGETHER?

Some of the strongest feelings that Kylie could not hold onto were her feelings about separation. She showed this throughout her sessions, in various representations. So much of the time in her sessions involved cutting, as if nothing could stay in one piece. Separation issues were especially intense when she knew that an ending was near—then she would start cutting and continue with great intensity, as if she would never be able to stop. It was as if, for her, when the therapist told her they were finishing soon, she felt the therapist had cut her off. She could not cope with the ending. Separation was obviously full of meaning for her. Very likely these meanings were sadness and abandonment, and being left alone.

Separation was difficult for her, even in the first session.

> I again mentioned that we only had a few more minutes and straightaway she asked, "Can we have some more water?" She then spotted the scissors and said, "I want to cut" (pause) "the lines out," almost frenetically, meaning the lines of the drawings we had just done together. (I wondered at the significance of picking the scissors as I was struggling to cut the session to an end.)
>
> She started by cutting along the lefthand side of the page from the bottom to the top. I sat beside her, as the paper sagged under its own weight, as she was cutting it unsupported. (I wanted to support the page but instinctively stopped myself. It seemed important that she do this on her own, at least at this point.) "I need to cut out the lines," she informed me. "I'm not going to cut out my family," she went on to say. I asked her if this was her family, she said "Yes, that's my family." I did go on to ask who was in this family but she went on to quickly say "I'm just going to cut out this little bit" as she started cutting fairly energetically. I wondered about the significance of these two figures "side by side."
>
> As she still was cutting the paper in the air, neither she nor I could see which part of the drawing she was cutting. She then told me, "I'm not going to cut out my face," "I'm not going to cut on the inside (pause), the outside." "I'm not going to cut on my head, no I'm not," she added quickly.

This was the picture (discussed earlier) that she drew when she was told that there was only five minutes left in the session. The fact that it had to be cut as soon as she was told that the session was finishing, and the way in which it is cut (the two people are cut into pieces) as well as her acknowledgment that one of them was herself, suggests that maybe this drawing represented herself and her therapist (the one whose legs went right down to the ground, providing stability for her). Perhaps from her perspective, when she and her therapist have to separate and lose the closeness and warmth of the session, the two of them (and their relationship) are cut into pieces. It made the therapist wonder about the lack of continuity of her relationships, and how she might feel cut into pieces (fragmented) when she feels left by a carer.

The session continued:

> I noticed that the paper then became more unmanageable for her as she was cutting so I offered to hold it for her. This seemed to be the right time for me to support this cutting. As I held the paper I repeated that we had to finish and that I would be back next Monday and again that there would be six more times. She just kept cutting. "What about some more?" she asked, and I repeated that we would do more when we met again next week. "We do more." "Not today but next time we'll do more." "What about five minutes," she said. I smiled slightly as I quietly replied "We finished five minutes." She continued cutting and asked, "Can you get another piece of paper please?" quickly followed by "five more minutes." I replied that we had one more minute and still she kept cutting. It seemed like the cutting was a parallel to the dripping, running water—she couldn't stop cutting.

The anxiety of finishing, and of separating from her therapist, was overwhelming for her. She was cutting as if she was compelled, almost as if she was being controlled by something else. There was indeed something controlling her: her anxiety about separation. Again it seemed that no one had helped her to manage her feelings about separating, and they couldn't be held or thought about. Rather they had to be enacted, through cutting. Her behavior suggests that she has an insecure attachment—a fear that she won't be remembered, and that her caregiver might not return after leaving (Ainsworth and Bell, 1970; Ainsworth and Bowlby, 1991). We could assume that separation for her seemed to be about being left and abandoned, or cut off, and that she did not hold the security that there would be a reunion again, or that separation could be a temporary state of affairs, before meeting again. It seemed that she held a fear that it was more likely to be a permanent cutting off. For little children, who depend so totally on their caregivers, a fear of their caregiver not returning after a separation creates enormous anxiety.

> Again I struggled to finish the session "We'll make this the last cut," I said. "One more cut," she replied, "two more cuts." I counted down the last cut, and then she said "Three more cuts" knowing that she was pushing the limits. I smiled as I said, "No, this is the last cut." She kept cutting and then said "I want to cut out with my friends" and still she kept cutting, the pieces falling into the pile on the floor.

If indeed these pictures were of herself and her therapist, then the message is well and truly clear—she had shown exactly how fragmented everything becomes on the inside when someone leaves her.

> She then started putting the textas [colored markers] back into the jar on the floor. I said I would tidy that up later. (It seemed it was unbearable for the time to finish.) She then picked up the biggest piece of paper (with "my head" on it, the piece to the right of an image with a pink head, one eye, and an oblong

> mouth) and would not let go of it. I showed her the folder that I put all the other pieces in. This was a safe place that I would keep it in, I said, and it would be here next week for her, when we met again. She insisted on taking the piece with her as we walked back to the playroom, and she was still holding the scissors. She needed to keep something of this with her. It was intolerable to let go, it seemed. She ran ahead of me as we finally walked down the stairs into the main room.

In the second session, she showed surprise and great delight that her art therapist had not only remembered her, but had returned to see her. Her insecure attachment meant that she did not completely trust an adult who said she would return.

> I arrived at the preschool for my second session with Kylie entering via the playground and was greeted by one of the care workers at the door. As we were chatting at the gate Kylie ran up to us eagerly so that we both looked down at her. "You came back," she said, looking up at me with brightness and expectancy. I smiled down at her "Yes, I came back, I said I would." She seemed so eager that I felt she wanted to go to the room straightaway. "I'll just set everything up and I'll come back and get you." She seemed reassured but I still added "I won't be long," as I could feel her anticipation. I wondered about her expectations of people coming back to her, especially those that touch her feelings.

It could be imagined, after such excitement that her therapist had come back, that she would have been in a rush to get into the room. However, her insecurity led her to respond differently.

> When I returned the care worker informed me that they had just had morning tea but reminded me to take Kylie to the bathroom before the session started. I thanked her for this, remembering how she had wet herself during the last session. As we left the bathroom she walked away from the direction of the art therapy room and sat at a little table next to the pigeonholes full of the children's bags. "I've got sultanas," she informed me, and sat down and started eating out of her pot. I asked if she would like me to sit down with her at the table. (I was struck by the fact that I had felt her eagerness to start the "art time" as I had arrived only a few minutes earlier yet it seemed like she was almost stalling now. Was the anticipation too much for her? I also wondered whether she had to "feed herself" in response to her needy, hungry feelings.)

It was as if Kylie's need to have her therapist was so intense that she had to pretend to herself (and to others) that she didn't really need to see her at all. We can only wonder if the fact that her therapist wasn't able to stay with her immediately felt like rejection. When she rushed up, full of eagerness ("You came back!"), she was showing her pure joy and delight that she had been remembered, and (consequently) was wanted. Perhaps when the therapist had to delay taking her into the room it felt like she wasn't wanted as much as she thought, and she may have felt embarrassed that she showed just how needy she is. By stopping to eat her sultanas, she was giving the impression that she didn't really need the therapist at all, as if she could take or leave the whole therapy session.

This behavior is another sign of an insecure attachment. Children who have an insecure avoidant attachment are worried that their caregiver will not be there when they need them, but do not show it (Fonagy, Gergely, Jurist, and Target, 2002; Fonagy and Target, 2009). Unlike children who have an insecure anxious attachment, who show clingy behaviors, avoidant/resistant children show a lack of concern, and appear to be unaffected by separation, frequently ignoring caregivers when they return. However, Ahnert, Gunnar, Lamb, and Barthel (2004) demonstrate that the cortisol levels of such children are elevated, showing that these children are actually experiencing high levels of stress in relation to separation, even when they are behaving as if they felt the opposite way. It can be surmised that they do not feel secure that their attachment figure will return when needed, and that it also does not feel safe to show their neediness. It seems the urgent need for sultanas was Kylie's way of hiding her insecurity.

We can also wonder if her choice of avoidant activities gave her away. By eating, while pretending that she didn't need her therapist, she may have been betraying just how "hungry" she was feeling—her initial reaction to the therapist shows that she was actually hungry for her art therapy. She was actually a very needy little girl who, like all insecure avoidant children, had learned to cover up her hunger and need for attachment figures. (This behavior could be compared to adults who "comfort eat"—eating food when really they are hungry for emotional comfort and attachment.)

Her subsequent responses indicate that the memory of the end of the previous session was clearly uppermost in Kylie's mind. She was so focused on the separation with the therapist that it dominated not just the end of the first session, but also the beginning of the second session. It was as if the session itself was not as important to her as the ending of one and the beginning of the next—the separation and rejoining held greatest salience for Kylie.

> She finished her sultanas and as we walked toward the room I said, "We're going to do some art together, maybe some painting," and quickly she chimed in "and cutting." "And cutting" I said, with emphasis on the word cutting. We entered the room and she ran ahead, straight to the pile of papers, turning to me as she asked for a piece of paper. I knelt down next to the "birds on the tree branch" that represented the number of sessions. She picked off the bird for that day and then she counted the number still on the branch "1, 2, 3, 4, 5." "Yes that's how many more times we have after today." I pointedly put today's bird and last week's bird on the table "So they can watch from over

> here." She quickly replied "Can you get the cutters?" and again I felt the urgency of the statement. She gathered a jar of black paint, the scissors, and the paper and we sat on the floor on the carpeted area. She then said, "I'm going to cut the lines out" as she started cutting the blank sheet of paper. (I was struck by how well she was able to link the two sessions together.) As she started cutting I was surprised that she cut in the same direction and line as she had cut the previous week. This week's paper was blank, yet she was telling me she was going to "cut the lines." I replied, "You're cutting along the edge. That's what you did last week, isn't it?" At this point I showed her the folder where I had put the remnants of last week's cut image. She did look up but I could see no emotion or even any recognition that these scraps of paper were important today. She was intent on her cutting, and the big sheet of paper seemed a little bulky and unwieldy. "You're cutting all the way to the edge, aren't you?" "I'm cutting round to make a curve" she said as the line curved around to the left of this first long cut. It was almost an identical distance, shape, and even consistency to last week's first cut.

The end of this session was also very intense. As they approached the end of the session, Kylie tried to deal with her fear of rejection by ending the session herself, asking if they could finish early. The therapist said she could, but Kylie then continued with the therapy, emptying paint tins into the water bucket. When the therapist tried to keep some paint in the tin, Kylie informed her "It's supposed to be empty," as if she were describing her feelings about finishing—she felt empty when she was left by her therapist, who could acknowledge and listen to that deep part of her which seemingly was so much in need of being heard and held. After doing some more cutting she then showed just how difficult and permanent separation feels for her:

> She quickly picked up the basin of clean water and upended it all over the floor. There was a large amount of water and it ran slightly downhill, under the clean, unused table and under the door down the drain. It was quite a surprise to both of us as we watched the water run away, down the hill. "It's not ever coming back, ever again," she said with vehemence in her voice, almost defiant with a little stamp of her foot. "It's not coming back ever again," as we both watched the water.
>
> She said, "It's still watching us." She gestured with her hand as if she was pushing an invisible door; "You want to push it outside," I said, meaning pushing the water. "Yes" she nodded.

Again in the following session she struggled with the ending, and felt safer to create her own ending than wait to feel rejected:

> I announced that we had five more minutes left. With this she announced that she would like to return to the room. She quickly pulled off her apron and dropped it to the ground. Again I got the impression that she was "retreating" as she backed away from the apron as well.

A similar experience occurred at the beginning of her fifth session. She ran up to the art therapist as soon as she saw her arrive, and greeted her with enthusiasm and joy. A care worker also approached the therapist and engaged her in conversation about some important logistics to do with the school. The therapist was unfortunately not in a position to give her full attention to Kylie. Kylie walked away. When the therapist was ready to start the session, Kylie was no longer interested, seemingly engrossed in another task and told the therapist "Not yet."

Similarly, at the beginning of another session she was reluctant to come to the therapy room, despite having enjoyed her previous sessions, telling her therapist "I've got painting at home." She was showing yet again how she clearly struggled with beginnings and endings. Separation was full of intense feelings for her: Was she wanted? Would she be remembered? Is it possible to leave someone and trust that they will return? Her fears of separation were so strong, and they could not be held. Her feelings spilled over, as did the materials in her art therapy sessions, time after time:

> As the water spilled over the edge of the containers onto the table, it started to drip down the back of the table. I said "It's hard when it all spills over isn't it, it's hard to hold it all in." She then became aware of the dripping and said "It's all going outside," as the water dripped into the drain outside. She bent down and actually waved. "Bye-bye water," she said (as we had said in previous sessions, but this was the first time she had waved to the water). "The water's running away, it's hard when you don't know when the water's coming back," I continued. She replied, "It can't come back."

CONCLUSION

Kylie's art therapy sessions showed clearly that she was not able to hold onto her emotions inside herself, in a way that could be helpful to her. The paints, water, and other materials represented her feelings and thoughts—they spilled everywhere, had to be thrown and dripped and wiped all over her. It was as if she was showing that none of her feelings could be held inside and managed. There was no "tap" to call upon that could keep them inside for the moment and then be relied on to let them out safely at an appropriate time and in an appropriate way. As they built up, so they leaked out. We can surmise that she had no one to help her hold onto her feelings, no one to contain them and help her to sort out what she thought and felt and how to deal with it.

Containment comes from an attachment figure, or caregiver, noticing and naming the child's emotions, and being able to stay connected to the child while he is experiencing strong emotions, so that that the child learns to be able to stay connected to himself and others while he is having strong emotions. When this occurs time after time throughout the early years, the child gradually develops a container on the inside—it is almost as if a little bit of the caregiver can stay inside of him (and becomes a part of himself), holding onto the feelings when they build up. Usually this means that he holds onto them until he can get a caregiver to take over (for example, until you get home to mummy or daddy, and they give you a cuddle).

It follows therefore, that if the attachment figure does not have the capacity to tune into (or is frightened of) the child's feelings, then the child is not given the experience of having his feelings held. He will not build up a container on the inside, and will have no way to manage the feelings. When it is felt, it has to come out. For many children this means an explosive tantrum, or impulsive behavior, like hitting or kicking. But for this little girl, her method of communication was not anything so obvious. It wasn't exploding—rather it involved spilling. Her emotions spilled out, just as her paint did, and just as her wee and poo did. They all flowed out of her, as if she had no control over whatever happened on the inside, emotional or physical. Without someone to hold onto her deepest worries, she was left with them all on her own. She couldn't hold onto them by herself, so they flowed out of her and she was left with the mess.

She showed that she could make use of her art therapy sessions to express herself, and to show how deeply she was defined by her lack of containment, and the insecurity of her attachment. She was very definite that she was making the water flow out because "she needed to." She showed how much she needed help to name, contain, and hold her feelings.

For this little girl, without a secure attachment and no one to hold onto her feelings, nothing could be held.

REFERENCES

Ahnert, L., M. R. Gunnar, M. E. Lamb, and M. Barthel, M. (2004). Transition to child care: Associations with infant–mother attachment, infant negative emotion, and cortisol elevations. *Child Development* 75(3): 639–650. doi: 10.1111/j.1467-8624.2004.00698.x.

Ainsworth, M., and S. M. Bell. (1970). Attachment, exploration and separation: Illustrated by the behavior of one-year-olds in a Strange Situation. *Child Development* 41(1): 49–67.

Ainsworth, M., and J. Bowlby. (1991). An ethological approach to personality development. *American Psychologist* 46(4): 333–341.

Bion, W. (1962). A theory of thinking. *International Journal of Psychoanalysis* 33: 306–310.

Bromberg, P. (2008). "Mentalize THIS! Dissociation, enactment, and clinical process." In E. L. Jurist, A. Slade, and S. Bergner, eds., *Mind to mind: Infant research, neuroscience, and psychoanalysis*, 414–434. New York: Other Press.

Fonagy, P., G. Gergely, E. J. Jurist, and M. Target. (2002). *Affect regulation, mentalization, and the development of the self.* New York: Other Press.

Fonagy, P., and M. Target. (2009). Attachment, trauma and psychoanalysis: Where psychoanalysis meets neuroscience. In N. Midgley, J. Anderson, E. Grainger, T. Nesic-Vuckovic, and C. Urwin, eds., *Child psychotherapy and research*, 15–49. London: Routledge.

Fraiberg, S., E. Adelson, and V. Shapiro. (1975). Ghosts in the nursery: A psychoanalytic approach to the problems of impaired infant–mother relationships. *Journal of the American Academy of Child Psychiatry* 14(3): 454–421.

Hodges, J., M. Steele, J. Kaniuk, S. Hillman, and K. Asquith. (2009). Narratives in assessment and research on the development of attachments in maltreated children. In N. Midgley, J. Anderson, E. Grainger, T. Nesic-Vuckovic, and C. Urwin, eds., *Child psychotherapy and research: New approaches, emerging findings*, 200–213. London: Routledge.

Mayes, L. C., and P. K. Thomas. (2009). Social neuroscience and theories of therapeutic action: Some implications for child psychotherapy. In N. Midgley, J. Anderson, E. Grainger, T. Nesic-Vuckovic, and C. Urwin, eds., *Child psychotherapy and research: New approaches, emerging findings*, 214–228. London: Routledge.

McDougall, J. (1989). *Theatres of the body: A psychoanalytic approach to psychosomatic illness*. London: Free Association.

Siegel, D. J., and M. Hartzell (2004). *Parenting from the inside out: How a deeper self-understanding can help you raise children who thrive*. New York: Tarcher/Penguin.

Slade, A., L. Sadler, C. De Dios-Kenn, D. Webb, J. Currier-Ezepchick, and L Mayes. (2005). Minding the baby: A reflective parenting program. *Psychoanalytic Study of the Child* 60: 74–100.

Stern, D. N. (1985). *The interpersonal world of the infant: A view from psychoanalysis and developmental psychology*. London: Karnac.

Trevarthen, C., and K. J. Aitken. (2001). Infant intersubjectivity: Research, theory, and clinical applications. *Journal of Child Psychology and Psychiatry* 42(1): 3–48. doi: 10.1017/S0021963001006552.

Part 3

Treating Trauma for the Aboriginal Preschool Child and Family

Chapter Nine

Mr. Carrots Counts the Time

Judy King and Celia Conolly

This is the story of a little girl who was fragile and unsure of how much things in her world could be sustained. She was unsure of herself as a person who could continue "going on being" (Winnicott, 1956b, p. 303), and she was unsure of relationships, holding on tight for fear they would not survive. Part of her survival strategy was to "merge" with others, in order to give herself some sense of strength from the outside (Winnicott, 1956a). Her therapy provided her with an opportunity to explore some of these feelings—to explore the fragility of her sense of self, and to explore how she could feel stronger within herself when she was given consistency and reliability. She took to the sessions in a remarkably playful and open manner, using the art activities, the relationship with the art therapist, and the materials themselves in ways which helped her to explore her fragile feelings and to express her need for reliability and consistency. The art therapy sessions helped her to develop a stronger sense of self.[1]

Lola was a three-year-old girl who appeared small and frail. Her preschool teacher described her as reserved and "emotionally tender," and she found it hard to let go of her mum when it was time to say goodbye. Lola was given the chance to be part of an art therapy project, with seven weekly art therapy sessions to be held in a room at her preschool. At first she was cautious and hesitant, as was to be expected, but she soon took to the opportunity with enthusiasm. The most remarkable thing about her therapy was that when her therapist used a special technique of hanging little birds on a tree branch to count the number of sessions remaining (in order to provide some consistency and reliability), Lola seemed to recognize the importance of this concept to her own sense of self and began using the birds as part of her therapy. The birds, far from being static reminders of how many sessions there were to go, became active participants in the therapy, being "bathed," painted, dried, and even named. Lola had taken the symbol of consistency and played with it—she had used the symbol itself to explore the concept more fully. In doing so, she enabled herself to express her needs and to explore where that might lead her.

For any child who has experienced trauma, the need for consistency and reliability is paramount. Ainsworth and Bell (1970) describe the importance of a "secure base" to provide security and safety for the child. Children who have not had the advantage of a reliable, capable caregiver to provide a secure base, or who have experienced other trauma in their lives, need the safety of predictability. Trauma robs children of their fundamental right to feel trust in good things being sustained in their world; it leaves them vulnerable to the feeling that at any time things could go terribly wrong again and it could all be lost. If there is nowhere to put your feet on solid ground, then it's hard to learn how to stand on your own two feet. Similarly, if you can't trust that good things in your life will be sustained and strong, including your relationships, then it is almost impossible to develop a strong sense of yourself as a worthwhile person who will also be sustained.

The themes of Lola's sessions show the fragility of her sense of self, her mechanism of merging to compensate for her fragility, her need for consistency and reliability, and her growing sense that she could actually become stronger as she explored these concepts and feelings. Over time she began to play with the concept of continuity, and herself as a continuing person, wanting to "make her mark" in the sessions, and upon the external world. She could begin to incorporate different parts of herself, including her Aboriginal identity. By the end of the art-therapy sessions there was some sense that she felt emotionally held by the therapist, and hence could cope much better with many situations. Her preschool teacher said that she benefited most of all the children involved in the art-therapy project, becoming more confident, and much more expressive in her language, and that the changes had lasted over the next year. She had begun to feel that her world could have some consistency and reliability, and hence she could be a stronger person who would continue and survive.

FRAGILITY OF IDENTITY

The fragility of Lola's identity is shown in her choice of materials and the way in which she used them, as described by her art therapist:

> Lola asked for orange paint and some paper. She picked a big sheet of pink tissue paper off the pile and as she lifted it the wind made it billow as she carried it across to the table. She immediately poured the orange paint straight onto the tissue paper.

And in another session:

> First she poured some paint from one jar into a fresh new jar. She then went to pick out a piece of tissue paper. (I wondered about the fact that she continues to choose this fragile tissue paper that won't survive, especially when laden with paint and rubbed and smeared so hard on top.)

She repeated her now familiar pattern in yet another session:

> She then walked over to the pile of papers and picked out the tissue paper (as she had done each week so far). She got the glue pot and squeezed that out into the middle of the tissue paper, then looked for the spoon to smear it from side to side. (I noticed that this had been the theme of her art making at the beginning of a number of sessions. It was as though these were her "scales" before playing the piano concerto.)

The art therapist felt that her choice of materials was a way for her to show her just how little, frail, and emotionally tender she felt, not just on the outside but also on the inside. The fact that she then treated the tissue paper with such a strong impact—pouring paint directly onto it and then rubbing it firmly around and around with her hands until the tissue paper gave way and disintegrated under the onslaught, made the therapist wonder about Lola's experience. Did the world impact upon *her* so strongly, making her feel as if she had got lost on the inside, swirling about in the world of big, powerful emotions, and other people's wants and needs? Was this a symbolic representation of how easily things could disintegrate inside herself? The therapist wondered if she was showing how hard it was to hang onto her sense of herself as a separate person, with the capacity to continue "going-on-being" without being overwhelmed by others and their emotions.

MERGING

Unsurprisingly, one of the themes of Lola's sessions, which became apparent very early, was the theme of merging. So many of her activities and behaviors seemed to have some form of things becoming merged with each other, blending into each other, or overflowing so that there was no sense of separate identity. Winnicott (1956b) describes the process of an emotional "merging" between the mother and baby as a normal part of development early in the baby's life, in order to protect the baby from the onslaught of stimuli from the outside world. Slowly, however, as the baby develops and grows, the mother helps the baby to separate and individuate, that is, to slowly become his or her own person. Those children who do not successfully negotiate this stage are left with a fragile, undeveloped sense of themselves, and can retreat to the safety of the merged state.

Lola's sessions demonstrated merging in a multitude of ways. For example, she always made her paints overflow so they would merge into the materials and art space:

> She then got the jar of blue paint and emptied it into one of the bigger portions of the palette tray. She poured the paint right to the lip of that compartment. As I commented on that, she said "It's a really, really, really lot."

And later:

> She started pouring red paint from the "almost empty jar" into the blue jar. More purple was poured into the palette as it was almost overflowing.

In another session the paint was seeping into the paper:

> As the paper rolled over she peeked under the roll ahead of it. "What's under there?" I asked. "They're coming through," she informed me as the paint started to seep through.

In her third session the merging between herself and her materials became apparent:

> As we washed hands and rubbed them together, slightly away from the table and the image, she hummed a little song under her breath. As I picked up on the tune and hummed a little back she looked up at me. I echoed the tune a few times and she smiled. She had been lost in her hands, rubbing the paint around and around.

She was "lost" in the rubbing of the paint around her hands. It was as if she had become merged into the world of the paint, going around and around, singing as she did. Similarly, on more than one occasion there was some merging behavior with her therapist that was reminiscent of the merging between a mother and a very young baby:

> She repeated that I had paint on my face, pointing out where I had the different spots. We then had a little bit of a game as she "directed" me to clean my face. I dabbed on one side and she laughed "No, this side," so I dabbed the other side of my chin and up to my ears pretending to clean all over. Finally she said, "All gone," and I remarked that she had paint on her face too. I asked "Would you like me to clean it . . . or would you like to clean it?" She giggled with each dab, as I named each color that I softly rubbed off. She seemed to really enjoy this.

She also used the paints on herself, merging the painting materials and herself:

> She returned to the task of painting her hands with combinations of colors. Her concentration was intense as she layered the paint. . . . She then started painting my hands with the paintbrush, layering the different colors onto my palms. She painted my hand, then her own hand, and then "stroked" with the brush across my wrist and up my arm. We were now both thick with paint on our arms.

And later in the same session:

> She grabbed the paintbrush and painted on her arm and then onto my arm. As in previous sessions, I noted that she sometimes did not differentiate between the edge of the paper and the table. So I now felt that my arm and hers were together in the way she painted on them both, and although they were not right next to each other, they were close. She then concentrated on painting all the different colors on my arm and I sang each color as it was painted on.

Her therapist had become an extension of her work (and her world):

> She wanted me to put a little tin on my knee and asked me to hold it for her. At one point I had a glue bottle, tin, paintbrush, and cloth all balanced on my knee as I sat beside her on the small chair. This was where she put her things, as the table was already quite full of all the paint jars. It seemed that I had become an extension of the table, a working surface, somewhere to hold the things she needed. It seemed I was now part of the art; I was in her world.

It makes sense that for a child who feels vulnerable on the inside, and whose sense of self could easily disintegrate, then the most sensible survival mechanism is to find your strength in the outside world—merge into others, lose yourself in their world. Strength from the outside is better than no strength at all. This is the world of followers, of those who get swept up in peer pressure or mass movements, or who end up following the opinions of stronger, more self-directed individuals. Lola was doing her best to survive, but merging with other forces or people undermines the development of a sense of self. What Lola needed was help to come to know her own thoughts and feelings, to know that she, as a person, could survive. To do this she first needed to be known, and then to gain strength and security through consistency and reliability in her world and her relating.

CONTINUITY OF SELF

Lola's art therapist had prepared a technique to show the children about the number of sessions they would have together. While all the children receiving similar art-therapy sessions benefitted from this hands-on, age-appropriate method of recognizing how many sessions they had left to go, Lola used it in a way completely different from the other children.

Young children cannot grasp the concept of time in the same way adults do, and helping them to feel some sense of control and continuity about the timing of the sessions can lower their anxiety and help them to process the passing of time. In the first session the therapist showed each child the number of sessions they would have together by counting the relevant number of fingers together. However, from the second session onward, the therapist had prepared a small branch of a tree with seven small birds (robins made from felt, bought from a local shop) hanging from the tree, one for each session. At the beginning of each session she and the child counted the robins left hanging on the tree as a reminder of how many sessions they had left to go. The bird for that week was then placed on the table for that session. In this way the children were helped to cope with their feelings about the sessions finishing.

While the other children who had art-therapy sessions used the birds to count the sessions remaining as had been expected, Lola responded in a much more personal way to the little birds. She counted them with her therapist, like the others, but then began to include the birds themselves in the sessions. Gradually they became central to the session material. It seemed that Lola needed to explore and work through *the concept of continuity itself*. The little birds represented the continuity of the sessions, and, within the safety of this concept, she could explore the continuity of her relationship with the therapist, and consequently the continuity of her sense of herself as someone who could be valued and thought about, at a deep level. Through the highly symbolic play with the birds she was able to find some sense of continuity of self.

Lola showed that she was mindful of the number of sessions she was having with her art therapist from the beginning. In the first session, the therapist indicated the number of sessions they would have together by using her fingers:

> I introduced the premise that she and I would be having this time together for the next seven Tuesdays, after today, and held up my seven fingers to show her that number. I pointed out that we had textas [felt-tip markers] and crayons as well as the paints. (I still felt her hesitation as I heard myself welcoming her to the space and materials.) She walked slightly behind me as I led her into the room.

In her second session the therapist introduced the birds on the tree to Lola:

> We entered into the room together, side-by-side, and then she ran to the little table and quickly sat down. I was struck with how ready she was for whatever we were going to do together this week. I then redirected her from that table to the middle of the room to point out a tree branch that I had hung seven felt robins on (this had not been there the previous week). I explained that the

> previous time we had met was represented by one red robin, and I picked that one off the tree as I said it. I counted the birds, saying that there was a bird for every Tuesday that we were to meet together. I asked her to pick a bird off the tree, and told her that would be for this week. This she solemnly did, looking at me for reassurance that she had "picked the right bird," I thought. I smiled, counting how many birds were left. We walked together over to the little table and I put the two birds to one side on the table explaining that they would wait there with us and watch.

Soon into the session she showed that the number seven (that is, the remaining number of sessions) was on her mind:

> As she was pouring paint into the palette she said "This looks like a number," talking about the shape of the compartment. I looked again in surprise. I asked her what number it looked like (as I could not quite see it) and she replied "seven." "Ah, yes I can see that now too, it does looks like a number seven."

It seemed that the continuity of the sessions, and the counting of the seven remaining sessions, was important to her, even from very early on in the therapy.

When the therapist arrived at the preschool for session three, it appeared that Lola had been anxious about the session:

> As I walked into the dimly lit room through all the sleeping children I was struck by the peacefulness in the room. I walked straight to Lola's bed in the corner. The worker, Deborah, was sitting on the floor next to her. Lola's head popped out of the blankets as Deborah said, "Here she is, here's Judy." Deborah informed me that Lola had been asking over and over that morning: "When's my painting time? When's my painting time?" We both turned to Lola and smiled.

Lola needed to be reassured about the continuity of her sessions. She struggled with the idea that her therapy, and her relationship with her therapist, were not like the tissue paper, which could so easily fly away or be destroyed.

> As we walked into the room we visited the tree-branch birds. She gently picked off "this week's bird" and I walked over to the table to place him with the other two birds, saying that they were waiting "so they could watch from here."

The process of being able to have some sense of control of continuity through counting seemed to be important to her, and she applied it to other areas of the session:

> She then systematically worked her way along the jars of paint, pouring each color into the palette. She mastered the screw-top lids and poured each color, sometimes naming it: "It's on top of the yellow." When there were only two paint jars on the shelf, she said "There's only two left." I felt that our counting of birds for each week, exemplifying the structure, had perhaps influenced this reduction in the number of paint jars available to her. The rhythm of these "color pourings" continued with each colored paint handed to me and put to the side of the paper with the lid left off.

Later in that session she showed how the structure of counting the birds gave her a way to think about how hard it is to wait. It had been hard for her to wait for her therapist to come to see her (asking the teacher "When's my painting time?"), but now the birds gave her a concrete way to cope with such big, abstract feelings:

> She then looked over to where the three birds had been "waiting and watching" for this session. She picked one up with her painterly hands. I said "Ah, we need the birds for the next week." "Why do they have a little tree?" she asked, and then answered her own question, "So that they can wait for me to come," she continued.

In her mind it was the birds that had to cope with waiting, not her. In therapy, as in life, it is often so much more palatable to firstly see feelings and behaviors in others that we struggle with in ourselves. Being able to think about the birds' difficulties with waiting was an important step along her own journey of coping with her own feelings of having to wait (Rose, 2000), and experiencing the fear and worry that maybe the sessions might not continue.

Now that the birds were carrying her worries, they became important players in her session. They could become a way to explore her own (as yet pretty scary) feelings of worry about continuity—whether or not her relationship with her therapist could continue, and whether or not her own, fragile sense of self could continue. Toward the end of session three she was concerned about the impending ending:

> She went on to say, "We're going to go soon." I said that yes we would, but not just yet, "in ten minutes." With this she then walked over to the birds on the table, picked one up and said she wanted to put it back on the tree. I wondered whether she was preparing for next week, whether she wanted it to be back so that next week might be closer if the bird was waiting on the tree already. "He's flying," she told me as she picked him off the tree. "And he's looking at me" as the bird bobbed around on his thread toward her. She brought him over to me to show me and then "flew" him back to his tree, walking him back to the middle of the room. "So that he'll be waiting for you next week," I said. "His name is Mr. Carrots," she informed me. "Why is there

> this one here?" she asked, gesturing to all of the birds. "Well, there are five more birds because we have five more times together."

Two points are important here. Firstly, she spoke about the five birds as if they were one single bird. In her mind, they are all merged into one. She speaks as if she has one long session, rather than seven separate sessions. It could be inferred that separation and individuation are relevant issues for her. Secondly, she needs to ask why they are there, even though she has been told and really does know the answer. It is as if she can't quite grasp the concept that the sessions will actually go ahead each week that they really will continue. She needs to check that her now-special relationship with her therapist will actually continue and survive the weekly separations.

The session continued:

> She picked off another bird and informed me that he was going to walk over, as she trotted him from side to side. "Why can't I put him in the water?" she asked. "He can have a bath in the clean water" I said, so she dropped him in the water delightedly. She picked him out and told me "He needs to dry." She then went on: "Why can't I put him in there?" gesturing toward the paint pot. I knew she was testing the boundaries of how far the bird could go. How "dirty" could he get?

She was testing the therapist to see how far it was possible to use these birds as a way of exploring her own feelings. The therapist recognized that this was important for her, and knew that she identified with the birds as a way of thinking about continuity—whether she had to stay fragile, like the tissue paper, always ready to be blown away or destroyed by the impact of stronger people, or whether she could "wait" and stay connected to others. Was she strong enough, in herself, to be herself? Was she sure enough of herself to stay connected to her art therapist?

They continued:

> "You want to put him in the paint?" I inquired, and then said "Yes, you can put him in there," and Mr. Carrots became covered in red paint. She then picked him out of the paint and put him into the dirty-water pot. As we "dried" Mr. Carrots I said "Hello Mr. Carrots" and she said loudly "Hello" back. I felt she was giving Mr. Carrots a voice to reply back. She then dropped him back in the dirty water, telling me "He's having a bath."

The bird had to be submerged, and totally covered in paint. It could be surmised that this is a girl who has felt "submerged" in other's feelings—the fragility of her own sense of self had meant that she was at the mercy of other people's very strong feelings. By identifying with the birds, she showed what this felt like: it was the same as being submerged. This is consistent with her use of the tissue paper—also overwhelmed by the world—submerged and smothered in paint and rubbed until it couldn't hold out any longer. It disintegrated. Over and over, in all different ways, she showed her therapist how her world felt sometimes: overwhelmed, submerged, and fragile, a world often in danger of disintegrating.

> She picked up the wet bird and I asked if she wanted to hang him back on the tree. As she did so she said two other birds needed a wash. When I asked what their names were she said, "Mr. Carrots, they're all called Mr. Carrots." She "washed" these in the dirty water, saying that they were "having a bath," and then hung them back on the tree "to dry."

The birds did not have individual identities—they were all "Mr. Carrots," as if they were all merged into one. They, as she did, struggled with their individuality. There were no gaps between them—and as they represented her weekly, individual sessions, we can wonder if they represented her wish to have no break between her sessions—she would prefer that it was one long seven-week session, which would feel more secure and solid for her. Having gaps and breaks reminded her of her own fragility, her need to wait, and her fear that her (emotional) world might not continue. Without gaps things can be assured of continuing and everything feels much safer.

"Transitional objects" (Winnicott, 1953, p. 89) solve the problem of filling in the gaps. They are a useful and ordinary part of a child's development (like a "blankie" or teddy that is carried everywhere), and also a useful tool within therapy, helping children cope with the gap between their wishes, hopes, and desires, and their real world (Horne, 1999). The seven Mr. Carrots were no longer simply the art therapist's tool for counting weeks; they had become transitional objects, functioning halfway between the real world (counting the weeks of the real sessions) and the play/fantasy world (carrying her feelings/exploring her fears). She had made them an integral part of her therapy work, where they played a vital role in helping her explore continuity of being.

"MAKING HER MARK"

The therapist reminded Lola twice that they were finishing soon, as she "washed" the birds.

> After the second time she put her hands back into the paint and swirled it around singing a "mixing song." I knew she was prolonging the session and sat with her while she did this. She then asked if she could put her handprint on the wall. She really did want to "make her mark," perhaps leave something behind that was on the building, on the physical structure of this session. When I denied her this she informed me that she "was a good cleaner." As she rubbed her painterly hands together she looked down, saying "It's dropping on

> the ground" and she clapped her hands together, splattering the paint further. (She had made her mark here after all, I thought.)

It is interesting that she was so determined to "make her mark" at this stage in her therapy. She had had an experience of showing her therapist how easily she felt submerged or overwhelmed, first by destroying the tissue paper(s) and then by submerging the birds in paint. Maybe the opportunity to express her feelings about being overwhelmed and fragile, in the presence of a person who was interested and thinking about her experience, had given her hope that she could be stronger, and remembered and noticed. Perhaps she was freer now to explore the possibility that she could continue, and that she could begin to contemplate leaving her mark—a permanent, personal reminder that she did exist here in this special room. The simple expression of feelings which have been held inside, in a safe, empathic environment, becomes a very powerful force inside an individual, giving her an awareness of her own experiences, and hence a feeling of a sense of self. In a later session she persisted with her desire to place her handprint on the brickwork.

This experience is similar to the process of "mirroring" by the mother with her baby, described by developmental psychologists (e.g., Stern, 1985), and further developed by research into the role of mirror neurons (Mayes and Thomas, 2009). An attuned mother will spend time watching her baby, responding to the baby's emotions with her own appropriate comments and facial expressions, using words and noises to mirror the baby's thoughts and feelings. For example, when the baby giggles and smiles, the mother will look directly into the baby's face, laughing and smiling, and saying in an exaggerated voice things such as "You like it, don't you? That makes you happy, doesn't it?" Similarly, when the baby is frowning, the mother will look directly into his or her face with an exaggerated frown, saying, "That really upset you, didn't it? Ooohhh. You're very upset!" The baby learns to put together his internal experience with the mother's words and expressions. "When the mother reflects, or mirrors, the child's anxiety, this perception organizes the child's experience, and he now 'knows' what he is feeling" (Fonagy, Gergely, Jurist, and Target, 2002, p. 35). In a similar way, when the therapist gave Lola the opportunity to use the birds to express her feelings of being overwhelmed, and joined in the play with her, this helped Lola to know what she was feeling inside.

We can surmise that having her unrecognized thoughts and feelings expressed through the art activities, and then noticed and named in an empathic manner by the therapist, gave her some sense of organizing her internal experiences. The consequence would be that she may have felt capable of recognizing her desire to be stronger, to be sustained, and to continue, and not to be swept away or forgotten. She wanted, then, to leave her mark, both in the room, and in the mind of her therapist.

Interestingly this encounter led to a very warm separation (which was different from her separations in previous weeks):

> We walked together past the tree branch and I said "We'll see Mr. Carrots next week, okay." With this we walked back down the stairs. She ran ahead to be greeted by the teacher, and then turned and said goodbye with a smile. Later she saw me leaving the preschool and yelled "Bye-bye Judy" and I waved back, "See you next week."

It was as if she could feel more confident that she would be remembered by her therapist, and that she could be sustained in her therapist's mind. She seemed to have gained the confidence to build her own bridge to her next session by reminding the therapist that they would be reconnecting again next week. Secure in the knowledge that the relationship would continue, she could separate happily.

The following session began with a return to the birds immediately. They (and she) had continued, and been remembered:

> Straightaway she walked up to the birds hanging from the tree. I linked the sessions quickly by introducing "Mr. Carrots" from last week. Having picked off the bird to represent this week, she walked over to the jars of paints.

And later,

> She then walked over to pick one of the birds from the tree and place him in the painterly water. As she lifted him out she wiped the base of the bird, "washing his little bum bum," she informed me. She went on to tell me "his feet are clean," and then he was put back into the water. She then spooned purple painterly water from the container into the hand-washing basin. All of this spooning and cleaning seemed important to "clean" and "nurture" these birds. They had so much more meaning than just birds on a tree. These were the sessions we had shared and the sessions to come. This was her one-on-one time with this stranger who appeared to "allow" her to be.

She was nurturing the birds, which by now seemed to represent her sessions, and her relationship with her therapist. It seemed she was nurturing the relationship, doing her part to make sure it continued and survived.

> "I'm going to wash Mr. Carrots, and put him over there to dry," she informed me in an authoritative tone. She hummed as she did this, walking over to the tree and picking another bird, telling me that he needed a bath as she put that bird into the black paint. She then squeezed the bird and the excess went all over the floor onto my feet.

She was so determined that Mr. Carrots was totally submerged. He was completely overwhelmed by his bath. Her experience of being overwhelmed by her world and her emotions was being acted out and displayed very clearly. Then he is squeezed out almost violently—as if she can't hang onto her feelings because they are expelled so quickly. It is as if nothing can be digested or sustained. The therapist was very aware of the intensity of the emotions being played out during the sessions.

> She pulled the bird's short thread apart and said, "How come you can't put it here?" as she tried to put Mr. Carrots over her head as you would a necklace. I pointed out that it wasn't big enough, and pondered that this painterly, sodden bird was so meaningful that she wanted to wear it.

Lola had identified very strongly with the creatures that represented the stability and continuity of her sessions. Perhaps she had wanted to wear it on her body because they had become almost like a part of herself—overwhelmed and fragile—yet in this setting they could survive and last through the experience with the art therapist, who was interested in her and her thoughts and feelings. They would survive together: sodden and battered, but surviving, and continuing.

In the next session (session five) Lola chose the bird for that week. It seemed that remembering (which could be thought of as "continuing to exist in someone's mind") was an important theme now:

> She then walked over to the tree of birds and picked off one of the birds that represented the session week. "You remembered it was Mr. Carrots?" she asked, "Yes," I said, "you told me it was Mr. Carrots last week." She seemed quite pleased with this and put Mr. Carrots right into the green paint jar so that he disappeared. This was more of a submerging than a "bath." "Ah, he's covered," I went on to say. "I'm going to leave him in there," she continued, promptly pulling him out and carrying him toward the bucket to "wash him." "You remembered it was Mr. Carrots?" she commented again. "Yes," I said, "you told me." I guessed from her tone that she needed to remind herself that I had remembered it from last week.

Being remembered was important to her. Knowing that the therapist had held her in her mind over the past week was vital to her growing sense that she could actually "continue on being." She had not disappeared from her therapist's mind. She continued to show how overwhelmed she felt by making many of the Mr. Carrots go through the experience, over and over:

> "I'm putting him underneath" she said, as she held the green-clad Mr. Carrots at the bottom of the bucket. "Stay underneath," she went on. I wondered what was being buried down there and felt that whatever it was it needed to come up. I then gave Mr. Carrots a squeaky voice: "I don't want to be down here, I don't want to be in the dark, Mr. Carrots says." Immediately she allowed him to rise to the surface and looked up at me. "There" she said in a quiet voice.

> There was a relief in her face that was apparent in her handling of the bird. "Ah he's come out again. You're squeezing him out," I said. She gently squeezed him, to release the water, and placed him next to the other ones on the table, humming under her breath. As she did this she turned to me. They could all watch from there.

This seemed to be an important moment for Lola. The therapist had understood that she was showing how deep the submerging was—how sometimes she was totally overwhelmed by strong feelings, and by other people's emotions. She felt she had no choice—she had to "stay underneath." The therapist named her desire, as yet unspoken, to be able to break out of this pattern—to be able to escape from the pressure, and for someone to notice her and her feelings. When the therapist did notice and name Lola's wish to be free of the sense of being overwhelmed, it seemed to unleash some hope. She showed relief in her face, and the sodden, drenched Mr. Carrots could be rescued and "squeezed out." He didn't have to feel that he had to stay underneath forever. Neither did she, when someone was interested in her and her feelings.

"YOU'RE ALL HERE TODAY": THE NEED FOR HOLDING

Immediately before the following session (session six), the preschool informed the therapist that unfortunately there was going to be a clash of activities, and Lola would have to miss one session. The therapist was particularly concerned about how Lola would react to this news, as she was very attached to the therapist and to the sessions, and she had made such a point of helping Lola to be able to predict the number, regularity, and continuity of the sessions. Lola did have sad, disappointed feelings about missing out on her promised session, and the subsequent loss of her art therapist, but the use of Mr. Carrots helped the two of them negotiate these feelings.

> As I went to collect Lola for her sixth session, I noticed her standing up from her bed, almost standing to attention. She was ready for me that was clear. It was almost as though she was "reporting for duty." Due to preschool logistics there was going to be one less session for Lola. There were three birds on the tree, but the children were booked for a special circus performance the following week that clashed with our time. I explained that we should pick a bird for this week and a bird for the circus performance the following week. It was a difficult negotiation (particularly for me). She quietly picked one bird off and we walked together to put him on the table with the previous session birds, as was the routine. I then had to prompt her to pick another one, for the special performance the following week that prevented me from coming. I felt my discomfort (and guilt) a little as we did this. We then walked back and looked at one sad and lonely bird on the tree, "We have one more time together after today," I said (in a rather too upbeat voice I later thought). "Mmmm" she said,

> "but you're All here today?" she asked. "Yes I am All here for you today, for the time we have together . . . now." "I'm gonna go All here," she replied, although it was a little difficult to hear. "Yes" I continued, "I am all here for you now," hoping that was what she had meant in her second question. As I listened back to my dictaphone after the session, over and over to be sure I had the correct words, I heard her repeat back the "All here today" phrase twice. Yes, she was right, she wanted to get on with the "All here today."

This is such a moving encounter. Lola was clearly ready and waiting for her therapist—she had managed to hold onto a sense of continuity in their relationship, and the image of her as "almost standing to attention" suggests a sense of purpose and strength. So it is no surprise that she becomes quiet when she hears that she will be missing one of her important sessions, and has to be prompted to remove the "circus"-bird prematurely. It would be very understandable for this fragile little girl to give up, because she has shown through her play how easily her world falls apart, or is destroyed. However her words are remarkable: "But you're All here today?"—and then her response: "I'm gonna go All here today." Despite her disappointment, she knows at a deep level that it is the therapist's focused attention to Lola's mind, and her thoughts and feelings, that has made things different. She had already internalized some sense of her therapist being able to stay with her, to continue with her, to hold her as a continuing, valuable person.

Winnicott (1960) describes the importance of the "holding environment" for the baby—that is, of the the outside world (that is, the parent) being able to provide conditions that hold together the inside, emotional world of the infant/child. We can guess that Lola's fragility demonstrates that, for reasons we don't know, she did not receive enough of a holding environment for her to feel strong on the inside. Developmental psychologists describe this deep, sustained thinking, or being held in someone's mind, as essential to emotional development. Winnicott (1956b) also describes "primary maternal preoccupation" as a state of heightened sensitivity by the mother, in which "the infant's going on being is sustained by the mother's continued preoccupation" (Phillips, 1988, p. 122). In other words, the mother's capacity to be deeply attuned to her child literally holds and nurtures the child's *mind* just as her arms hold the child's body. When a developing mind is safely held, it can begin to develop and grow, just like the rest of the body.

The holding environment that the art therapist provided gave her not only the chance to express her feelings through the art activities, but also, maybe even more importantly, the experience of being "held in mind." She knew that the art therapist was "all here" for her today—she knew that she was being thought about in a deep and sustained way, and this seemed to hold her together enough to cope with the disappointment: *"You're All here today?" . . . "I ' m gonna go All here ."*

Perhaps because she felt safe to have her own thoughts, she could then show the therapist how she felt about missing the session due to the concert. Her treatment of the "circus bird" demonstrated how she felt about missing the session due to preschool logistics:

> She carried the "circus bird" over to the table, saying "put him in here?"—meaning the bucket—and she promptly dropped him straight into the water. I said, "Ah, Mr. Carrots is having a bath." "He's really cold," she said. So I pretended to shiver with the "cold" that Mr. Carrots was feeling.

Her art therapist recognized that Lola felt left out in the cold by having to miss the circus session, and saw that she could express it through the game. So she played along with the concept, pretending to shiver, thus augmenting the feeling and showing that she understood its significance. In this age-appropriate way, Lola could feel that her feelings of disappointment were known, validated, and had a place in her therapist's mind. She was being held.

IDENTITY AS AN ABORIGINAL GIRL

As Lola began to address issues of her identity as an individual, she gradually began to address specific issues of herself as an Aboriginal girl.

> She walked over to the bird and picked him off the branch and took him over to the paint, not the water. "I'm gonna wash him, and paint him," she informed me, "and put him back on the tree," she repeated. He needed to be back on the tree so that he was there for her next week. She dipped him into the darkest color (black), and pulled him out of the jar with a "ta dah!" She jauntily bobbed his thread up and down to "walk him through the air" back to his tree. Lola asked me to help her put him "back on the tree." "He's going to wait until next week," I repeated.

It is interesting that this time she chose the black paint. He became a black bird. Her therapist wondered if this was because Mr. Carrots was becoming more and more of a representation of herself, and she was identifying herself as an Aboriginal girl. Her behavior after this session seemed to confirm these thoughts:

> We walked back down to the playroom and she ran up to the worker, Deborah. She called her name a couple of times before she turned around, so that Deborah knew she was back. Lola brought over a book from the shelf to show me. The worker pointed out that this was a book about "little white kids and little black kids." Lola wanted to show me the page with two figures on it and was pointing to the "black kid." Deborah pointed out that Lola associated strongly with her Aboriginal identity, apparently reminding her, the worker,

> and other children that they were Aboriginal. I thanked Lola for this and, seemingly satisfied, she put the book back on the shelf.

It does seem that Lola was trying hard to make a point to her art therapist (who was not Aboriginal), that she, Lola, was an Aboriginal girl. She was intent on showing the therapist the picture of the "black kid" directly following on from the session with the black Mr. Carrots. It could be surmised that, having spent so much time working through issues of identity in her art-therapy sessions, she was making sure that her art therapist knew this central part of her identity. Maybe now she could begin to integrate the different parts of herself—the fragile (tissue paper) part, the part which was getting stronger and felt she could make her mark (literally, on the wall), and the Aboriginal part of her, which was so important to her sense of self.

In the very first session she had felt the need to state this part of her identity:

> As she daubed the dots she said, "I'm Aboriginal" (stumbling over the word Aboriginal). I replied "Yes, you're Aboriginal." "I do dots," she told me, "You do dots when you're Aboriginal." She then informed me, "You don't do dots when you're not Aboriginal." Her sense of identity appeared to be important and she repeated this a number of times to make sure I got it.

The therapist wondered if her use of handprints, both in some of the tissue-paper paintings and on the wall, also reflected her identification as an Aboriginal girl. Being clear and certain about her Aboriginal identity seemed to provide a source of strength for Lola as she began to develop her own personal identity.

ENDING

A child coming to any form of therapy is always subject to the issues experienced by their caregivers. We could assume, from some of Lola's problems, that she had experienced some difficulties with being held in her caregiver's mind. Her behavior showed that, for reasons that we don't know, she has struggled to believe that her caregiver has the capacity to think about her feelings and thoughts, and remain present with them, showing that they can be survived. It was surmised that this may have led her to have developed a very fragile sense of self, and very little belief that her "self" could continue and survive strong emotions. Within this context, the circumstances surrounding the ending of her therapy provided further challenges for her and her therapist, and are important to consider.

> I arrived for my final session with Lola and checked in with the worker, Deborah. She rang her mother to see where they were as they were usually in

> by this time, and left a message. I sat in the back room for the duration of the session, with a lonely Mr. Carrots on the tree branch as my only company. Lola had been emphatic in the last session that he should have a wash in black paint and so he was slightly hardened from this experience, with the paint having dried. She had specifically hung him back on the tree to wait for our last session together. An hour and a half later Deborah rang again. Lola's mother answered the phone and thanked Deborah for reminding her and said she would be in shortly. I showed Deborah the Mr. Carrots that were sat on the table, representing the previous six weeks of sessions.
>
> I explained to Deborah that I would offer Lola the opportunity to take one of them home today and that I had an envelope prepared that we would put him in, staple it up and pop him in her bag to take home. Deborah again told me how much change she saw in Lola after our sessions. Another hour and a half went by and I finally packed up and said goodbye to Deborah. As I was walking out of the door there was another confused message from Lola's mum via the phone.
>
> I decided to return to the preschool a couple of days later to see Lola, to say goodbye and to let her choose a Mr. Carrots. For the sake of consistency I chose the same time-frame that I normally saw her, so I crept into the room during their naptime. Deborah informed me that Lola's mother had mistaken the call for a reminder to take Lola to the circus performance. She had rushed there in the rain, apparently flustered to find that she was a day early and that Lola had missed her final session with me. Deborah told me that Lola's mother was very angry with herself. As we were talking I became aware that Lola was listening and watching from afar. I walked over to her little bed and knelt down by her, explaining that I had waited for her on Tuesday, but that she wasn't there so I had come back today to say goodbye.

We can only guess at the circumstances that led to Lola missing her final session. Certainly it seemed that her mum was trying hard to get her there, but that the anxiety was so high that she became flustered, and everything became confused. It may have been possible that her mother had her own feelings about the therapy, or about it ending, and these may have interfered with her ability to get her little girl there for the final session. We can only wonder if this is related to the themes of Lola's play, of feeling she could fall apart at any time, feeling that she might not continue, and feeling submerged or overwhelmed, which were so apparent in the art therapy. We could wonder whether sometimes the feelings get overwhelming and confusing, and maybe this contributed to going to the wrong place. It would be possible to imagine that, in Lola's world, things were not always being held together very securely.

> I asked if she wanted to walk back to the room with me so I could give her a little gift. I said that we wouldn't be doing art today but Mr. Carrots wanted to see her, and that he had been sad on Tuesday not to see her. She took my hand and we walked together. As we got to the room she ran ahead but the room was empty of materials except for Mr. Carrots hanging on the tree (which she

> had painted black last week) and his mates (the ones from the previous sessions) lined up on the table. I asked if she would like to choose one to take home, and she chose the last Mr. Carrots from the tree. As she picked him off she said "He's hard," as the paint had dried and hardened him. I felt it was "hard" for both of us. I said that I had enjoyed my time with her and that it was hard when you had to say goodbye. With this she moved toward me and I gave her a hug. She stayed standing there for some time and we did not move. I then got the envelope and we put him in there and stapled the top to "keep him safe."
>
> We then walked back down the stairs and she ran ahead to put him straight into her bag in her pigeonhole. Deborah had wanted to take a photo of us together so I sat on the ground near Deborah, and Lola sat on my lap. As Deborah wanted to send me a copy she asked for my details. Lola still sat on my lap and had picked up the stapler while I was writing on the paper. She quietly asked if she could "put it," meaning use the stapler. I got the paper that I had written my name on and folded it over, similar to the envelope that Mr. Carrots was in. She struggled to close it and kept almost catching her fingers in the mechanism. Eventually between the three of us she put a "lovely staple" in the paper and she looked genuinely pleased with herself. With that I prepared to leave and said goodbye again; she quietly walked back to her little bed, gave me a smile, and waved.

Lola had chosen the black Mr. Carrots—the representation of herself as an Aboriginal girl—as her lasting memory of her art therapy sessions. The therapist felt this was an important factor in her coming to feel a little more secure about herself as a continuing, stronger person: she was more confident in herself as an Aboriginal girl. It could be surmised that feeling strong in her sense of Aboriginality provided strength in discovering the rest of her identity.

Being able to take a Mr. Carrots was a concrete reminder of the concept of continuity that she had explored throughout the therapy. Mr. Carrots would continue with her, even after her therapy had finished. When planning the therapy, and the use of the birds to count the weeks remaining, it had not been the therapist's intention to give one of the birds to the child at the conclusion. However, the way in which Lola had turned them into the therapy itself showed the therapist just how important it was for Lola to take one with her afterward, as a symbolic reminder of the work she had done in exploring her feelings of continuity of self.

The ending itself was very moving, as she hugged her therapist for a long time without moving. They had shared some very important moments and feelings, and she, in her fragile but brave way, had embraced the relationship with the art therapist as a way of exploring her difficult feelings of being submerged, and her fears of disintegrating, and of not being remembered. Together they had played with and expressed such feelings, and in the process she had been mirrored and enabled to feel more aware of her feelings and her fears. Most importantly, she could feel there was someone else who was there with her in all of it ("You're All here today? . . . I'm gonna go All here"), reliable and consistent, just like Mr. Carrots.

CONCLUSION

Lola's use of the sessions was remarkable. She took to the sessions with enthusiasm, openly involving herself in the process. At the beginning of each session she was ready for work. She was able to use not only the materials and the therapeutic space, but also the special relationship with the therapist. She seemed to be reaching out for connection, and was able to use it for her own benefit.

She showed how fragile she felt inside through her choice of fragile materials, and the way in which she used them, making sure they disintegrated under the onslaught of what was done to them. The therapist could hypothesize that her survival method up to now had been a form of psychological merging—how she felt some sense of safety in losing herself in others, and becoming whatever they were. Yet she was so readily able to respond when offered a different opportunity. Her therapist gently followed her, rather than leading her, and stayed very focused on her world, her mind, and her feelings, thinking about them deeply and responding with what she felt needed to be expressed. The seven Mr. Carrots gave her consistency and reliability. Each of these concepts seemed to give Lola great relief, and her teachers commented on more than one occasion how she had become more confident and more expressive due to her art therapy sessions. They said she had benefited most of any of the children involved in the program.

Indeed, within the sessions themselves there was an enormous contrast between the issues she was exploring at the beginning, and the progress she had made by the end. The first few sessions clearly showed things disappearing and disintegrating—the tissue paper was so fragile, and the merging when painting her arms and the overflowing of the paint containers was so pronounced. However, with the opportunity to incorporate the counting birds into the session she discovered a way to challenge her own sense of fragility and merging. Initially the birds had been used as a technique, a way to show the passing of time and sessions. However Lola had been so ready to grasp the concept of her art therapy, and so ready to utilize it to its fullest potential, that she used the Mr. Carrots as a way of exploring her feelings: they became representations of the sessions, of the relationship between herself and her art therapist, and sometimes parts of herself. The Mr. Carrots proved to be not so fragile—they could withstand being damaged without disintegrating, they could survive whatever was being done to them. With the confidence that her art therapist would be "All here" for her while she did this exploring, she felt capable of investigating the possibility that their relationship, and ultimately she herself, could withstand the storms and damage of others' feelings on her emotional world. She felt she could maybe even "leave her mark" on someone else's world, as long as there was someone fully engaged to receive the message, someone who was "All here today." Between the therapist and Mr. Carrots, this could be provided. The therapist was fully engaged when they were together, and Mr. Carrots was a concrete reminder that the reliable, constant therapist would be there for the coming sessions too. Even when she had to face missing a session, she could cope because her therapist (and Mr. Carrots) helped her to explore her feelings about missing out. The session might be missed but her feelings about it were allowed to have space and expression.

Even this short therapy experience enabled Lola to explore very deep psychological concepts of identity, and her need for consistency and reliability in developing her identity. The inspired use of the birds on the tree, and the therapist's openness to being fully available for Lola and thinking so deeply about her thoughts and feelings, gave her space and confidence to know her own mind better. She could then feel more confident as a person who would continue "going on being." Mr. Carrots not only counted the time, he (and they) also helped her to explore how much she needed consistency and reliability, enabling her to feel stronger in herself, and to become more in contact with some of the different parts of herself, including her Aboriginal identity.

NOTE

1. Judy King was the art therapist for this case, with clinical supervision provided by Celia Conolly. Sessions were recorded, transcribed, and discussed in detail after each session.

REFERENCES

Ainsworth, M., and S. M. Bell. (1970). Attachment, exploration and separation: Illustrated by the behavior of one-year-olds in a strange situation. *Child Development* 41(1): 49–67.

Fonagy, P., G. Gergely, E. J. Jurist, and M. Target. (2002). *Affect regulation, mentalization and the development of the self.* New York: Other Press.

Horne, A. (1999). Normal emotional development. In M. Lanyado and A. Horne, eds., *The handbook of child and adolescent psychotherapy*, 31–41. London: Routledge, 1999.

Mayes, L. C., and P. K. Thomas. (2009). Social neuroscience and theories of therapeutic action: Some implications for child psychotherapy. In N. Midgley, J. Anderson, E. Grainger, T. Nesic-Vuckovic, and C. Urwin, eds., *Child psychotherapy and research: New approaches, emerging findings*, 214–228. London: Routledge.

Phillips, A. (1988). *Winnicott*. London: Fontana.

Rose, L. (2000). *Learning to love*. Camberwell, Victoria: ACER Press.

Stern, D. N. (1985). *The interpersonal world of the infant: A view from psychoanalysis and developmental psychology*. London: Karnac.

Winnicott, D. W. (1953). Transitional objects and transitional phenomena: A study of the first not-me possession. *International Journal of Psychoanalysis* 34(2): 89–97. In *Through paediatrics to psycho-analysis*, 229–242. New York: Basic Books, 1975.

Winnicott, D. W. (1956a). On transference. *International Journal of Psychoanalysis* 37: 386–388.

Winnicott, D. W. (1956b). Primary maternal preoccupation. In *Through paediatrics to psycho-analysis*, 300–305. New York: Basic Books, 1975.

Winnicott, D. W. (1960). The theory of the parent–infant relationship. *International Journal of PsychoAnalysis* 41: 585–595. In *The maturational processes and the faciltiating environment: Studies in the theory of emotional development*, 37–55. Madison, CT: International Universities Press, 1965. Reprinted London: Karnac, 1990.

Chapter Ten

The Five Big Ideas

A Road Forward

Norma Tracey and Shiri Hergass

In Australia in 2007 the Labor party won the election and Kevin Rudd was sworn in as Prime Minister on December 3. One of the Rudd government's first acts was delivering an apology to indigenous Australians for the Stolen Generations. Following this national apology, and as part of the Council of Australian Government's Closing the Gap strategy, $26.6 million was provided in the 2009–10 budget to establish an Aboriginal and Torres Strait Islander Healing Foundation to address the harmful legacy of colonization, and in particular the history of removing children from their families that continues to impact on today's generation. On October 30, 2009, the Aboriginal and Torres Strait Islander Healing Foundation was established, "An Independent national Aboriginal and Torres Strait Islander organisation with a focus on healing our community."[1] It was their funding that supported Gunawirra and allowed it to carry out the Trauma Project described here.

From this was developed a project of eighty interviews with traumatized Aboriginal children. This book is the result of that work. That work became a cornerstone, which made us think again, within a psychoanalytic model, about practical, doable ways of healing trauma.

Our quest was to find a solution to the pervasive effects of trauma, both firsthand and transgenerational, that we got to know intimately and painfully, and not just in the children, but also in the teachers, parents, and wider communities. Our challenge was to make the wealth of knowledge available to us through psychotherapy relevant and accessible to the Aboriginal people while combining it with the deep jewels we discovered in their culture. From this was born the *Five Big Ideas*, which will be explained in more detail further on. First, here is some background on how we got here.

HEALING TRAUMA IN ABORIGINAL PRESCHOOLS: A GUNAWIRRA BEGINNING

It was with some degree of temerity that we approached the idea of working in the preschools. Some of these were community preschools that had at least a third of the children from Aboriginal families; some were Government preschools in local public schools where all students were Aboriginal. In hindsight we may even have been "fools rushing in." We were in no way prepared for what we were to find. We saw firsthand the results of transgenerational trauma, we saw eager little children using as best they could the environment so purposely and well created in the preschool, but we also saw children who were already so traumatized that curiosity, imagination, and play were simply not available to them. We also saw a great many burnt-out teachers.

TEACHERS IN NEED

In preschool teachers, what we initially took to be a kind of fatigue or malaise was, as we later came to recognize, a response to receiving the underlying trauma from the children in ways that they could not have had a conscious awareness of. This hidden projection of the children's trauma presented itself as a pervasive nothingness, a non-happening "no event." We came to know and identify this as a mask, a cover hiding a mass of emotions too painful to be experienced or to suffer.

What we did not understand was that many of these teachers had themselves suffered traumatic childhoods, and that no person, professional or otherwise, was present to guide, direct, or support them. We tried telephoning weekly, and for some this was a really good opportunity to make a link and not to have to experience so much of the senseless isolation they were suffering in the nation's outback towns. There are twelve preschools that we continue to call every week or every fortnight. The weight of those calls still remains with us each week as a proof of how much these teachers carry of the trauma around them. For some we were aware it was simply too late. They had already emotionally closed down, were living in a passive state, or had escaped emotion in a flurry of overactivity, a kind of practical tasking that would never end and would eventually exhaust them. Many however used us very well and taught us more than we could hope to teach them. They became our guides.

CHILDREN IN NEED

What of the children? We knew all too well—as child therapists, art therapists, social workers, and psychotherapists—that this was an age of intense curiosity and joy in living, and that everything had the potential to be fun, play, and experimentation. But this was in marked contrast to what we often saw. A small child, invisible in the corner, her presence unnoticed since she troubled no one, for example, or the opposite—children so overactive they were almost in a frenzy, with no goal or meaning other than to be active as a way of avoiding stopping and feeling what was to painful to feel. At first it surprised us that a child who already by the age of 4 had established a false self was able to present in a way that might gratify the world around them, and yet even at such a young age could not be in touch with their real internal self. Our research identified these as children traumatized as a result of their home situation. In seeing their parents and the problems they had in negotiating any sort of a meaningful life for themselves, we realized that there was no way that the vulnerable ego of a small child could be capable of handling such a degree of pain, pain often inflicted by those entrusted to care for them.

THE CAUSE OF SUFFERING

What we began to create in our minds was a model of what we thought might have happened in the minds of these children. Some small children faced trauma day after day, others were traumatized by the sudden impact of a father leaving (sometimes due to being put in jail), or by coming home to a mother who was stoned and emotionally unavailable to them. Not having enough food in the house was often an expression of this problem; many children came to school without having eaten any breakfast.

Along with considering problems arising from a lack of basic care, we also looked at problems that were deeply psychological and rooted in transgenerational trauma. In every case, the trauma initially had an impact too severe to be experienced, and the responses were either a crazy acting-out, or a retiring closedown. The joy, curiosity, and imagination so available to children when the space is created for it were already lost to them. Instead of painting they created black messes. They didn't play with the paint; they used it as a tool for acting out. They couldn't create an outside world from their inside world, as their inner world was too chaotic or too frightening to be expressed.

We were further burdened by a degree of denial in the parents, as well as in the other Aboriginal workers, who could not bear the pain of what their own subjugated race had been reduced to by generations of oppression and racism of the worst kind—a racism that denied their existence as human beings and part of the human race.

Presenting at an Aboriginal preschool conference in my first months of working with preschools, I was immediately afterward assailed by one of the teachers, an Aboriginal elder from Brewarrina whom I greatly respected. She said, "How could you shame us like that? Who do you think you are?"

I knew at that moment for the first time how one can make trauma worse by publicly naming it. I knew I would work to never again create an experience of shame in a people who had already been shamed beyond anything that was tolerable. I thought she was going to tell me that what I said was untrue. But she did not. She said, "Do you know that when you were talking of domestic violence there were women in the audience who had that morning been beaten and had bruises from being beaten by their husbands?"

I was stunned. These were Aboriginal preschool teachers—professionals. What that elder taught me that morning was not that the trauma was untrue, as so many tried to say, but that it was too true to be named.

FINDING A PATH TO HEALING

So what could we do to help, and how carefully would we need to tread in the wake of others who had trod with no concern at all on a fragile and dispirited people? It took us some years, but it was to our credit that no Aboriginal person or organization had any reason to complain about us in Gunawirra. Not one disagreement has occurred with a single one of the forty centers we serve. This came about because of the respect we learned, the understanding we developed of their pain, and our determination to deal not only with their pain but also with our own inner psychic pain, so often exposed in the work we did.

We learned too of the wonderful gifts inherent in their culture, gifts that we could bring into the present, and also of the many hidden, extraordinary capacities their way of life had enriched them with. We learned of their Dreamtime stories, and, as we learned, our respect grew—along with our determination to marry this rich past with a disenfranchised present. We also learned the value of the preschool as the perfect space in which to learn, become, imagine, and regain a sense of self-respect and pride in their culture.

There is a kind of imperial philosophy in Western culture that is born out of a mistaken idea of superiority. *They* are the poor and suffering, *we* are not—we are the kind benefactors. This is nonsense! We, all of suffering humanity, are one; it's just that our own good-enough childhood, or our own good-enough analysis has helped us cope with the pain better. We cry for our brothers and sisters, but we cannot suffer another person's suffering. Only they can do that, but we can know it, and identify with it, knowing that one of our limitations as humans is that we can only suffer our own pain. We can only cry with and out of our own pain.

With this awareness, and whatever funding we could initially muster, we cut our cloth accordingly. We were greatly surprised when our psychotherapy colleagues looked down on us for doing such practical things as developing the ideas for growing gardens in preschools. We think they considered that our professionalism had deteriorated, as if we were inferior for not doing pure psychotherapy or analysis.

What we in Gunawirra have learnt is that analytic thinking—one of the most powerful ways of thinking the world has experienced—cannot possibly belong only to an intelligent, insightful middle class able to afford it on the couch each day for months or years, it is too powerful for that. Instead it must inform every thought and action that works toward understanding human suffering, if we are to understand and ease that suffering. And so in our preschools we grew gardens. We had enough funding to grow about twenty gardens in twenty preschools in that first year, and from this we learned so much, even while acknowledging that our psychoanalytic thinking gave us the underlying basis for every thought we had and action we made.

GARDENS AS A PSYCHOTHERAPY COUCH

Gardens, a way of communicating with nature, so important to the spirituality and culture of the Aboriginal people; gardens, a nonthreatening way of our entering the center and giving it something, without criticism or judgment of any kind; gardens as a way of connecting with the parents, guiding them into the preschool center and linking them into that center. A little boy leaning against the wire fence telling another little boy, "That's my dad working there!" as his father, who the child had never known as a working parent, was helping create a garden. A garden, food to eat, to experiment with, to learn about!

In one center some ruffians broke in and pulled out every plant. The parents were devastated, but said to the teacher "Don't call the police; we know who did this and we will go and see them ourselves." They did, and threatened the parties that if they did it again they would "run you out of town." The mother cried as she told them her teenage children had indeed done this because there was no space for her young child in the preschool. Other parents then marched her and her child down to the preschool, and, to the surprise of all, the headmistress enrolled her child. Such a big deal was made of replanting the plants that the little children thought, "What fun!" and as soon as they planted them they pulled them out so they could plant them again. The teachers enjoyed showing them how: "Once you put them in you leave them there to grow." The depth of meaning contained in that small phrase—"to allow happening; to leave something to be; to trust"—was something this decimated culture had lost.

THE WEBSITE—TRACKING THE MILKY WAY

In 2011 Gunawirra called a meeting of several of our Aboriginal preschools in the area of Gunnedah, Kempsey, Inverell, and Kootingal—all in New South Wales. We asked them to come, and to think with us and plan ideas for a website that every preschool working with Aboriginal children could access. The teachers from Radford College Preschool, and the Director of the TAFE College preschool Bankstown,[2] came with us to Tamworth to chair the days, for which Radford College preschool in particular had prepared so much foundational material. About thirty teachers from surrounding preschools joined us in Tamworth, in the Northern Rivers region of NSW. About half of these visitors were Aboriginal; the other half worked with Aboriginal preschool children. With us was Jeff Nelson, a special Aboriginal cultural advisor, who helped us, and indeed created our name. Those three historic days' work created a program based on the *Reggio Emilia* early learning philosophy. Although originating in Italy, it nevertheless seemed to have a great fit with Aboriginal culture in so many ways. We found it easy to weave it together with Aboriginal culture and our own basic philosophy, which we saw as an interface between healing trauma and education. In Reggio Emilia thought, the child is seen as an active participant in learning. The Reggio approach sees a child as a very competent initiator who interacts with his or her environment, while the environment of the school is seen as the third educator. Most Reggio classrooms are filled with materials such as clay, paint, and writing materials and implements. Children use these materials to represent concepts that they are learning in a hands-on way. The teacher, parent, and child are collaborators in the process of learning. The Reggio approach views the parent as an essential resource for the child's learning. To foster community, Reggio schools host a variety of events throughout each school year, including conferences and special lectures for parents. In Reggio-inspired classrooms, teachers use a variety of documentation methods, such as cameras, tape recorders, and journals, to track children's thoughts and ideas as they play together or work with materials.

Our purpose with the creation of the Milky Way website[3] was to create a model of excellence that was culturally sensitive to all preschool children. What has now evolved is a website created by early childhood educators, social workers, and child and family therapists in order to bring the best tools, knowledge, resources, and assistance to those who need it the most.

Our content came from the workers of Gunawirra, Radford College, Werris Creek, Kempsey, Quirindi, Inverell, Gunnedah, Tingha, Little Yuin, Kootingal, Inverell, and the Bankstown TAFE. Our site aims to give educative and emotional support to preschool teachers, so they can in turn give it to the children.

THE FIVE BIG IDEAS

Arising from our psychoanalytic knowledge, our experience of getting to know the preschool center staff and children, and of discovering the incredible depth and breadth of the Aboriginal culture, we have created easily doable activities that we have called *The Five Big Ideas*. The five themes are: *Health and Hygiene*; *Nutrition*; *Healing and Resilience*; *My Culture, My Identity*; and *My Land, Our Environment*.[4]

Our aim for the Five Big Ideas was to make learning stimulating, interesting, interactive, and fun. We hoped to give isolated preschools and their teachers a way of communicating with and helping each other through the website.

The Five Big Ideas were developed over the last five years of working with the preschools that Gunawirra supports, and in constant collaboration with the preschool teachers and directors. A child who has had no breakfast does not have the capacity to play. Kids that are coming to school with bruises and open cuts will find it hard to be emotionally available, to say nothing of the children who come to school without the physical proof of the daily trauma they live with. A teacher who is worried because two sisters are sharing one pair of underwear finds it more difficult to put her full energy into the teaching syllabus, while at the same time trying to deny her own history of trauma and abuse. Between working within the context of their own emotional pasts and caring for the basic needs of the children in their care, there often isn't much space left for education. Gunawirra works on the interface between emotional health and education. And the Five Big Ideas evolved holding all of this in mind.

In our approach we seek to gently enlist the enthusiasm of the preschool teachers and hope that they then can do the same with the children at their school. The aim is to help the children celebrate the experience of childhood, the joys of play, the urges of the imagination, the struggle to make meaning, and the challenge of growing and developing through the complex phases of their lives.

There are many programs that are available for the preschool staff to use to deal with nutrition, health, and hygiene. These are free resources, books, DVDs, and even trainings where the teachers are given information and asked to teach the kids.

Our program differs from most others in that we spend a lot of pre-rollout time in the schools getting to know the staff, and hearing about the children, their families, and their community. We create a relationship, a space in which to try and understand the specific needs and challenges of the children and their teachers, and how best to address these.

Often the teachers know what is needed. Giving them the space and ownership to use it allows them to develop understanding, to see the children, to see the families, and to have ideas of what could be done. In this way the Five Big Ideas were born out of the community, our thinking, our analytic understanding, and out of Reggio Emelia and other theories. But for each teacher it becomes *their* program. And they involve the families and communities. Each of the five modules has a "community day," and the ideas that come from this are as diverse and as different as the centers themselves.

The Five Big Ideas were essentially their own ideas given back to them, and in them we offer a powerful connection both to the inner lives of children and to the preschool teachers. We provide a safe space where the teachers can gain more understanding of the childrens' inner worlds, listen to them, and create experiences for their families and communities that bring some light and hope to their days. The end result is that the teachers gain an understanding not only of the children and their families, but often also of themselves and how their own personal history impacts the way they work.

THE FIVE BIG IDEAS MODULES

The modules that together make up the Five Big Ideas are:

1. Health and Hygiene
2. Nutrition
3. Healing and Resilience
4. My Culture, My Identity
5. My Land, Our Environment

Each of the Five Big Ideas has five activities, which include a two-minute video clip of the Gunawirra Puppets talking about that idea, an Aboriginal Dreamtime story, a community day, and two experimental fun activities.

The Five Big Ideas take normal mundane things, the fundamentals of every day, and turn them into experiences that allow children to rise above the ordinariness of daily life, which for many of these children is nowhere near ordinary.

Throughout the activities and thinking around the Five Big Ideas we provide a rich range of opportunities for children to explore, investigate, and be involved and engage in purposeful, personalized, and meaningful experiences. This covers the teachers' need for accreditation, which they are often desperate for, but it also helps them to create different types of play, thinking, reasoning, and understanding for the child. It puts the child's needs front and center, and invites the child's ideas to be heard and acted upon. But this is not so easy. Sometimes the children are so traumatized that their capacity for play and imagining has already been severely damaged.

THE IDEAS IN PRACTICE

For the purposes of illustration we will use the Nutrition module as an example to show how our thinking grew, how community grew, how children enjoyed, parents understood, and how teachers felt empowered instead of just burnt out.

For the Nutrition module there is a PowerPoint presentation that talks about healthy foods and gives teachers activities to teach the children about nutrition in fun and practical ways that they can understand. There is a game the children can play to reinforce what the teachers speak about, a Dreamtime story,[5] and art activities that allow the children to learn the concepts of health and nutrition using Aboriginal symbols. There are the puppets screaming in joyful unison, "Eat good food!" as they joyfully devour a tomato or a piece of watermelon. The message we want to give is that good food is better than the fast food that many of our families may eat up to seven nights a week.

DEVELOPMENT THROUGH COLLABORATION

The Dreamtime stories were written with the help of Graham Toomey, Gunawirra's Aboriginal artist, and have arisen as a result of our ongoing collaborations with the preschool center. We speak with each school and spend many hours with the directors and staff brainstorming ways to support them, finding out how the modules can best be delivered, and how to integrate the needs of the schools' specific families and communities. From the beginning they, together with the elders, have told us what those modules need to be and what to put in them.

One school, for example, initially wanted to run a barbecue for the families as they felt it was the only thing they would come to. This was wonderful because it meant also inviting the elders, and that led to creating a campfire around which the elders could sit and tell bush tucker stories from long ago.

Another director knows that if the elders are not involved the parents will not cooperate. So she has created a special day, once a month, where an elder comes to the school to cook with the families. They are creating a special cookbook in and of that community with recipes that the elders are passing down.

Other schools have decided to invite the mothers to come and go grocery shopping with a teacher, and then come back to the preschool and cook a healthy meal with the children. They complement the cooking with herbs and vegetables that they have grown in the garden. Everyone enjoys cooking the food they have grown themselves, and it also fosters a sense of community that is alive and well.

In another school the teachers stuck the wrappers from all the junk food the kids brought to school on one side of a poster, and on the opposite column included healthier options for an equal or cheaper price. Its impact was huge. It can start a new wheel turning when parents cook at home, as opposed to going out for takeaway. The kids get to teach their parents, and the parents are given new choices and healthy, creative ways to meet their children's needs.

In one of our country preschools, to our surprise, it was the first time some of the mothers had cooked such staple meals as lasagne, shepherd's pie, or spaghetti bolognese—meals they later adopted for cooking at home. Some mothers (sometimes very young ones) had never cooked before and thought it was much more difficult and expensive than what they found out it actually was. Learning by experience is fun; it is also easy to remember and to recreate at home.

Another school grew spinach. For many of the children this was their first experience of seeing and tasting this vegetable. They all swallowed with pride (and yucky faces) the vegetable that they grew themselves. They also decided to sell it at a stall in front of their school and used the proceeds to buy more veggie plants. Children who could not add suddenly knew exactly how much money they had to spend, and a generous nursery owner was so impressed that he put in enough plants for each to take one home. We soon learned that the most resilient Aboriginal households had bush tucker plants in a pot on their windows. Connection and pride like this may at first seem so far away from psychoanalysis. But Bion's key ideas around creating links and meeting internal needs were alive and well in our minds.

THE IMPORTANCE OF COMMUNITY

These examples all illustrate the importance of community, as re-created with teachers, parents, and children. This is the framework of an education that works—an education that addresses the particular needs and challenges felt by our individual families and communities. It shows the power of the child to start parents thinking about new healthy habits at home. As one mum said, "It might be too late for me, but it ain't too late for my kids." One school told us that after a few months of working with nutrition, they created a five-star certificate that they handed to children who came to school with a healthy lunch. One mother came into school one morning very upset that she had packed a healthy lunch and did not get the certificate!

Children are very perceptive and aware of their parents' reactions, and if a parent is on board with what the school is doing the child will be too. We learned that it was harmful to the child to place or find them in a kind of conflict between a culture at home and a school culture. This became central to all our thinking. We feel that divisions like these are what account for so much missed school later.

We speak with many schools, and often they have wonderful innovative and creative ideas. We love to share these, especially as some schools are so isolated and have to deal with so many traumas and day-to-day hardships they may not have the luxury to spend time creating activities. For this reason we created the Milky Way website,[6] where we post activities and ideas for the teachers to see and share with each other. Community once more for a communal people becomes a central thought around which our ideas develop. We are creating a community within a community. Each school is a part of a community and the schools together create a wider community to support each other.

THE NEED FOR EXPERIENTIAL LEARNING

Research has proven how vital hands-on experiences are to allow learning to take place. This is especially true when one is working with this group of children who are traumatized and who may be blocked, numb, and out of touch with their own needs. Hands-on experiences penetrate the bubble. Having different types of learning is also important because some of the parents we work with are illiterate. Therefore having experiences that are culturally appropriate, fun, easy, and engage the senses is very important if we want them not only to learn because they need to, but also to embrace and own the learning and use it for changes in their lives. We all know nutrition teaches us that it is important to eat healthy food. There are many programs that speak or write about the importance of this. But we want to allow the children, their families, and often the staff themselves, to expand their palates. If they do this consistently over the year, they can change and adapt their tastes and create more healthy eating habits.

To again use the example of nutrition, we found that after many discussions teachers often have an insight into their own relationship to food, and what they feel when they teach it to the kids. A director once told me that a teacher was telling the kids how healthy and delicious spinach was, while she herself had never tasted it. It is hard to teach what you do not know or believe in. This is more important than it at first appears. These teachers are part of the community the children belong to. They are parents themselves, and often a child's teacher can be a last lifeline for a child at risk.

THE CHALLENGE FOR ABORIGINAL TEACHERS

Aboriginal society pre-colonization provided optimal conditions for the health and well-being of families and children through its collective nature. Today, although Australia ranks as one of the healthiest developed countries, its Aboriginal population is among the least healthy.

It is important for us to empower the teachers, and to acknowledge their hard work. Often they are not only *not* acknowledged by the families, they are bullied by them, by the Department of Community Services, and even by the Board of Education, whom they spend hours writing and preparing assessments for. They are also themselves suffering from trauma. In seeing them and acknowledging them, we believe they can become more available for the children who really need them and their full awareness and attention. It is an integral part of our job to remind them how important their jobs are, and that often the relationships that the children form with these teachers can impact their entire lives.

By speaking with them on an ongoing basis we create a space and time for the teachers to think about activities. As one director told me with great embarrassment, "I have been working in this position for eighteen years. One just gets used to doing the work without thinking about it. When you come, I remember that we can do so much more, and that there are so many things we can do!"

We know that in extreme trauma what can often save a child is their relationship to a caring adult. Often this caring adult is the teacher. It is as if we share with them the developmental stage of the children—we reinforce their own ideas that the children need to play, to explore, to create, and to imagine. And in cases where they are not able to do this, due to their traumatic background, we support teachers to just be, and allow them to contain and have trust in the capacity of these children and their own skills.

THE TWO MAIN GOALS OF THE FIVE BIG IDEAS

One of the core aims of the Five Big Ideas is that these experiential activities be developed through community collaboration between teachers, children, parents, elders, and us. We want the ideas to belong culturally to a people who have been robbed of their culture, and we want this program and its activities to give them a sense of pride in who they are and where they come from. Kirra, one of the puppets, asks, "Why does knowing who my mob is matter?"[7] and the other puppets tell her, "So you can belong, so you can be somebody! Not nobody!" Exploring their stories, connecting to elders, to country and to themselves, makes them a Somebody.

Our other main aim is helping an exhausted staff member feel a value in his or her role. We want them to see themselves not only in the context of giving learning, but also as healers of trauma. We want to add the soul of Aboriginal spirituality to the learning process of preschool to foster a cultural renewal. And finally, we are advocating a way of education that dares to link in with psychoanalytic thinking, and to use it to understand both the trauma of the children and the possibilities that it opens for healing.

NOTES

1. See http://healingfoundation.org.au (accessed on 3-23-14).
2. TAFE refers to Australia's Technical and Further Education system.
3. Gunawirra wishes to acknowledge Sarah Boardman, the Frank Leyden Tot-Ed Trust, The Healing Foundation, and the Vincent Fairfax Family Foundation, whose funding made this website possible.
4. For more on the Five Big Ideas, see http://gunawirra.org.au/projects/preschools/five-big-ideas/ (accessed on 3-23-14).
5. Part of the PowerPoint information: "Today we are going to talk about fish. Eating fish is healthy. Children should try to eat fish two times a week because it's good for brain development. Fish are a lean, healthy source of protein—and the oily kinds, such as salmon, tuna, and sardines, give us the heart- and brain-healthy omega 3 fat."

And a related Dreamtime story, "Barramundi":

"A long time ago in the Dreamtime, there were no fish, so the people lived on animals, roots, and berries. The Aboriginal people were very happy. That is except Boodi and Yalima, for they wanted to marry. But the tribe insisted that Yalima marry one of the old men, to look after him. Boodi and Yalima decided to run away, and so they ran as fast as they could.

"Now, to go against the Elders of the tribe is breaking the law, and they probably would be punished. Soon the men of the tribe began running after them. Boodi and Yalima ran on and on, and soon they became very tired. They came to the edge of the land, where the water began, and they knew that to survive, they would have to fight. With the angry tribe descending on them, they quickly gathered wood, and made as many spears as they could.

"But the tribesman were too many, and soon the spears were all gone. Boodi turned to his beloved Yalima and said, 'For us to be together forever, we must go into the water to live.' And so they did. They are still there in the shape of the Barramundi hiding amongst the logs and reeds."

6. See the website Tracking the Milky Way at http://gunawirra.org.au/tracking-milky-way/ (accessed 3-23-14).
7. Among Aboriginal people "mob" means their community. "Our mob" is a very important concept for a communal people.

Chapter Eleven

Using the Weaving Thoughts Peer Method to Generate Meaning

Putting the Bits and Pieces Together

Ionas Sapountzis and Judy King

Therapists who work with young children are likely to frequently have the feeling of not being able to understand what is happening in the course of a session or of not knowing how to respond effectively to a child's actions. The multiple shifts in the child's mood, the games and projects that are started but quickly abandoned or dissolve into something else, the references to themes and characters that cannot be easily followed, and the seeming lack of continuity from one session to the next can leave therapists, as Chethik (1989, p. 23) noted, in a state of bewilderment. These emotions, which are quite common, are likely to be experienced more acutely by therapists who work with children who have experienced abuse in their lives, or who have been traumatized by the failure of their caretakers to provide them with a safe and validating environment. Present in the mind of every therapist who works with traumatized children is not only what to make out of their behaviors, but also how to use that understanding to offer these children an experience that is useful and lasting.[1]

The challenges involved in understanding the reactions and emotional states of children who have experienced trauma in their lives, and the need of teachers and therapists to feel that they are offering those experiences that are reparative and meaningful, were the topics of several discussions during some recent seminars held at Gunawirra with teachers and therapists from outback preschools. Over the course of several presentations and group discussions, the participants repeatedly conveyed that the experience of not being able to make full sense of the emotional states of these children can be very discouraging. However, the act of sharing these experiences with colleagues and listening to their work enabled them to create a space (Winnicott, 1971a) where they all felt validated and understood. In the discussions and presentations that took place at last year's seminars, teachers and therapists had an opportunity to reflect on their work and contemplate how the children they worked with were likely to experience their exchanges with them. Interestingly, the insight that was generated did not emerge in just one meeting but through a series of exchanges and discussions that gradually enabled the participants to explore different perspectives and to feel more hopeful and less constrained by their self-doubts.

The Weaving Thoughts (WT) peer group process is a method for eliciting insight that has the potential to create experiences for therapists and teachers that are similar to the ones that were created in the seminars. The process involves a group of therapists listening to a treatment case, and then sharing their reactions and associations without concerning themselves with whether they are right or wrong. The participants' reactions help broaden the therapist's understanding of the case and enable him or her to become mindful of possible blind spots and of additional areas to be more attentive to. I used this process with my students at Adelphi University to review the session notes from a case involving a 4-year-old girl that was sent to me by a therapist from Gunawirra, and I was surprised by the results. This chapter describes the method and gives an account of how the associations of group members to an individual case can contribute to a better understanding and appreciation of what a child's acts may indicate.

THE WEAVING THOUGHTS PROCESS

The Weaving Thoughts (WT) peer group process is one currently being used by analytic groups in Europe (see Salomonsson, 2012, for a detailed description). It is a method for generating associations and thoughts on a psychoanalytic case by peers who are not familiar with the case. The process involves the presentation of a therapy session to a group of colleagues who know nothing about the case except the age and gender of the patient. After the presentation of the session, a moderator—who is also not familiar with the case—invites all group members to offer their reactions and associations while the presenter refrains from making any comments. The process continues until the end of the agreed-upon time for reviewing the material.

The WT process does not aim to reach a level of consensus among participants as to what has transpired in the session they just listened to, or to generate an understanding that is superior to that of the analyst. Its underlying premise is that the participants' associations, regardless of how resonant and on-target they may be, contribute to a mosaic of possible meanings that give analysts multiple perspectives, which in turn enable them to contemplate thoughts and possibilities they may not have entertained until then. The WT group process does not serve as a supervising session for the analyst, and the associations and ideas that are voiced are not intended to be experienced as evaluative. The process simply involves the eliciting and sharing of associations without the members concerning themselves with their level of accuracy and concordance. For that reason, group members are instructed to not ask the therapist any clarifying questions but to simply respond to the case material based on their own reactions and thoughts, however random they may seem to be. The therapist is not expected to respond to his colleagues' comments at any time.

To teachers and early childhood specialists, as well as to psychologists who are unfamiliar with psychoanalytic thinking and group processes, WT may seem like a strange and perhaps convoluted exercise. One can easily question its relevance and applicability and wonder whether this method is useful to early-childhood teachers and practitioners who work with children from deprived backgrounds. To some, the process may feel too introspective and thus rather disconnected from the realities teachers face daily in their classrooms. However, although the WT group process has been presented in the literature as a method to be used in analytic cases, I have found it to be applicable in nonanalytic settings as well. In presenting and discussing material with intern students in psychology, practicing psychologists, psychotherapists, or teachers, regardless of whether the material presented involves a psychotherapy case, an excerpt from a child's behavior in the classroom, or a consultative meeting with parents or teachers, I have found that the associations shared by the other group members offer the presenter the opportunity to notice and contemplate dynamics that had, until then, been outside the realm of his or her awareness, and thus, to deepen his or her understanding of the case. Equally important, the experience a student or a teacher derives from presenting a case to a WT group is likely to be quite different from the experience of a one-on-one supervisory session.

Unlike the supervisor–supervisee relationship exchange, in which there is a built-in asymmetry with the supervisee reporting and the supervisor being the one with the "super-vision," the WT process helps teachers and therapists generate thoughts without feeling preoccupied by what is correct and what is not, and thus without having to feel exposed and perhaps criticized. The tone and feel of the supervisor–supervisee relationship can vary widely depending on the idiosyncrasies of each participant, the context in which they meet, and the level of trust they experience toward each other. But the WT process itself enables the therapist to listen to different associations and reactions and to create his or her own meaning and understanding. Furthermore, instead of an exchange between two people that is marked by the experience of one person, the supervisee, being evaluated, and the other person, the supervisor, being the one who assesses the supervisee's grasp of the case, the WT process can be experienced as an act of mutual exploration, a sharing of minds, and that can be quite liberating for all participants. In a sense, it is a process that fosters mentalization, the capacity to take in different perspectives and reflect on them at one's own pace and without feeling defensive or unduly critical of oneself.

The advantages the method offers and its effectiveness even when used in a nonanalytic context became apparent to me when I asked my students to comment on a case I presented. Unlike previous case discussions, which were typically characterized by the more outspoken students having the most reactions, I noticed that when I asked all the students to write their associations on an index card without including their names and to hand the cards to me before we discussed the case, all of the students shared reactions that were resonant and helped the group to better grasp the depth and richness of the case we were reviewing. Their reactions created a very rich tapestry that captured the core issues of the client, and also helped me notice aspects about the case that I had not paid attention to before. Feeling quite surprised by how perceptive and enlightening the students' associations were—after all, they were all students in the first year of their graduate studies—I started presenting other cases, including consultation cases from schools. In every case I presented in class, the students' associations broadened my perspective on the case and increased my appreciation of the students' innate capacities and clinical skills. More importantly, the students' participation in a WT group process enabled them to feel actively involved in the meaning that was generated and the possibilities that were explored in class.

To demonstrate the benefits of the method I will present below the associations offered by a group of students who listened to a session I read to them involving the case of a 4-year-old girl. The girl had been seen by a therapist who is affiliated with the Gunawirra group, and the summaries of all the sessions had been sent to me to review. Compared to the WT process group described by Salomonsson, the WT method presented in this chapter differed in terms of the level of training of the group participants, the way they expressed their associations, and the absence of the therapist from the group process.

The group consisted of first-year graduate school psychology students with only beginning knowledge of psychotherapy. In addition, in my role as the moderator, I had prior access to the case material and thus time to formulate my own ideas and reactions. Yet like the moderator in Salomonsson's article, I knew nothing about the child's background other than that she was a girl whose parents were Aborigines and who lived somewhere in North West New South Wales. The students did not have that information. Some had the association, which they shared in class, that the little girl was a Native American living on one of the reservations in the southwestern part of the

United States. Like me, the only information they had was the age and gender of the child. Although the students did offer additional associations in the discussion that followed in class, these were not recorded by me. However, their associations reflected the tone of the discussion in class, and each idea that was voiced contributed to the deepening of our understanding of the case and our growing appreciation for the complexities involved in addressing the needs of the little girl in therapy.

SIXTH TREATMENT SESSION SUMMARY

The sixth session from the girl's treatment was shared with the students. The session starts with the little girl walking into the art room and proceeding quickly to the art table. After slipping the apron on, she pours black paint into a palette and begins to paint the edges of the paper black as if she is creating a black frame. She then adds blue to the palette and uses it to fill the interior of the frame she has created. Finally, she adds red. She seems totally absorbed in what she is doing. She seems to be especially fascinated by the sensory experience of painting and by the colors that fill the page. She paints the palms of her hands red and then her fingers, and clenches and opens her fists to make a squelching sound. She looks at the therapist and laughs and watches the paint ooze through her fingers. When the entire sheet is colored she expresses her delight to the therapist by raising her paint-covered hands, and the therapist responds to the girl's gesture by raising her hands as well. The little girl seems to hesitate for a moment, but then, with delightful spontaneity, pushes her palms into the therapist's hands, covering them with paint. She seems thrilled by this exchange. She then goes to one of the buckets and begins to rinse the paint off her hands, humming softly to herself as she does so.

She gets some white paint and pours that directly onto her painting and makes a few playful childlike sounds followed by "Its amaaaazing!" and continues to cover her earlier painting with thick layers of fresh paint. She then begins an elaborate process of adding paint and glue into containers filled with water, mixing them around with a paintbrush, and seems absorbed in watching the water change colors. Her movements flow from one activity to the next without any hesitation, as she smells the paint, pretends that she is making dinner, pours painty water over the top of her painting, and mixes the colors of the buckets by pouring one container into another. She then cuts three pieces off the edge of her painting, dips one of the pieces into a bucket, swishes it around backward and forward while singing softly over and over and over "to eat, to eat, to eat, to eat," and tells the paper it has to stay in there forever and that it can't come out. She adds more paint and continues mixing everything, saying "not ready, it has to stay in there forever," then takes the sodden paper to one of the buckets on the floor, leaving behind the two bits of wet painted red paper she had previously cut off from the larger image; she does not seem to notice that she has left them behind. She drops the sodden painting into a bucket while saying "eeuuukkkk," lifts it out and drops it in a garbage can, takes it out again saying "eeeyuuuk!" again, dips it back in the bucket, squeezes it out and passes it to the therapist to hold, and then puts it back in the garbage bag for the last time. She then retrieves the flat bit that was "going to stay under the water forever" and rolls it into a little ball and drops it into a smaller white bucket placed on a chair.

She begins to clean up the surface of the table with wipes, and as she cleans she moves the two bits of paper she had left there over to the art materials table, as well as the palette and used brushes. For the first time in her sessions with the therapist the little girl starts directing her by telling her to put something in the bin and looks at her for help as she struggles to pull off the remaining shreds of paper towel to finish with her wiping efforts. She asks for help to clean the table but then pours more painty water onto it, making pretty patterns as she continues wiping its surface—a theme of spilling and cleaning away.

Having wiped the table clean, she notices some hardened bits of paper that are stuck on and tries to clean them off with the help of the therapist. In the little time that is left she selects another piece of paper, draws with a marker a diagonal stripe across the page, and cuts it and then cuts some tiny bits of paper off the end of the long thin strip of paper she has already cut and calls out "I've finished." Before she leaves she notices three bird puppets that have been hanging from the ceiling, names them "L and R and J," and removes the one that has the same initial as her first name. She brings it to the art table and says softly under her breath that she wants to keep it and allows the therapist to wipe off some leftover paint from the back of her arms while pointing out bits of paint for her, before she returns to class.

To me this is a wonderful session with a delightful little girl who finds "magic" even in routine acts and becomes absorbed in what she does. Her ability to find wonderment in what emerges when least expected is a wonderful quality to have. The little girl's interest in what begins to take shape and what *becomes* as a result of what she *does* may be a telling metaphor for how she experiences her sessions with the therapist. She is a girl who, under the warm and encouraging gaze of the therapist, finds enjoyment in being surprised by what she creates. Her progress in treatment is quite impressive. The little girl who was so unsure and guarded when she started treatment is much more lively now and seems to enjoy mixing colors, creating sensations, pouring paint, wiping surfaces clean, and finding the playful in whatever she chooses to do.

Much to my surprise, in reading the students' comments I noticed that they too responded to the little girl's spontaneity and playfulness and seemed as taken by her as I was. They commented on her openness and excitement and remarked on the trust she showed and the obvious enjoyment she conveyed in connecting with her therapist and making projects in her presence. But they also voiced associations about the little girl feeling "stuck" and unable to "undo," of feeling herself drowned and submerged. Their associations pointed to dimensions that may not be easily noticed because they are not as likely to rise to the surface unless one looks at the patterns that emerge when all the different associations, like the colors she was mixing in her palette, are treated as found objects (Winnicott, 1964, p. 302). The students' associations pointed to other possibilities and evoked themes of the little girl feeling "deep down" frightened and needing to create frames to face a chaotic world where things dissolve and change and are hard to make sense of. Interestingly, these associations were ones I instantly recognized and found myself nodding in agreement with as I was reading them. Yet, I also realized that although the "bits and pieces" my students noticed instantly resonated in me, I had not really thought of them, and they had not become part of my consciousness until they were brought to my attention through their eyes. I found myself thinking that the students' associations were like the bits and pieces the girl created in her sessions and cut off, leaving some to the side and one submerged in colored water, the discarded bits that became the objects of her fascination.

SUMMARY OF STUDENTS' ASSOCIATIONS

Student No. 1 commented on how trusting and excited the little girl seemed to be. For the student, the bits of papers the little girl submerged in the water evoked the association of how submerged the little girl felt herself and perhaps how unable to come to the surface.

Student No. 2 also noted how confident and excited the girl's play seemed to be and added that she thought the girl's play became chaotic and confusing toward the end of the session. This led the student to wonder what the girl's home life was like.

Student No. 3 commented on how connected the girl seemed to be with the therapist and how much she seemed to enjoy her exchanges with her. She also expressed the thought that the little girl's desire to keep one of the three birds at the end marked her need for permanence and stability, and also the unspoken wish to be remembered and not left unclaimed.

Student No. 4 also noticed how comfortable and even confident the little girl seemed in the presence of the therapist, and hypothesized—based on her play with submerging bits of paper in water—that the little girl may have felt drowned in life, and that her life may have felt messy and in need of a frame.

Student No. 5 suggested that the little girl wanted the therapist to feel her feelings through her gestures and high fives, and that the white color the girl used evoked the association of innocence and the wish for a new start.

For student No. 6, the little girl's act of leaving pieces of paper in cups of paint mixed with water suggested that things are missing from her life; these acts evoked for her the association of a girl who feels trapped or maybe feels like she is in a mess herself.

For student No. 7, the little girl's desire to cover all the space and leave no empty space or void evoked associations of wanting to keep away unsettling feelings and thoughts. The student also remarked how active and trusting the little girl seemed to be and how her play suggested that she did not want the session to end.

To student No. 8, the girl's play alluded to the possibility of a chaotic world at home. Her excitement as she tried to create a frame and fill it with colors and then clean up the mess suggested a wish to organize her emotions and to find some order in her life.

Student No. 9 pointed out that the girl's painting progressed from black to red, from dark emotions and thoughts she could not describe to more defined emotions, such as anger and love, and that the little girl became more connected with the therapist as she was doing this.

Student No. 10 also wondered why the little girl started with black and why she needed to start by creating a frame. Like student No. 9, for her the black paint evoked associations of dark, inarticulate emotions, and the frame the girl created at the very beginning indicated a need to contain these emotions and organize them.

Student No. 11 pointed out how frightened the little girl was by a sense of permanence, how she found herself unable to undo what has been created and exists in her life; her wish to clean created a sense of mastery and of taking care of her own mess.

For student No. 12, the openness the little girl showed toward the therapist and how absorbed she seemed to be in what she was doing suggested a growing trust and also a desire to connect with others. The student added that the little girl's acts suggested that she wanted things to stay the same forever and indicated a wish to have some permanence in life.

Student No. 13 also commented on the little girl's choice of black as the first color, and her seemingly being deliberate but becoming more excited and spontaneous as she gets carried away and lets her emotions "spill out." Like student No. 10, the student also commented that the little girl wants the paper to last "forever," suggesting not just a wish for stability but also an awareness of how precarious things are in life, an allusion, to some extent, of how short-term her therapy sessions felt to her.

For student No. 14, the little girl's playing made her think of a game of nourishment and oversaturation; she also noticed a duality in the girl's manner of engagement, specifically how careful and also how careless she was with the painting, as well as how serious and deliberate she seemed at the beginning and how "chaotic" and active she became at the end.

REFLECTIONS ON THE EXPERIENCE

When I read the students' associations, I became aware not of what I was missing, since their ideas resonated instantly in me, but of what I took for granted. I became aware of "bits" of information which, although they were lying there—like the hardened pieces of paper the little girl noticed at the end of her session—had not been "seen" until the students' associations put these bits one next to the other and they became "found objects" (Winnicott, 1964, p. 302) and, as a result, visible to me.

The students' associations made me pay attention to some other dynamics as well. I became aware that by focusing on the magical and enchanting feeling this girl created, which is certainly a gift that bodes well for the future, I was ignoring the trauma and anxiety she had most likely experienced in her life. This is not a matter of being wrong or right, but of capturing only a part of the possible meanings. Racker (1968) was the first analyst to draw attention to the different emotions a client can elicit in the therapist, from sympathy and sadness to annoyance and indifference. For Racker, any relationship triggers concordant and complementary emotions, feelings of identification with the patient's emotional state and also feelings of distance and "dis-identification," especially when the patient's acts are experienced by the therapist as offensive or painful and are not easy to identify with. For Racker, the issue is not whether these emotions are present or not—because, according to him, they are always present in a relationship. Rather, the issue is to what extent these emotions color one's perspective and how aware one is of them. My reaction to the girl's session was perhaps more concordant than complementary because I identified with her potential and not with what was missing. I responded to the evocative element of her acts and not to the fragility and possible emotional wounds that lay submerged and out of consciousness. A 4-year-old who creates a moment of hopefulness out of the colors she mixes up and the frames she paints is a girl whose creative gesture, as Winnicott (1971b) argued, needs to be noticed and acknowledged. But if one notices only the hopeful and delightful and not the possible fears and scars that may lie deep inside, one may end up missing an important part of the child's experience, and as a result be less attuned to the reality the child is faced with. By attending primarily to the dream and paying no attention to the trauma inside her, I risked missing the possibility of what the dream enabled her to keep submerged and out of consciousness.

It is indeed important to notice the spontaneous gesture of a 4-year-old and find delight in her delight. Mirroring a child's actions and delight is, after all, an act of validation. But when we fail to factor in what other realities may lie submerged, we are likely to fail to take in the *totality* of the child's life. One can argue that this act of "omission" (Levenson, 1995, p. 1) is likely to deepen the chasm between the wish and the fear because something fundamental about the child's experience is not being taken in by the therapist. In the case of the little girl, this is a failure to recognize the coexistence of her desire to be and experience, as well as her need to suppress and avoid, a split that is likely to exist in a child who comes from a chaotic household and who may have witnessed and experienced many traumatic incidents in her life. Unless the polarities that mark the life of such a child are understood and begin to be addressed, the little girl who at the age of 4 seeks excitement in the colors she mixes and the shapes she creates to keep a bleak reality at bay may, when she is older, seek to escape in acts that, however exciting, are likely to deepen the chasms in her life.

Allowing one's mind to take in the stuckness that characterized her life and even the trauma she may have experienced is a way of empathizing with her at a concordant level of being and experiencing that she could not communicate with words. On my end, I missed the sense of the little girl feeling submerged and perhaps trapped, a feeling that most likely reflected the state of her family as well. The students' associations made me also think that the girl might be ashamed at some level, and want to undo or create a frame to contain her emotions and control the messiness around her. The act of taking in and becoming mindful of the totality of the little girl's world is very important in enabling a therapist to create a therapeutic frame that would contribute to her feeling contained and held and, over time, convey to her the hopeful message that the messiness she experiences in her life is understood and that her experiences and emotions *do* make sense.

The students knew nothing about this girl and had no conception of her history. They had no information on who her parents were and what the possible family conflicts and developmental issues might have been. Their associations emerged from attending only to their own reactions and from allowing their minds to move freely and for different ideas, like the discarded pieces, to emerge. It is interesting how much on-target they were about a central aspect of the girl's emotional life, which was in fact a central aspect of the entire family: how stuck and perhaps discarded they all felt among all the colors around them. It is a core emotional experience that the girl could sense but was only able to articulate in the form of her creatively messy play.

It is also interesting how defensive I was, focusing primarily on the spontaneous and hopeful to avoid dwelling on the painful and, perhaps, her sense of drowning. Why is that? How is it that first-year graduate students were able to notice aspects of this girl's life that may not have figured as prominently in her therapist's thinking and certainly not in my thinking? To some extent that is the risk of working with a delightful girl. One might be so taken by her and her need to not dwell on the negative that one may take for granted, as I did, where she is coming from and the stuckness that I imagined has characterized her family's history. But there is another element that one can point to as well. That has to do with the freedom to associate, to let things rise to the surface unencumbered by other meanings that can weigh on us and make us become defensive. Not knowing her history or having "any images" about this girl enabled the students to play with meaning and to listen to the material in a way that a therapist or "super"-visor may not be able to. It enabled them to generate associations strictly from what the sessions evoked in them without their associations and thoughts being "framed" by background information and other specifics. And so, we were all able through this process to generate a kaleidoscopic view that is very hard for a single person to achieve. It is a process that requires multiple voices so that one can become aware of multiple possibilities and thus able to contemplate and play with multiple meanings.

What if we do that in the classroom? What if instead of focusing only on what is the right method of teaching, or how to break down a behavior or a lesson plan, we can also take into account the thoughts people have, and the emotions they feel but rarely pause to give voice to? Then, I suspect, what might emerge is not so much about what is right or wrong but instead about what else there is that we may miss seeing and experiencing. It is so easy to miss that, to find ourselves missing parts of what we experience in our lives and in our exchanges with others. It is easy to miss how likely we are to not fully take in the depth and breadths of another's experience out of our own need to not feel hopeless. That, I think, is the major advantage of the weaving thoughts method. The associations of the different group members when woven together can increase the potential space that exists in the therapy room as well as in the classroom. It is a process that can help a teacher become aware of other aspects about the child's behavior and being that are not usually attended to or thought of until a space is provided for the different thoughts to emerge and be woven together.

Of course, one can argue that my reaction to the girl's session was that of a reader—an experienced reader, but a reader nonetheless. Although the space does not allow me to offer a detailed account here, when I read sessions from my cases to my students and ask them to write their comments, I find myself becoming surprised, yet again, by what emerges and what they see and what I become able to see. It is a *humbling* process, one that deflates one's sense of omnipotence but that at the same time makes us not only more aware of dynamics we may be unaware of, but also of how perceptive the students are and how meaning can emerge when different perspectives and associations are mixed together. In retrospect, I should not have been surprised. For all the factual language one may use to describe the format and purpose of the WT method, the process is not only about weaving different meanings together but also about listening to our peers' reactions without any preconceived notions so that we can in turn listen to the associations their comments evoke in us. When we do that, we find ourselves not only listening but also seeing and thus finding the *bits and pieces* that, to paraphrase Winnicott (1963), are always there waiting to be found.

NOTES

1. We would like to thank the students of the Psychodynamic Perspectives course that was offered in the spring of 2013 at Adelphi University for reading the summary notes from the little girl's sessions and sharing their thoughts and reactions. This paper would not have been possible without their input.

REFERENCES

Chethik, M. (1989). General characteristics of the child patient. In *Techniques of child therapy*, 5–27. New York: Guilford.

Levenson, E. A. (1995). A monopedal presentation of interpersonal psychoanalysis. *The Review of Interpersonal Psychoanalysis* 1: 1–4.

Racker, H. (1968). *Transference and countertransference*. Madison, CT: International Universities Press.

Salomonsson, B. (2012). Psychoanalytic case presentations in a weaving thoughts group: On countertransference and group dynamics. *International Journal of Psychoanalysis* 93(4): 917–937.

Winnicott, D. W. (1963). Communicating and not communicating leading to a study of certain opposites. In *The maturational processes and the facilitating environment*, 179–192. Madison, CT: International Universities Press, 1965.

Winnicott, D. W. (1964). The Squiggle game. In C. Winnicott, R. Shepherd, and M. Davis, eds., *Psychoanalytic explorations*, 299–317. Cambridge, MA: Harvard University Press, 1989.

Winnicott, D. W. (1971a). The place where we live. In *Playing and reality*, 104–109. London: Routledge.

Winnicott, D. W. (1971b). Transitional objects and transitional phenomena. In *Playing and Reality*, 1–25. London: Routledge.

Chapter Twelve

Hitting the Wall

The Hidden Effects of Caring Relationships

Ingo Lambrecht and Aretha Paterson

Most of us entering a caring profession are never quite ready for the personal costs involved. If warnings appear, they are often brushed off in the enthusiasm of accessing the profession as a career. However, most of us as caregivers will have an experience in which we feel overwhelmed, shocked, or utterly drained when caring for someone. It is often a profound experience of reaching the limit of our energy and caring, like hitting a wall that stops us in our tracks. It is this moment of surprise, of standing still, that is being highlighted in this chapter. In this gap, one option is to ignore the inner pain, and to just push through, deny, and dismiss the draining anguish as weakness. The other option is to take the stunned moment as an opportunity to reflect, to ponder, and to be curious. This chapter seeks to capture this moment both in the form of personal experiences and in the reflections of a play therapist and a supervisor, with some backing of current research. The style of writing will be more direct to reach a wider audience. However, references cited in parentheses will allow anyone the option of exploring the relevant research literature. Three main sections emerged while we were exploring this topic. In the first section, a play therapy session is presented. This will be followed by the supervisor's reflections on burnout, compassion fatigue, and vicarious trauma. The third section explores more deeply the causes, triggers, processes, and dynamics involved. In the third section, the emphasis is on the recovery and vicarious resilience that lead to a rebalance of inner caring processes. Such a rebalance of our caring processes allows caregivers to be flexibile in caring for themselves and others after such difficult events.

Aretha Paterson is a social worker. She is new to the field and currently has two years' experience. At the age of 25, Aretha decided she wanted a rewarding career that has the potential to change lives and empower others. The session portrayed in this chapter was Aretha's very first experience in social work. She saw two preschool-aged Aboriginal children for ten art and play therapy sessions. One of them was Charlie, a four-year-old, fair-skinned boy who didn't even know his own age. As Aretha reports in her own words, "When I asked him how old he was, he would reply 'three.'" At first Charlie would not even come into the room for these sessions. He struck me as a boy who was stuck and could not connect. He had virtually no verbal communication.

Here it is important to note that in Aboriginal culture it is considered unacceptable or even rude to look a person directly in the eye. Their privacy of self forbids it. Such eye contact in Aboriginal culture can and does have a different meaning than in Western culture, and it is important for therapists and teachers and carers to have knowledge of this. Therefore the lack of contact is not related to the boy's gaze, but rather physical and verbal hesitancy.

Importantly, however, this chapter is not about the child in session, but rather the play therapist and her internal world in connection with the wider context. To make the sense of being in the therapy room more alive, Aretha is quoted directly about her experiences.

Ingo Lambrecht, as a clinical psychologist with more than twenty years of experience, has worked many years in the fields of child and adolescence, families, psychosis, and personality issues, as well as with the cultural-clinical interface. A large part of his practice is providing supervision, and he has studied the concerns of compassion fatigue, parallel processes, and vicarious trauma that arise when working with care professionals. Having worked both in South Africa and New Zealand with indigenous cultures, and trained as a *sangoma*, a South African shaman, he is acutely aware of indigenous people, their political history, and the long-term effects of colonization. He is currently working at a Māori mental health service in New Zealand. Ingo's reflections will follow Aretha's description of her experiences. Aretha writes about her important painful moment in the following way.

HITTING THE WALL

The play therapy session that affected me so deeply occurred at a preschool far outside Sydney, Australia, with a 4-year-old boy called Charlie [a pseudonym]. In this session my eyes were opened to the pain and suffering of a little boy in a painful family dynamic. It was the day I stopped being naive and lost a part of my innocence. Who would have thought that a week after such a sweet child was making me bracelets and necklaces that he would show me the dark side of his life? On the day of the session, the preschool had advised me that Charlie would not be coming in today as he had witnessed a violent incident outside his home, which I later found out was an incident that in fact occurred inside his home. I later heard that Charlie could not block out the violent fight between his parents as he usually does by watching television or a DVD. The electricity to his home had been cut off. At the beginning of the session, Charlie had picked out certain toys, which included trucks, helicopters, a plastic toy monkey with a removable head, and a box full of plastic hammers and plastic knives; I could not have imagined what would happen next. Charlie was a gentle child who would always greet me with a precious smile and a hug. He was always so happy to see me, but today he was different. As he began to unpack his box of toys he went into what could only be described as a frenzy, searching desperately to find one particular item while throwing everything else out. He then placed the plastic knives and the hammers on the table. I was told not to touch anything. He picked up the hammer and started hitting my head.

It was as though he wanted me to see and feel the unbearable pain he had experienced at home. Through my training, I had been told about children who had been through trauma. However, I was unprepared for the amount of feelings I encountered within him and myself. As he began to literally beat the toy monkey without restraint, I tried hard to engage him by pretending to be that monkey in pain. He did not respond or falter in his actions; it was as if his frenzied attack could not be stopped. I realized nothing could stop him from what he needed to do and to express.

I felt shocked; this was something I did not expect from Charlie. In looking back, I realize that what also played into my strong feelings of being shocked is that I was already exhausted and anxious. This was our ninth session together and to be honest while I was enjoying the experience of working with children, I was exhausted. Every week I would have sleepless, restless nights worrying that I would sleep in, miss my alarm, be stuck in traffic, and miss the flight that I would have to be at the airport for at 7:30 a.m. to fly to Charlie's preschool in a remote area of Australia. I wondered why this happened so late on in the process. I honestly felt sick, tired, and unsure of what to do. I had no one in the room with me to tell me what to do, I had to think on my feet, and it was terrifying. The shock of the attack came when I was already feeling vulnerable, burnt out, and unsure. So when the hammer struck, it hit me deeper than I realized, and deeper fault lines opened up. My way of finding some composure was to focus on him. I wondered whether he wanted to see what I could tolerate? He then began using a plastic knife to try and cut paper with a complete look of anger and frustration on his face. I would try to connect with Charlie with the acknowledgment that the paper felt the pain of the knife, I would get no response, he would just continue. At this point I did not know what to do, so I sat back, exhausted, confused, and just watched him. Had something snapped? I sat there with this overwhelming thought of "ten weeks is not enough; he needs more support he needs more help."

What came next is what shocked me the most, because my body began to respond to the feelings in the room. I had never felt so much anger, sadness, pain, and frustration all at once. Charlie began to hit a toy with utter rage, and in that moment it felt like play turning into reality. Charlie began hitting the toy monkey head with a plastic hammer and knife, hitting it so hard that he wanted that monkey to die. As I sat back in awe, shock, and amazement, I felt the intensity of his pain in my body. As he continued to literally kill that monkey he would say "die cunt." As if trapped in a trance, he continued to do this over and over again. The violence and the words ripped through me. Then he suddenly stopped, as he noticed paint on the knife. This seemed to snap him out of it. I felt a sigh of relief moving through me as I asked Charlie if he wanted to go clean it, as he seemed disturbed by the sight of red paint on that knife. Reflecting back, maybe at this point my interpretation, my words sought to contain what had happened for him and for me.

I felt Charlie's calm manner as we reentered the room after cleaning the knife in a basement outside of the room. At that moment I was able to breathe again. He began to reconnect with me by sharing his toys with me and playing with his trucks and motorbikes. As we played together with his trucks and some pick-up sticks, I tried to tell Charlie it was time to pack up for today, which he would usually comply with, but today was no ordinary day; he did not want to leave. Although it was hard for him to say goodbye and for me to digest what had just happened, he all of a sudden began talking, being quite talkative, which surprised me all over again. This session was just full of surprises. This had been the most talkative I had seen him, as if he had been allowed to express himself freely and now that he had let out his aggression, pain, frustration, and sadness, it was as if something had been holding him back for so long, and now that he had let go he could now speak. His silence was no longer needed.

I was so tired and I wasn't expecting this at all! If anything I had expected this from Michael, the other boy I saw; Charlie was the type of child who would not express this kind of rage. I honestly felt a little numb, exhausted; I felt so guilty feeling this, but I honestly could not wait for this session to end so I could process what was happening. I felt so confused given this was session nine, and in the previous session Charlie was the sweetest child I had ever seen, making me bracelets and necklaces and talking more. In this session, however, he was a completely different child. Even though I could see he became more settled toward the end of the session, because he was talking freely, I wanted this session to end so I could process what had just happened. I needed to write. I needed to get it out of me as soon as possible.

Upon reflection and for the next two weeks, the image of Charlie beating that monkey and saying "die cunt" with a growl in his voice, flashed back through my mind and body. This must have been so hard for him. What did he really experience? He must have felt as helpless as I did when witnessing his frenzy. As already stated, I had found out later that he had come to preschool because of domestic violence between his parents. Also, I heard that the electricity had been cut off, and knowing that Charlie would often watch DVDs to distract himself from his parents fighting, that too made me aware how this time he could not escape the violence in his home. It reminded me of when I was a child and going through my teenage years. My room was my sanctuary. My stepdad was a lovely person, but at night he would drink a bottle of wine. He would do so night after night. He would then begin to belittle everything we would say, so I would go to my room, eat dinner, watch television and videos, and just stay in my room all night. If the electricity had been cut out, I would have been stuck to deal with what was happening in reality. This is what Charlie triggered off in me. It is these personal memories that started resonating painfully. I could so relate to Charlie through my own experience, and at the same time, just because I could resonate with him, his hammer struck so deeply.

REFLECTING ON OUR INNER SPACES

When reflecting on Aretha's story, I can't help but wonder, as a supervisor, about the deep web of caring. Her story shows how complex caring can be, because the very inner space that allows Aretha to empathize with Charlie is also the place that brings up painful memories of her own wounds. This finding is not new to the field of caring. Across the ages and in many cultures there is the symbol or archetype of the wounded healer. In fact being a wounded healer is part of becoming a traditional healer in many cultures (Lambrecht, 2014a). Traditionally, the process of becoming a healer or care professional has meant accessing your own pain. In my personal and professional experience, there has always been a cost in caring. This cost has many names in modern times, be it "countertransference" (Hesse, 2002), "compassion fatigue" (Figley, 1995), "burnout" (Rosenbloom, Pratt, and Pearlman, 1995), or "vicarious trauma" (Pearlman and Saakvitne, 1995). These terms overlap, and although they have at times been used interchangeably, important differences exist (Trippany, White Kress, and Wilcoxon, 2004). In my experience, compassion fatigue or burnout is usually a slow process that can become inevitable. We try to avoid it, but it can occur due to exhaustion, long hours, and the endless drain of caring with people who are suffering. It is as if we are running on empty, feeling we have very little energy to give. It is more chronic than acute (Figley, 1995). The term "vicarious trauma" is a bit different. It basically means that we become traumatized by listening in a caring manner to someone else's story of trauma. Listening to stories of trauma, even witnessing the trauma of others, can trigger our own memories, our own personal trauma (Pearlman and Ian, 1995). We then feel traumatized, and so our body and mind react with shock, fear, and flashbacks. So this is more sudden, more surprising, more acute. Vicarious trauma seems to be a better fit for Aretha's story, because it was very sudden, and she felt shocked and surprised by her own experiences.

Of course, if some people become regularly traumatized by caring for others who are suffering, then that can lead over time to burnout (Pines and Arenson, 1988). So in this way burnout and vicarious trauma overlap (Devilly, Wright, and Varker, 2009). In psychology, these concerns are not new, and have been with us for more than a hundred years. Freud called this "countertransference" (Freud, 1910). Countertransference is a word used to describe what happens to us as caregivers and therapists who notice our own strong and powerful feelings toward a client. This can interfere with the caring. So when care professionals develop sexual feelings or angry feelings toward the client that can be dangerous for the client. Personal feelings can get in the way of being caring. In a way, vicarious trauma constitutes our own powerful feelings, and can, if we are not careful, get in the way of caring (Hesse, 2002).

In the session with Charlie, Aretha expresses her dismay, her shock, and how she is thrown by the sudden intensity of the attack on her. It triggers off her own personal sense of exhaustion and fatigue already present, but also her memories of her own childhood. In other words, her personal dynamics have been triggered, which understandably leaves both client and therapist vulnerable. It is clear from the session that Aretha is able to contain her own feelings and thoughts so that it would be safe and secure for Charlie. She did not allow her own dynamics to spill out into the session. Although traumatized, Aretha held and contained her inner turmoil in a good-enough manner. It is worth reminding supervisees and therapists that this is the real work of the care professional or therapist. Having personal feelings about those we care for in our work is normal, it is what we do with these specific feelings that may help or hurt our clients. What is important to remember is that such shocks as Aretha experienced don't just pass in a day. They can linger and affect us for a long time. They can make us not want to work anymore, or we can become distant and scared. It can even affect our personal life (Stamm, 1997). In this way, vicarious trauma can lead to burnout and compassion fatigue. With that in mind, let us consider more closely the trauma for Charlie and the vicarious trauma for Aretha with the aftershocks that come with such experiences.

THE RESONATING AFTERSHOCKS

It all started with Charlie witnessing a violent incident at home. As Aretha states in her own words: "Although this fact may be a small thing for some, it resonated strongly with me as a child who would hear her own parents fighting, I would often lock myself in my room watching videos and television in order to escape my reality and live in a fantasy world. I often wonder whether parents and adults know that children are always listening and can strongly feel other people's pain, anger, and sadness. For a child who hears and sees their parents fight, how do they express this pain when they can barely speak?"

For a supervisor, this linking of what happens in sessions to Aretha's own personal experiences matters. The reason for this is that there is some research that shows that when we as care professionals have experienced our own trauma or post-traumatic stress disorder (PTSD), then we are more likely to experience vicarious trauma with clients (Bloom, 2003; Catherall, 1995). The causes of vicarious trauma are as complex as the causes for trauma and PTSD in general. The person experiencing vicarious trauma with a client has the same experiences as anyone else experiencing trauma. It affects our body, our mind, and our relationships. Listening with empathy to stories of violence, sexual abuse, and torture can shatter our positive illusions about people and the world, creating a deep questioning, as trust is lost in people. Feelings of powerlessness can come up, and sometimes we want to avoid therapeutic engagement, leading to a distancing from clients or those that suffer. This can also make us feel ineffective as care professionals. If there is no supervision or support from others, then this can become engrained and habitual. We can then slip into feelings of failure and shame about ourselves as caregivers, and we can push such feelings underground (Sabin-Farrell and Turpin, 2003).

For some that I have worked with, experiencing vicarious trauma means that the care professional can become jumpy and very anxious. They might struggle with falling asleep and either not eat enough or overeat. Obsessing about a client or thinking endlessly about them at night is common. Care professionals can have terrible flashbacks of the client's stories or images. Such intrusive thoughts or images can even disrupt other sessions with different clients. For Aretha, Charlie's words, and the image of him hitting her, kept recurring, as is common with trauma. Emotionally, feelings of being overwhelmed, anxious, unable to feel pleasure, numbness, despair, resentment, exhaustion, and of being flooded by our own personal memories of our own traumas from the past are very difficult to work with. This then can lead to feeling trapped at work, having no choice but to continue to work. This is what Aretha reported in regard to feelings of avoidance and exhaustion when working with the traumatized Aboriginal children in outlying places. As a supervisor, I find it important to acknowledge the suffering due to the extreme experience of vicarious trauma, especially when working with vulnerable clients such as children. This is especially true for those just beginning in a care profession, as with Aretha. For Aretha, both just starting off with the usual optimism, and at the same time not feeling that confident, makes her vulnerable to vicarious trauma. Often care professionals who have been in the field for far longer will usually comment on how they "harden up" and distance themselves from their work, but for a new worker this is seldom the case.

In my experience as a supervisor, I have noticed certain risk factors that make some care professionals slightly more vulnerable than others to vicarious trauma. One important risk factor is overwork and too long hours. This was especially true for Aretha, who needed to get up very early in the morning in order to drive to the airport. From there she would to fly a few hours to the preschool in the outback. After providing play therapy, she would then need to fly back by the end of the day, and such traveling every week, session after session, is exhausting. Just the tyranny of distance and travel is exhausting, and will lead us to becoming vulnerable. In fact, one study showed that sometimes work-related stressors, such as long work hours and organizational pressures, as well as being new to the profession, could be more important in making us vulnerable than our own personal trauma history (Devilly et al., 2009).

Importantly, it also matters who your clients are and what they have suffered. Many studies have found that caregivers or care professionals who mainly work with severe trauma, torture, sexual abuse, sexual violence, and child abuse, seem to be more vulnerable to vicarious trauma and burnout compared to other caregivers (Anderson, 2000; Chouliara, Hutchison, and Karatzias, 2009; Mouldon and Firestone, 2007; Van Deusen and Way, 2006). To a certain degree this fits, as Aretha was working with vulnerable children that have high levels of personal and intergenerational abuse and trauma. Other risk factors the research suggests are those of being female, as well as being a younger or inexperienced mental health professional. This would also apply to Aretha, who, in beginning in her career, is working with very profound deprivation and long-term intergenerational trauma.

Importantly, I have found that care professionals who have experienced their own personal trauma are more vulnerable to vicarious trauma. This is backed up by a considerable amount of research (Adams and Riggs, 2008; Baird and Jenkins, 2003; Bell, Kulkarni, and Dalton, 2003; Lerias and Byrne, 2003). Here are some more studies that drive home this relation between personal and vicarious trauma. In studies of therapists, counselors, and social workers who had experienced vicarious trauma, more than half of the participant samples for each study identified as having a personal trauma history (Baird and Jenkins, 2003; Slattery and Goodman, 2009). In a recent survey of service providers working with survivors of family and sexual violence (Choi, 2011) more than 80 percent of the workers identified as having experienced at least one personal traumatic event, and more than 70 percent of workers identified as having experienced traumatic events related to family violence or sexual assault. As with Aretha, family violence experienced by the therapist is strongly related to vicarious trauma (Ben-Porat and Itzhaky, 2009). This does not mean that if one has experienced personal trauma, then vicarious trauma is inevitable, nor does it mean that those who do not have a personal trauma history escape the experiences of vicarious trauma. It does, however, suggest that those who may be vulnerable to vicarious trauma deserve to take their own personal traumas seriously enough to work on becoming resilient.

In my supervision, I often prefer to go a bit deeper into why this is so. What are the reasons for this, and what could the dynamics be within us that can lead to vicarious trauma, burnout, and compassion fatigue? In my experience, the more aware we are of our own personal dynamics in being a care professional—or, in other words, of how well we have worked through our own past emotional pain—the better. This does not always protect us from vicarious trauma, but we are more likely to move through it more easily, and with some kindness. Interestingly, in one study, therapists in training had a greater tendency to be self-sacrificing, and were less self-aware of the style of their defense, as compared to those with more experience in trauma work (Adams and Riggs, 2008).

This brings us to the notion of the care professional as a rescuer (Berne, 1975), a role that I find central when working with care professionals and within myself. Here is the challenge that is often hard for us to face as care professionals. The very tendency within us that brings us to become caregivers is also the very same process that can make us vulnerable to vicarious trauma. This is something so often overlooked in the caring profession. In my experience as a supervisor, we are in the caring profession because of our own dynamics, and that is a positive thing. We can understand our client's pain through the empathy of our own wounds. We become the living expression of the ancient symbol of the wounded healer. However, our own personal dynamics are at the same time the very source of our responses that can lead to certain risks for the client and ourselves. Due to our own histories, it becomes very easy to possibly overidentify with our clients, seek self-sacrifice, and maybe attempt to "rescue" the clients to fill our own unmet needs. For example, if I don't recognize my own personal feelings of being abandoned when I was younger then I can overreact to clients who have been abandoned. I might be tempted to rescue them, get overinvolved, or maybe shun and avoid them, because it is too similar to my own pain. If this dynamic remains unrecognized, sooner or later this leads to an exhausting burnout, where compassion for the client shifts into cynicism and apathy within us.

We can become irritable or distancing when with clients. It can also lead to guilt in having such feelings. These guilt feelings are important to recognize, because otherwise we will then attempt to rescue even more, which again brings about the vicious cycle of burnout and guilt. This is something I have found to be important to address in my own personal work in regard to being a psychologist. As a supervisor for more than twenty years, I have too often witnessed this process in those who have not carefully explored on a personal level why they want to be in this caring but also demanding profession.

There are some studies on helper or rescuer personalities and burnout that back this up (Guggenbühl-Graig, 1998; Hawkins and Shohet, 2000). No one acts out of only pure altruistic reasons when entering a helping profession. It is the dark side of a carer's personality that can lead to early burnout, if suppressed and left unprocessed. This shadow side can also be a hidden urge for power on the part of the rescuer or helper, as the "healthy" carer feels superior to the "sick and helpless" client, all in the name of caring of course. I have noticed as a supervisor that a feeling of having power over the client helps the therapist or care professional to conceal and avoid his or her own feelings of helplessness and incapacity. Thus, for example, a care professional will attempt to overcome such feelings of helplessness by setting up hectic activities for clients, endlessly fighting for them with the authorities, and, in response to the carer's role as the omnipotent rescuer or hero, the client becomes forced into the helpless role of the victim. Such rescuers seldom acknowledge or work with the strengths of the client, which could allow the client to solve the issues themself. There are always exceptions of course, but here we are focusing on general tendencies. As stated, this is often a challenge for care professionals, and they can become quite defensive around this topic.

To give an example, such rescuing care of a cancer patient can help a nurse to avoid her own fear of death. She or he becomes too preoccupied with activities, rather than listening to the feelings of the cancer patient. A caregiver who takes on too many clients, groaning under a too-great workload and refusing to accept the support and help of colleagues, is trying through addictive overactivity to defend against his or her own neediness. One way to understand this rescuer role is to consider that this could actually be an unrecognized selfish and narcissistic process within us, which care professionals rarely wish to admit. The way care professionals achieve power and social recognition is to be caring. So to be super caring often marks a hidden drive for power. It is a dynamic we need to face. If we don't acknowledge this part in us, then the rescuing "selfless" carer will seek a subtle selfish or narcissistic lust for glory and honor, and to be idolized by thankful organizations, colleagues, or clients (Pross, 2006).

POLITICAL ASPECTS OF TRAUMA

There is another aspect of vicarious trauma that is rarely mentioned in the literature, namely the political aspects of vicarious trauma. That Charlie is an Aboriginal boy in Australia cannot be denied. Aretha was traumatized by Charlie's expression of his own trauma. And so trauma is transmitted from person to person, from generation to generation. Charlie's trauma is very likely the result of complex trauma from past generations, of generations being traumatized by the effects of colonization on his people in Australia. Personal trauma is political trauma when the intergenerational aspect of trauma is acknowledged. This is especially true in working with indigenous people, when family trauma is often caused by the political processes of colonization in the past (O'Loughlin, 2013), be it among Native Americans in the United States, the Aboriginal people of Australia, the many indigenous people of South Africa, or the Māori in New Zealand. In working with indigenous people, as with any other people, the intergenerational trauma reveals the political aspects of personal trauma. Unraveling the political aspects is helpful in strengthening the healing process (Lambrecht and Taitimu, 2012).

This is also true for Aretha's own intergenerational trauma that was triggered. Her heritage is both Mauritian and Australian. Although Aretha did not witness any domestic violence, domestic violence occurred throughout her family. In Mauritius, Aretha's mother married young to a man who would often exert power over her, and so at a young age her mother was extremely vulnerable. Her mother ended up in a refuge and studied community welfare. She now works with clients who experience domestic violence. Aretha's own father used more subtle forms of domestic abuse. In addition, her sister has been involved in a physically abusive relationship, and Aretha's first partner was involved in domestic violence. Therefore domestic violence cycles through Aretha's family through the generations. Charlie's own personal and political trauma vicariously resonated with the intergenerational trauma in Aretha. Thus it is clear that vicarious trauma has important social and political aspects.

FINDING THE REBALANCE

Aretha writes, in reflections on her vicarious trauma, that "the only thing that helped me through this was being able to talk and talk and talk and talk. What eased the pain was removing what I had inside of me, what I witnessed, what I heard, what I felt, piece by piece to anyone that would listen, unloading parts of this session onto anyone who would hear it. Having supervision with a wonderful psychotherapist named Marilyn Charles, who had such a caring understanding and empathetic voice, was very healing. Also, having a fellow colleague down the road run up to give me a hug and hold me while I cried really helped. What also mattered was knowing that I somehow had helped Charlie. Seeing him wave at me at the end of the session, with that smile on his face, as if to say thank you, my burden is no longer mine but yours. And it felt like a disease, being touched by so much pain and rage; it was now mine to deal with and the only way I could deal with it was to pass it on to others to deal with it, and the cycle could continue either negatively or positively."

Vicarious resilience is achieved by working through vicarious trauma. This working-through means that the difficulties related to vicarious trauma are openly talked about in a safe environment within a caring organization, together with supportive supervision, and being held within a caring home life and friends. Research supports this, in that many care professionals going through vicarious trauma in a positive way notice positive changes (Jenkins, Mitchell, Baird, Whitfield, and Meyer, 2011). Supporting healers is important in the process of being able to heal themselves.

An essential part of this healing is to normalize the experiences and processes of vicarious trauma. In supervision, I focus on the stigma of being a failed and pathetic care professional. We need to address the loss of status in being seen as a vulnerable or sick caregiver, one who cannot handle the clients they work with. The literature strongly suggests the importance of vicarious trauma being normalized in the work environment (Brady, Guy, Poelstra, and Brokaw, 1999; Bride, 2007). It is in and of itself a therapeutic intervention when staff in an organization feel understood and heard, and so then experience almost immediate relief (Maltzman, 2011). Aretha definitely received this care and understanding at Gunawirra, and I am aware of how caring this organization is under the supportive leadership wings of Norma Tracey. Norma clearly holds the culture of respecting the powerful effects of vicarious trauma, and such a culture of care toward care professionals at Gunawirra has a profound effect on healing the hard-working care providers.

Considering our work, one of the primary predictors for vicarious trauma is the number of hours per week we spend working with traumatized people. Therefore, part of the solution may be more structural than individual. That is, organizations must determine ways of addressing vicarious trauma. Gunawirra is very effective in this manner. Other protective factors for vicarious trauma include working with clients who do not suffer from trauma (Brady et al., 1999). Having a more diverse caseload with a greater variety of client problems is also helpful, along with participating in research, education, and outreach (Bell et al., 2003).

Regular, supportive, and empowering supervision is very protective against the long-term effects of vicarious trauma. The research clearly shows how important regularly scheduled supervision is for workers in the field of violence and trauma (Berger and Gelkopf, 2011). Supervision has been shown to lessen the incidences of vicarious trauma and is essential to alleviate the painful effects of trauma work (Slattery and Goodman, 2009). When working with a supervisee, as I have stated above, it is important to normalize vicarious trauma, and to celebrate their achievements (Baird and Jenkins, 2003). Only then is it important to work through the darker side, as I have discussed above, together with the rescuing aspect and the person's own personal trauma (Adams and Riggs, 2008). In my experience there is no doubt that once the care professional understands what she or he went through, how well they managed, how common this is, and what amazing work they have done, that then the impact of the vicarious trauma decreases (Ben-Porat and Itzhaky, 2011). Another factor worth mentioning is that the support of colleagues and peers matters. This has a very positive effect when it comes to vicarious trauma. It normalizes the experience, validates the care professional, and allows for venting and some objective reflections (Berger and Gelkopf, 2011).

As a supervisor, I also check in on the self-care of a care professional, including their diet, their sleep, the support of friends and family, the ways they de-stress, and so on. I explore whether personal therapy might be helpful, if it is necessary. For the same reasons, being aware of our personal limits is central. The rescuer has a tendency to ignore these in the name of care, and then burn out. We are not useful to our clients if we are a burnt-out wreck, so knowing our limits and watching our self care matters to our clients. It is important to know our own levels of tolerance. A life–work balance becomes central in addressing a rebalance (Bloom, 2003).

Aretha's last comments, on noticing that she made a difference despite her exhaustion and shock, relate to the spiritual component of vicarious trauma. For me as a supervisor, it is crucial to support care professionals, after the first supportive work, in finding meaning in such pain. This is central in being on the path to recovery and rebalance. Yet not all the vicarious effects of trauma are negative. This is sadly often not discussed in the literature. There are some who experience vicarious resilience when working with trauma (Engstrom, Hernandez, and Gangsei, 2008). It is worth noticing what Aretha said, that it mattered to her that her therapy was valuable, no matter how traumatizing it was for her. This experience will change her for the rest of her career. This is her legacy of the human capacity to survive and thrive, and that is the reason to highlight the immense value of the clinical work she provided.

Interestingly, there is some suggestion that trauma work can lead to an increase in spirituality and meaning in the care professional (Baker, 2012). Spirituality, mindful self-awareness, meditation, and breath work have been shown to be helpful for vicarious trauma (Berceli and Napoli, 2006; Harrison and Westwood, 2009; Sommers, 2008). Also, trauma-specific education can diminish the potential for vicarious trauma. Training in trauma and vicarious trauma can help individuals to name their experience and respond to it (Bell et al., 2003). In my view, it is important that formal trauma training is not just a one-time happening; rather, the training needs to be ongoing. Holistic approaches to healing trauma, and therefore the vicarious trauma of the healer, include addressing meaning and spirituality. This is in fact part of the traditional healing practices of indigenous people (Lambrecht, 2014b). This is particularly relevant when working with indigenous cultures; in Aretha's case, she is part of Gunawirra, an organization that I have witnessed pays particular attention to this holistic approach, seeking and finding important links to cultural healing practices. There is no doubt that Aretha has benefited from such cultural-political sensitivity in all the people involved with her.

CONCLUSION

In this chapter, vicarious trauma came alive in a play therapy session with a little boy in the depths of his own traumatic agony. It moved across the therapeutic space, and left a profound impact on the play therapist. The traumatic event and its expression resonated and activated old memories of the therapist's own painful childhood memories. Although she was able to contain the impact in the session, tears began to flow later. It is clear that, for Aretha, the exquisite support of her organization, as well as her insightful and kind supervision, made all the difference in leading to healing her vicarious trauma. Under the leadership of Norma Tracy, Gunawirra holds a strong culture of sophisticated support for the therapists along with a full awareness of the complex personal, cultural, and political trauma these therapists face every day in their work with preschool Aboriginal children. Gunawirra intuitively and consciously is providing best practice support for vicarious trauma. The research presented in his chapter supports similar findings, and indicates that Aretha's experiences of vicarious trauma are not uncommon for many care professionals. Equally, the immense positive support she received held exactly the positive protective factors that the literature suggests. Caring has a cost, and at the same time, through the wounds of caring, care professionals find greater depths and increase their subtleness in the caring process. It is in this way that inner changes within the professionals become possible. The cost of caring can in certain circumstances enhance the healing capacity of the care professional. It can then lead to more effective and in-depth caring, which can only benefit patients, clients, and children of all cultures and histories.

REFERENCES

Adams, S. A., and S. A. Riggs. (2008). An exploratory study of vicarious trauma among therapist trainees. *Training and Education in Psychology* 2(1): 26–34.

Anderson, D. G. (2000). Coping strategies and burnout among veteran child protection workers. *Child Abuse & Neglect* 24(6): 839–848.

Baird, S., and S. R. Jenkins. (2003). Vicarious traumatization, secondary traumatic stress, and burnout in sexual assault and domestic violence agency staff. *Violence and Victims* 18(1): 71–86.

Baker, A. (2012). Training the resilient therapist: What graduate students need to know about vicarious traumatization. *Journal of Social, Behavioral, and Health Sciences* 6(1): 1–22.

Bell, H., S. Kulkarni, and L. Dalton. (2003). Organizational prevention of vicarious trauma. *Families in Society* 84(4): 463–470.

Ben-Porat, A., and H. Itzhaky. (2009). Implications of treating family violence for the therapist: Secondary traumatization, vicarious traumatization, and growth. *Journal of Family Violence* 24(7): 507–515.

Ben-Porat, A., and H. Itzhaky. (2011). The contribution of training and supervision to perceived role competence, secondary traumatization, and burnout among domestic violence therapists. *The Clinical Supervisor* 30(1): 95–108.

Berceli, D., and M. Napoli. (2006). A proposal for a mindfulness-based trauma prevention program for social work professionals. *Complementary Health Practice Review* 11(3): 153–165.

Berger, R., and M. Gelkopf. (2011). An intervention for reducing secondary traumatization and improving professional self-efficacy in well baby clinic nurses following war and terror: A random control group trial. *International Journal of Nursing Studies* 48(5): 601–610.

Berne, E. (1975). *What do you say after you say hello?: The psychology of human destiny.* London: Corgi Books.

Bloom, S. L. (2003). Caring for the caregiver: Avoiding and treating vicarious traumatization. In A. Giardino, E. Datner, J. B. Asher, B. W. Girardin, D. K. Faugno, and M. Spencer, eds., *Sexual assault: Victimization across the lifespan*, 459–470. Maryland Heights, MO: G. W. Medical Publishing.

Brady, J. L., J. D. Guy, P. L. Poelstra, and B. F. Brokaw. (1999). Vicarious traumatization, spirituality, and the treatment of sexual abuse survivors: A national survey of women psychotherapists. *Professional Psychology: Research and Practice* 30(4): 386–393.

Bride, B. E. (2007). Prevalence of secondary traumatic stress among social workers. *Social Work* 52(1): 63–70.

Catherall, D. R. (1995). Coping with secondary traumatic stress: The importance of the therapist's professional peer group. In B. H. Stamm, ed., *Secondary traumatic stress: Self-care issues for clinicians, researchers, and educators*, 80–92. Lutherville, MD: Sidran Press.

Choi, G. (2011). Secondary traumatic stress of service providers who practice with survivors of family or sexual violence: A national survey of social workers. *Smith College Studies in Social Work* 81(1): 101–119.

Chouliara, Z., C. Hutchison, and T. Karatzias. (2009). Vicarious traumatisation in practitioners who work with adult survivors of sexual violence and child sexual abuse: Literature review and directions for future research. *Counselling and Psychotherapy Research* 9(1): 47–56.

Devilly, G. J., R. Wright, and T. Varker. (2009). Vicarious trauma, secondary trauma stress or simply burn-out? The effect of trauma on mental health professionals. *Australian and New Zealand Journal of Psychiatry* 43(4): 375–385.

Engstrom, D., P. Hernandez, & D. Gangsei (2008). Vicarious resilience: A qualitative investigation into its description. *Traumatology* 14(3), 13–21.

Figley, C. R. (1995). Compassion fatigue: Toward a new understanding of the costs of caring. In B. H. Stamm, ed., *Secondary traumatic stress: Self-care issues for clinicians, researchers, and educators*, 3–28. Lutherville, MD: Sidran Press.

Freud, S. (1910). *The future prospects of psychoanalytic therapy*. Standard Edition 11: 139–151. London: Hogarth Press.

Guggenbühl-Graig, A. (1998). *Power in the helping professions*. New York: Spring.

Harrison, R. L., and M. J. Westwood. (2009). Preventing vicarious traumatization of mental health therapists: Identifying protective practices. *Psychotherapy: Theory/ Research/ Practice/ Training* 46(2): 203–219.

Hawkins P., and R. Shohet. (2000). *Supervision in the helping professions: An individual, group and organizational approach.* Buckingham, UK: Open University Press.

Hesse, A. R. (2002). Secondary trauma: How working with trauma survivors affects therapists. *Clinical Social Work Journal* 30(3): 293–311.

Jenkins, S. R., J. L. Mitchell, S. Baird, S. R. Whitfield, and H. L. Meyer. (2011). The counselor's trauma as counseling motivation: Vulnerability or stress inoculation? *Journal of Interpersonal Violence* 26(12): 2392–2412.

Lambrecht, I. (2014a). *Sangoma trance states*. Auckland, NZ: AM Publishing.

Lambrecht, I. (2014b). *Healing transgressions of Tapu: Re-membering the body sacred.* In M. O'Loughlin and M. Charles, eds., *Fragments of trauma and the social production of suffering.* Lanham, MD: Rowman & Littlefield.

Lambrecht, I., and M. Taitimu. (2012). Exploring culture, subjectivity, and psychosis. In J. Geekie, P. Randal, and D. Lampshire, eds., *Experiencing psychosis: First-person and research perspectives*, 44–54. London: Routledge.

Lerias, D., and M. K. Byrne. (2003). Vicarious traumatization: Symptoms and predictors. *Stress and Health* 19(3): 129–138.

Maltzman, S. (2011). An organizational self-care model: Practical suggestions for development and implementation. *The Counseling Psychologist* 39(2): 303–319.

Mouldon, H., and P. Firestone. (2007). Vicarious traumatization: The impact on therapists working with sex offenders. *Trauma, Violence, & Abuse* 8(1): 67–83.

O'Loughlin, M. (2013). Reclaiming genealogy, memory and history: The psychodynamic potential for reparative therapy in contemporary South Africa. In C. Smith, G. Lobban, and M. O'Loughlin, eds., *Psychodynamic psychotherapy in contemporary South Africa: Contexts, theories and applications*, 242–271. Johannesburg, South Africa: Wits University Press.

Pearlman, L. A., and Ian, S. M. (1995). Vicarious traumatization: An empirical study of the effects of trauma work on therapists. *Professional Psychology: Research and Practice* 26(6): 558–565.

Pearlman, L. A., and K. W. Saakvitne (1995). *Trauma and the therapist: Countertransference and vicarious traumatization in psychotherapy with incest survivors*. New York: Norton.

Pines, A. M., and E. Arenson. (1988). *Career burnout: Causes and cures.* New York: Free Press.

Pross, C. (2006). Burnout, vicarious traumatization and its prevention. *Torture Violence* 16(1): 1–9.

Rosenbloom, D. J., A. C. Pratt, and L. A. Pearlman. (1995). Helpers' responses to trauma work: Understanding and intervening in an organization. In B. H. Stamm, ed., *Secondary traumatic stress: Self-care issues for clinicians, researchers, and educators*, 65–79. Lutherville, MD: Sidran Press.

Sabin-Farrell, R., and G. Turpin. (2003). Vicarious traumatization: Implications for the mental health of health workers? *Clinical Psychology Review* 23(3): 449–480.

Slattery, S. M., and L. A. Goodman. (2009). Secondary traumatic stress among domestic violence advocates: Workplace risk and protective factors. *Violence Against Women* 15(11): 1358–1379.

Sommers, C. A. (2008). Vicarious traumatization, trauma-sensitive supervision, and counselor preparation. *Counselor Education and Supervision* 48(1): 61–71.

Stamm, B. H. (1997). Work-related secondary traumatic stress. *PTSD Research Quarterly* 8(2): 1–3.

Trippany, R. L., V. E. White Kress, and S. A. Wilcoxon. (2004). Preventing vicarious trauma: What counselors should know when working with trauma survivors. *Journal of Counseling and Development* 82(1): 31–37.

Van Deusen, K. M., and I. Way. (2006). Vicarious trauma: An exploratory study of the impact of providing sexual abuse treatment on clinicians' trust and intimacy. *Journal of Child Sexual Abuse* 15(1): 69–85.

Chapter Thirteen

Art as an Opening of a Door to Aboriginal Culture and Identity

Graham Toomey

My name is Graham Toomey, and I am an emerging Aboriginal artist who is a descendant of the Aboriginal Wiradjuri and Wongaibon peoples of western New South Wales.

The creative works I make express my powerful spiritual connection to my people, my ancestors, and my homelands. I have described my work this way:

> My work reflects and symbolizes my people's traditional values, beliefs, and stories. It can be seen as educational while also holding and describing the importance and the magic of our spirituality. When I work I strongly feel the presence of my ancestors. My ancestors provide the ideas, thoughts, and emotions for me to create artworks. They guide my hands and they inspire me to create work; it's as though I'm their voice, I'm their connection to the world they have left behind, it's their way of staying in touch with me, their people, and their homelands.

ON TRADITIONAL LIFESTYLES

The managing of my *homelands* has always been both physical and spiritual. The natural environment of my homelands was and is an Aboriginal landscape, not a wilderness. The Aboriginal environmental knowledge base has played a central role in the development of strategies to conserve biodiversity in sustainable ways. For thousands of years there has always been an ongoing purpose to value, nurture, and protect the land, for it is the means for survival. Since the time of the Spiritual Creators from The Dreamtime, when everything was created, there have always been beliefs, laws, protocols, and behaviors that protect these values for Aboriginal culture and society. They had to have a balance, an "ecological balance," and there had to be infrastructure.

Tribes from my homelands could only be large enough, not too big to jeopardize the natural resources. If they were too big, there would not be enough food and fresh water to go round. Between the coast, forests, inland river systems, and the desert, there were differences in quality, number, availability, and variety of food sources. Aboriginal people had to move from place to place around the seasonal cycle and The Dreaming cycle to fully utilize these resources, following the breeding, feeding habits, and patterns of the migration of fauna and plant life. Usually an elder, or someone of high degree, who was spiritually attuned, or had knowledge in management of land use, would make the decision to move along.

THE SEASONS

The start of the new season would be a time for ceremonies, a time when neighboring tribes would gather to celebrate, trade, to give and receive gifts, and to catch up. Tribes were divided by religious beliefs into "moieties," and thus usually this was a time for marriage, for women and men were promised to each other through this system. Aboriginal people have always moved this way for food or land management reasons, for it was also a time of connecting with spiritual creators from The Dreamtime or the creation time, the mythology. Each time they made their sacred journey they encountered their history, so that their current time was imbued with their past. It was important for this to be in a natural cycle, so that its circle from place to place could be completed, and then it would occur again and again.

In addition to their intimate knowledge of the land and the seasons, Aboriginal people used knowledge of animal physiology, using strategies and tricks. They would hunt from downwind; they would also cover themselves with clay and oils to change their own smell. They were also great at mimicking animal sounds, like clicking their tongues, which would attract crabs out of holes, or making the sound of a hawk that would make the *goannas* scared and freeze in one place, or other bird noises for attracting game out of their hiding places.

While seasons varied over the years, with some years having more rain than others, or sometimes drought, it was important before moving around that you left enough for others, or for your own tribe. Tribes or clans were always restricted in numbers, and certain areas did not have large families, especially in the top end and desert regions of Australia. Otherwise it would put too much of a burden or strain on the natural resources One tribe of twenty people may have enough food resources in a twenty-mile circular area for a season. Part of this area might be shared with neighboring tribes, overlapping on the fringes of those boundaries, so it was important that they all shared and did not drain all the food sources.

For plant foods such as wild fruits, nuts, berries, leaves, and other plants, it was necessary to leave enough seeds to allow for regrowth. When hunting it was important not to kill the young animals, or the females, whenever possible. It was the same when collecting bird eggs, and other eggs from animals: always leave some for the future, which would also assist in not making animal and bird life extinct, or rare. This is what makes "Aboriginal land use" so unique: they were always thinking ahead, they would not deplete the natural resources but protect them, and their country, just like their elders, and ancestors did for thousands of years.

All these incredible stories and facts of how my ancestors survived remain inside my mind and my heart always. I value the knowledge and it inspires me to teach non-Aboriginal people about our culture daily. If they don't learn or understand us and our culture how can they ever really know about us or understand us?

CEREMONIES, CUSTOMS, INITIATION

Ceremonies are valuable because they provide my people with a means of recreating and contacting our Creators and contacting our Ancestors from the Ancestral world. The meanings of ceremonies are for initiation and fertility, for the living and the dead, and contain themes and events that hold myths, family, and rituals. Burial is the final stage of the life cycle, and the beginning of another life. A ceremony will play this out and then play out the first initiation into another life. As a person grows older and participates in more and more ceremonies he or she establishes a continuing relationship with the clan's Ancestral beings. In ceremonies he or she will reveal sacred objects, paintings, and body paint that define their link to their Ancestral past. They believe the more times one goes through ceremonies and initiations, the more the spirits of the ancestors witness them doing their steps toward being fully initiated. Saying and singing the power words of the songs sung also represent steps.

SPIRITUALITY

Aboriginal spiritualty is characterized by having creators or gods who created the people, language, flora, fauna, and the environment during a particular creation period at the beginning of time.

My people and I are very religious and spiritual, but rather than praying to a single god they cannot see, each tribe generally believes in a number of different beliefs whose images are often depicted in recognizable forms. These forms may be that of a particular landscape feature, an image in a rock art shelter, or in a plant or animal form.

For an example of this, many Aboriginal communities believe that the Rainbow Serpent, at the time of the Dreamtime or Creation Period, created the mountains, rivers, and landscape as she weaved her way across their homelands.

Another example is that a depression in a rock or in the ground may represent the footprint or sitting place of an Ancestral Being. Or that there may be a rock formation that can also be seen as a Creation Being or beings.

Down the south coast in Yuin country, there are three rocks that sit on top of each other. The Yuin people believe that the bottom rock symbolizes where we come from (the land), the middle rock symbolizes where we are now, and that the top symbolizes and points to the stars and that is where our destiny awaits.

THE MOTHERS GROUP

For me personally I love art and love sharing my knowledge, skills, and creativity. Art takes us away from the worries and the negatives and gives us a purpose and also the ability to create something that is about ourselves and our culture. In 2012 I started teaching and guiding indigenous and non-indigenous mothers from Gunawirra in Redfern, Sydney, about my incredible culture and art. I have seen the amazing transformation with them. When we started there was negativity, words like "I can't do that," or "It's too hard." Now I hear laughter and positive remarks, and it's hard to drag them away from what they are creating.

I incorporate in these sessions talks and information about Aboriginal history, survival, and spirituality, so as to give them knowledge, feelings, and ideas to create their own artworks. We also learn about and create ceramic art pieces using clay, which is a way to see that the clay is part of the land which belongs to and is part of us. We have come a long way in a short period, and it has been so rewarding for me to see them grow as artists but also to see them understanding more about themselves and their culture. The mothers now have skills, ideas, and interests that can be used in the future to make themselves stronger and more knowledgeable about their art and culture, but more importantly to teach their own children about art and their culture, which will sustain our culture into their children's generation.

Index

About the Contributors

Marilyn Charles is a staff psychologist at the Austen Riggs Center and a psychoanalyst in private practice in Stockbridge, Massachusetts. A Training and Consulting Analyst at the Michigan Psychoanalytic Council and the Chicago Center for Psychoanalysis, she is a contributing editor for *Psychoanalysis, Culture & Society*, and a member of the editorial boards of numerous other psychoanalytic journals. She has presented her work nationally and internationally, publishing more than eighty articles and book chapters, and four books, including *Constructing Realities: Transformations Through Myth and Metaphor* (Amsterdam: Rodopi, 2004); *Learning from Experience: A Guidebook for Clinicians* (Analytic Press, 2004); and *Working with Trauma: Lessons from Bion and Lacan* (Lanham, MD: Jason Aronson, 2012). A fifth book, *The Stories We Live: Life, Literature, and Psychoanalysis*, is in progress.

Celia Conolly is a psychologist with twenty-five years' experience in the public and private sectors. She trained as a Child and Adolescent Psychotherapist with the Institute of Child and Adolescent Psychoanalytic Psychotherapy (ICAPP) and currently consults in private practice in Maroubra, Sydney, with children and parents. Celia has trained and supervised psychologists and counselors for more than sixteen years. At Mandala Community Counselling Service, which offers free counseling for the disadvantaged in Sydney, she was a founding member and is now Manager of Clinical Supervision. She has taught at the University of New South Wales, the University of Western Sydney, and the University of South Australia, and is currently completing her PhD, which investigates intergenerational issues with parents and children.

Jeffrey L. Eaton is a graduate of the Northwestern Psychoanalytic Society and Institute, in Seattle, Washington, and a full member of the International Psychoanaytic Association. In 2006 he was awarded the 10th Frances Tustin Memorial Lecture Prize. His writing appears in several edited books, including *Living Moments: Essays in Honor of Michael Eigen* (Karnac, 2015), as well as in his own first book *A Fruitful Harvest: Essays after Bion*, published by The Alliance Press in 2011. Eaton is also a member of INSPIRA, the International Seminar on Psychoanalytic Intervention and Research into Autism. He lives and works in Seattle.

Shiri Hergass has an MA in Clinical Social Work from Tel Aviv University, Israel, and a postgraduate diploma in Art Therapy; she is now a PhD candidate at Australian Catholic University. Her experience has involved children and women in both the public and private sector, in work with Ethiopian mothers and children newly arrived in Israel, in reconciliation efforts between Bedouins and Jews, and in other conflict-resolution groups. In New South Wales she ran a group for mothers and their children in Emu Plains Correctional Centre. She also developed groups for parents and children who have experienced trauma, called Free to Be Me. At Gunawirra she serves as the country manager, working with forty preschools all over NSW, and has a small private practice where she sees women and children.

Ursula Kim is Director at Minimbah Preschool, Armidale, North Western NSW, where she cares for about one hundred twenty Aboriginal children. An Aboriginal woman, she is a valuable board member of Gunawirra, where she plays a particularly significant part in educating non-Aboriginal teachers in their understanding of Aboriginal culture and transgenerational trauma. She is also in charge of the choice of pre-literary books for as many as twelve preschools in her area, and is a speaker at Gunawirra's annual seminar on what it means to be an Aboriginal preschool teacher. Strongly aware of the problems of Aboriginal families and children, she is devoted to working closely with them, just as she honors her culture's links to the country in her respect for the land of her ancestors.

Judy King has an MA in Art Therapy from the University of Western Sydney, a BA in Fine Arts from the National Art School, Sydney, and has been a registered nurse for more than thirty years, working with trauma in varying capacities. Her therapeutic work has encompassed early intervention, children in foster care programs, and at-risk adolescents in the school system. Through Gunawirra she worked intensively at an urban Sydney preschool with some of the Aboriginal children discussed in the clinical material described in this book. Judy works as the art therapist at Prince of Wales Hospital, Sydney, in palliative care and with clients suffering chronic pain.

She also runs ongoing community-based art therapy workshops for seniors and people living with mental health issues.

Ingo Lambrecht, PhD, has been a clinical psychologist and psychotherapist for more than twenty years. After training in Europe and South Africa, he has for many years worked in a Māori mental health service in Auckland, New Zealand. His special interests include children and adolescents, psychosis and personality issues, as well as trauma and mindfulness. He has also written on the cultural-clinical interface through clinical work in different cultural settings, and was privileged to undergo an intense shamanic training as a *sangoma*, a South African traditional healer. In addition to his recent book, *Sangoma Trance States* (AM Publishing, 2014), he has contributed articles and chapters on the relationships between culture, psychosis, and spirituality, and has also presented at national and international conferences.

Maria Losurdo grew up in the Blue Mountains in New South Wales, where she has had close connections to Aboriginal families since childhood. For more than thirty years she has worked in the community sector in children and family services, battered women's shelters, and in community development roles. She currently works in Western Sydney providing training and resources to support community workers in helping bring social justice and cross-cultural awareness into the heart of their practice. Influenced by her Italian heritage and her experiences of separation and connection that come from our differences, Maria's work with Gunawirra came about through her work alongside Jackie Stewart, with its focus on naming and healing from the impacts of generational trauma for Aboriginal people in Australia.

Aretha Paterson holds a Masters in Social Work from Australian Catholic University, where she was a student at the time she carried out a significant part of Gunawirra's research project. There, with the benefit of supervision, she worked closely with two young children each week over a semester for an hour each session, and through the use of art and in creating a safe space for expression was able to initiate a valuable process of healing. Her French Caledonian background gives her a special awareness of and sensitivity to the needs of children from other cultures, and she is now employed full time in Sydney as a social worker in the public sector, helping families who are facing difficult mental problems that may include psychosis.

Ionas Sapountzis is an Associate Professor at the Derner Institute at Adelphi University in Garden City, New York, and the director of its School Psychology program. He is also a faculty member and a supervisor in the Psychoanalytic Psychotherapy and the Child, Adolescent, and Family Psychotherapy programs at the Derner Institute. He has published a number of articles on working with children in *Psychoanalytic Perspectives*, the *Journal of Infant, Child, and Adolescent Psychotherapy*, and the *Psychoanalytic Review*.

Jackie Stewart is an Aboriginal woman from the Kongabula tribal group of Southern Queensland. She currently lives in the Blue Mountains and works in Western Sydney in the community sector creating and delivering cultural training and resources to support cross-cultural understanding for both Aboriginal and non-Aboriginal workers. Jackie's deep connection to her Aboriginal culture and the spirits of her Ancestors guide her in her work and life. Jackie's connection with Gunawirra came through her work on naming and healing from the impacts of generational trauma for Aboriginal people in Australia, which she carries out in partnership with Maria Losurdo. Jackie is currently working on Tribe of Life, an art-based storytelling and healing process. When completed it will be available for use by both Aboriginal and non-Aboriginal people.

Graham Toomey, an Aboriginal artist, designer, and educator belonging to the Wiradjuri and Wongaibon tribes of Western New South Wales, is currently on the staff at Gunawirra, where he works with its Mothers groups and leads its art therapy project. His background includes diplomas from the Eora Technical and Further Education Institute in Sydney in Aboriginal Studies, Aboriginal Cultural Arts, and the Aboriginal and Torres Strait Cultural Arts program. An established artist, his works are now in a number of notable collections. He is also a director at the Boomalli Aboriginal Artists Cooperative in Sydney, and at Croana Aboriginal Consultancy Services in Mascot, NSW, and is a member of the Metropolitan Local Aboriginal Land Council in Sydney.

Norma Tracey has been a social worker for fifty-three years and a psychoanalytic psychotherapist specializing in work with mothers and infants up to age 5 for thirty-five years. She was assistant to the professor of Child Health, Sydney University; senior psychiatric social worker in the Department of Child and Family Psychiatry, Children's Hospital, Camperdown; and later her research was on the internal world of parents with a premature infant. In conjunction with her private practice of many years, she began work with Aboriginal families and preschool children fourteen years ago and founded Gunawirra five years ago. The author of more than thirty internationally published papers, several booklets, and books, Norma is CEO of Gunawirra, is active clinically with children and parents with infants, and designs Gunawirra projects with its brainstorming teams.

CPSIA information can be obtained at www.ICGtesting.com
Printed in the USA
BVOW04*1433311014

373072BV00003B/3/P